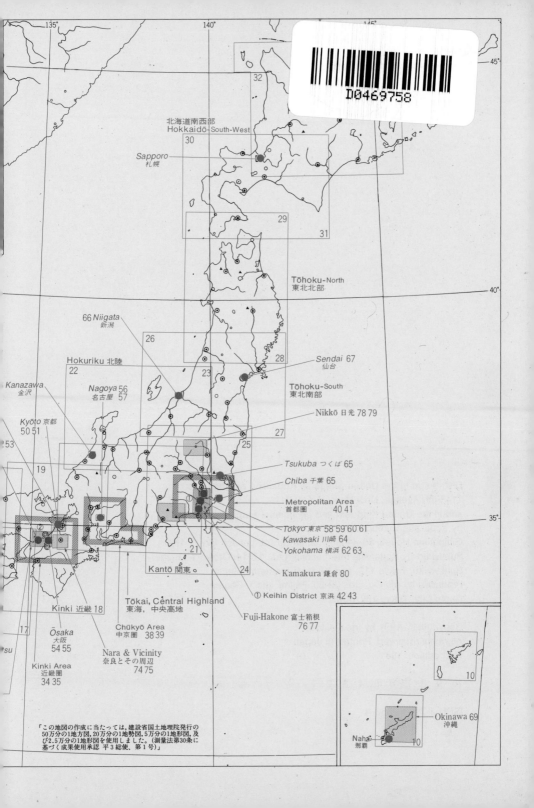

135°   140°   145°

45°

32

北海道南西部
Hokkaidō-South-West

30

Sapporo
札幌

29

31

66 *Niigata*
新潟

26

Tōhoku-North
東北北部

40°

28

Sendai 67
仙台

Hokuriku 北陸

22   23

Kanazawa
金沢

Nagoya 56
名古屋 57

Tōhoku-South
東北南部

Nikkō 日光 78 79

Kyōto 京都
50 51

25

53

27

19

Tsukuba つくば 65

Chiba 千葉 65

Metropolitan Area
首都圏   40 41

35°

Tōkyō 東京 58 59 60 61
Kawasaki 川崎 64
Yokohama 横浜 62 63

21

Kamakura 鎌倉 80

Kantō 関東

24

① Keihin District 京浜 42 43

Tōkai, Central Highland
東海，中央高地

Fuji-Hakone 富士箱根
76 77

Kinki 近畿 18

17

Chūkyō Area
中京圏 38 39

Ōsaka
大阪
54 55

Nara & Vicinity
奈良とその周辺
74 75

10

Kinki Area
近畿圏
34 35

Okinawa 69
沖縄

su

「この地図の作成に当たっては、建設省国土地理院発行の
50万分の1地方図，20万分の1地勢図，5万分の1地形図，及
び2.5万分の1地形図を使用しました。(測量法第30条に
基づく成果使用承認 平3総使、第1号)」

Naha
那覇

10

Distributed in the United States by Kodansha America, Inc.,
114 Fifth Avenue, New York, N.Y. 10011.
and in the United Kingdom and continental Europe
by Kodansha Europe Ltd.,
Gillingham House, 38-44 Gillingham Street, London SW1V 1HU.
Published by Kodansha International Ltd., 17-14, Otowa 1-chome,
Bunkyo-ku, Tokyo 112, and Kodansha America, Inc.
Produced by Iris Co.,Ltd., 39-30, Fujimi-cho 1-Chome,
Chofu City, Tokyo 182, Japan.

10 9 8 7 6 5 4 3 2 1

ISBN 4-7700-1536-4

JAPAN

A Bilingual Atlas
日本二ヵ国語アトラス

KODANSHA INTERNATIONAL
Tokyo·New York·London

CONTENTS 目次

PART I | Area Maps 地域図

South-West Japan 南西日本 ·········· 4
Central Japan 中央日本 ·········· 6
North-East Japan 北東日本 ·········· 8
Kyūshū South 九州南部 ·········· 10
Kyūshū North 九州北部 ·········· 12
Chūgoku 中国 ·········· 14
Shikoku 四国 ·········· 16
Kinki 近畿 ·········· 18
Tōkai,Central Highland 東海, 中央高地 ·········· 20
Hokuriku 北陸 ·········· 22
Kantō 関東 ·········· 24
Tōhoku South 東北南部 ·········· 26
Tōhoku North 東北北部 ·········· 28
Hokkaidō South-West 北海道南西部 ·········· 30
Hokkaidō North-East 北海道北東部 ·········· 32
Kinki Area 近畿圏 ·········· 34
Hanshin District 阪神地方 ·········· 36
Chūkyō (Nagoya)Area 中京(名古屋)圏 ·········· 38
Metropolitan Area 首都圏 ·········· 40
Keihin District 京浜地方 ·········· 42
Fukuoka Area 福岡圏 ·········· 44

PART II | City Maps 市街図

Naha 那覇 ·········· 45
Fukuoka 福岡 ·········· 46
Kitakyūshū 北九州 ·········· 47
Hiroshima 広島 ·········· 48
Okayama,Takamatsu 岡山, 高松 ·········· 49
Kyōto 京都 ·········· 50
Kōbe 神戸 ·········· 52
Ōsaka 大阪 ·········· 54
Nagoya 名古屋 ·········· 56
Tokyo(1) 東京(1) ·········· 58
Tokyo(2) 東京(2) ·········· 60
Yokohama 横浜 ·········· 62
Kawasaki 川崎 ·········· 64
Chiba,Tsukuba 千葉, つくば ·········· 65
Niigata,Kanazawa 新潟, 金沢 ·········· 66
Sendai 仙台 ·········· 67

Sapporo 札幌 ·········· 68

PART III | Sight-Seeing Maps 観光図

Okinawa 沖縄 ·········· 69
Beppu, Aso, Unzen 別府, 阿蘇, 雲仙 ·········· 70
Kyōto & vicinity 京都とその周辺 ·········· 72
Nara & vicinity 奈良とその周辺 ·········· 74
Fuji, Hakone 富士, 箱根 ·········· 76
Nikkō 日光 ·········· 78
Kamakura 鎌倉 ·········· 80

PART IV | Transportation Maps 交通図

Metropolitan Hiking path 首都圏自然歩道 ·········· 81
Metropolitan Rail System 首都圏電車路線図 ·········· 82
Tokyo Subway System 東京地下鉄路線図 ·········· 84
Kinki Area Rail System 近畿圏電車路線図 ·········· 86
Keihanshin,Nagoya Subway System 京阪神名古屋地下鉄路線図 ·········· 88
Chūkyō(Nagoya)Area Rail System 中京圏電車路線図 ·········· 90
Major Roads 主要道路 ·········· 92
Major Railways 主要鉄道 ·········· 94
Major Air Route 主要航空路 ·········· 96

PART V | Thematic Maps 主題図

Active Volcanoes 活火山 ·········· 97
National Park 国立公園 ·········· 98
Quasi National Park 国定公園 ·········· 99
Marine Park 海中公園 ·········· 100
Special Scenic Spot 特別名勝 ·········· 101
Special Historic Spot 特別史跡 ·········· 102
Special Natural Preserve 特別天然記念物 ·········· 103
National Spa resorts 国民保養温泉 ·········· 104
Bird Watching spots 探鳥地 ·········· 105
Ceramic kiln areas 陶磁器産地 ·········· 107
Lacquerware areas 漆器産地 ·········· 109
Textile,Dyeing 織物, 染色 ·········· 110

INDEXS 索引 ·········· 112

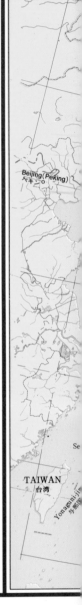

Beijing(Peking) ペキン

TAIWAN 台湾

Yonaguni-jim 与那国

Se

KEY
地域図凡例

CHIBA千葉 Prefecture 都道府県
◎ City 市
⊙ Town 町
○ Village 村
Prefectural Boundary 都道府県界
J.R. Line JR線
Bullet train line *shinkansen* 新幹線

Other Railway その他の鉄道
National Road 国道
Expressway 高速道路
Ferry フェリー
Other Sea Route 一般航路
National Park 国立公園
● Prefectural seat 都道府県庁所在地

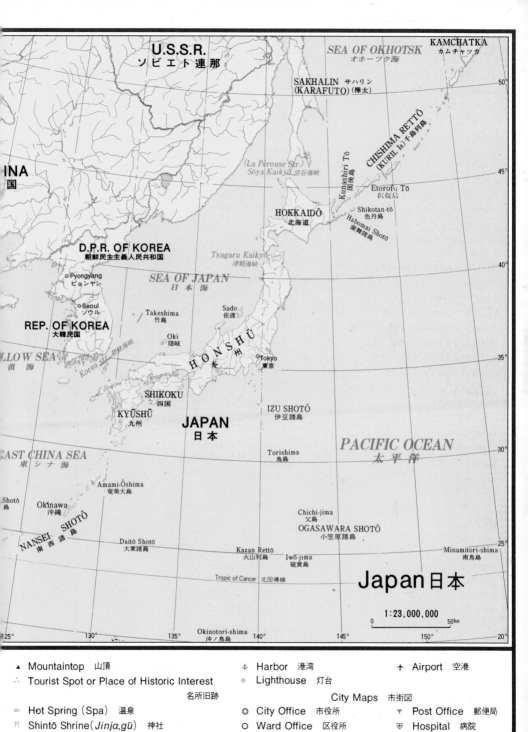

	Mountaintop 山頂		Harbor 港湾		Airport 空港
	Tourist Spot or Place of Historic Interest		Lighthouse 灯台		
	名所旧跡		**City Maps** 市街図		
	Hot Spring (Spa) 温泉		City Office 市役所		Post Office 郵便局
	Shintō Shrine (*Jinja,gū*) 神社		Ward Office 区役所		Hospital 病院
	Buddhist Temple (*-ji,-in*) 寺院		Government Office 官公庁		School 学校
	Church, Cathedral 教会		Embassy 外国公館		Factory 工場

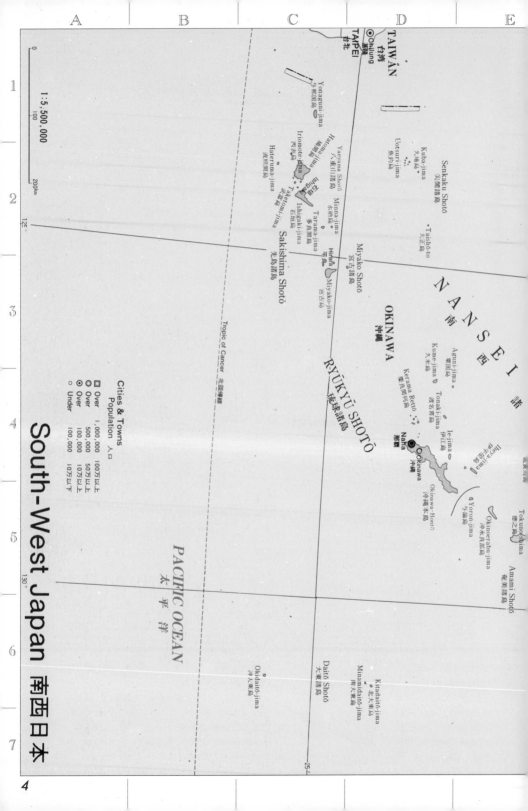

1

2

3

4

5

6

7

TAIWAN
台湾

◎Chilung
基隆

TAIPEI
台北

1:5,500,000

0
100
200km

125°

130°

25°

Yonaguni-jima
与那国島

Yaeyama Shotō
八重山諸島

Iriomote-jima
西表島

Hateruma-jima
波照間島

Hatoma-jima
鳩間島

Kohama-jima
小浜島

Taketomi-jima
竹富島

Ishigaki-jima
石垣島

Kuba-jima
久場島

Uotsuri-jima
魚釣島

Senkaku Shotō
尖閣諸島

Taishō-tō
大正島

Minna-jima
水納島

Tarama-jima
多良間島

Hirara
平良

Miyako-jima
宮古島

Miyako Shotō
宮古諸島

Sakishima Shotō
先島諸島

N A N S E I
南西

Aguni-jima
粟国島

Kume-jima
久米島

Kerama Rettō
慶良間列島

Tonaki-jima
渡名喜島

Ie-jima
伊江島

Iheya-jima
伊平屋島

OKINAWA
沖縄

◉Okinawa
沖縄

Naha
那覇

Okinawa-Hontō
沖縄本島

Yoron-jima
与論島

RYŪKYŪ SHOTŌ
流球諸島

Okinoerabu-jima
沖永良部島

Tokunoshima
徳之島

Amami Shotō
奄美諸島

Daitō Shotō
大東諸島

Kitadaitō-jima
北大東島

Minamidaitō-jima
南大東島

Okidaitō-jima
沖大東島

PACIFIC OCEAN
太平洋

Tropic of Cancer
北回帰線

Cities & Towns
Population 人口

□ Over 1,000,000 100万以上
◙ Over   500,000   50万以上
◉ Over   100,000   10万以上
○ Under   100,000   10万以下

South-West Japan 南西日本

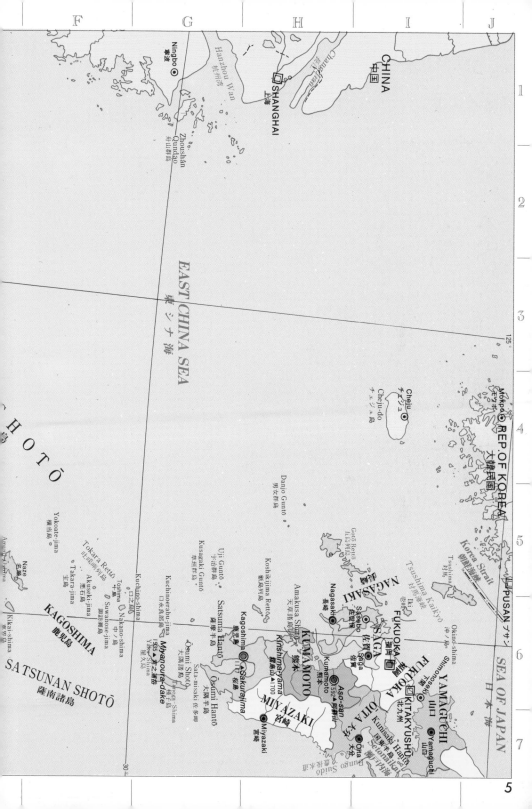

F G H I J

1

CHINA
中国

Ningbo
宁波 ⊙

SHANGHAI
上海 □

Hanzhou Wan
杭州湾

Zhoushan
Qundao
舟山群岛

2

EAST CHINA SEA

東シナ海

3

125°

Cheju
チェジュ
Cheju-do
チェジュ島

REP. OF KOREA

大韓民国

Mókpo
モクポ ⊙

4

SHOTŌ

Danjo Guntō
男女群島

5

Yokoate-jima
横当島

Naze
名瀬

Tokara Rettō
吐喇列島

Takara-jima
宝島

Akuseki-jima
悪石島

Kuchino-shima
口之島

Toshima
十島

Nakano-shima
中ノ島

Suwanose-jima
諏訪之瀬島

Kuchinoerabu-jima
口永良部島

Koshikijima Rettō
甑島列島

Uji Guntō
宇治群島

Kusagaki Guntō
草垣群島

Gotō Rettō
五島列島

Amakusa Shotō
天草諸島

Nagasaki
長崎

NAGASAKI

Sasebo
佐世保

SAGA

Saga
佐賀

Iki
壱岐

FUKUOKA

Tsushima Kaikyo
対馬海峡

Tsushima
対馬

Korea Strait
朝鮮海峡

Okino-shima
沖ノ島

Shimonoseki
下関

PUSAN
プサン

SEA OF JAPAN

日本海

KAGOSHIMA
鹿児島

SATSUNAN SHOTŌ

薩南諸島

Kikai-shima
喜界島

Satsuma Hantō
薩摩半島

Kagoshima
鹿児島

Sakurajima
桜島

Miyanoura-dake
宮之浦岳
1935 ▲ 屋久島
Yaku-Shima

Tanega-shima
種子島

Ōsumi Shotō
大隅諸島

Ōsumi Hantō
大隅半島

Sata-misaki 佐多岬

Kirishimayama
霧島山 ▲1700

KUMAMOTO

Kumamoto
熊本

Aso-san
▲阿蘇山

MINYAZAKI

Miyazaki
宮崎

ŌITA
大分

Ōta
大分

FUKUOKA
福岡 □

Kitakyūshū
北九州

KITAKYŪSHŪ

YAMAGUCHI

Yamaguchi
山口

Kunisaki Hantō
国東半島

Hachō
八丁

Shikoku Hantō

Bungo Suidō
豊後水道

30°

5

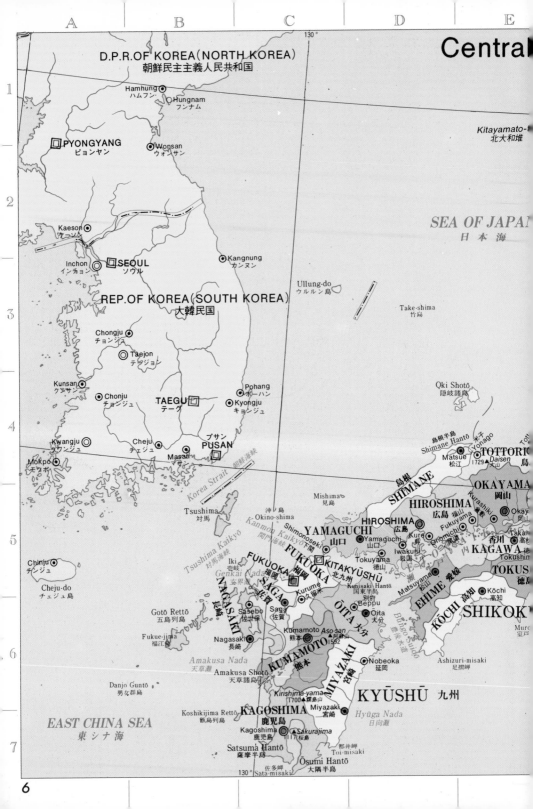

Central

D.P.R.OF KOREA (NORTH KOREA)
朝鮮民主主義人民共和国

Hamhung
ハムフン
Hungnam
フンナム

□PYONGYANG
ピョンヤン
Wonsan
ウォンサン

Kitayamato-
北大和堆

SEA OF JAPAN
日本海

Kaeson
ケエソン

Inchon
インチョン
□SEOUL
ソウル

Kangnung
カンヌン

REP.OF KOREA (SOUTH KOREA)
大韓民国

Ullung-do
ウルルン島

Take-shima
竹島

Chongju
チョンジュ

Taejon
テジョン

Kunsan
クサン

Chonju
チョンジュ

TAEGU
テーグ

Pohang
ポーハン
Kyongju
キョンジュ

Oki Shotō
隠岐諸島

Kwangju
クァンジュ

Cheju
チェジュ

プサン
PUSAN

Mokpo
モクポ

Masan
マサン

島根半島
Shimane Hantō
米子
Yonago
Tottori
TOTTORI
鳥取

Matsue
松江
Daisen
1729 大山

島根
OKAYAMA
岡山

Mishima
見島

SHIMANE

Okay
岡

Chinju
チンジュ

Tsushima
対馬

沖ノ島
Okino-shima
Shimonoseki
下関

HIROSHIMA
広島

HIROSHIMA
広島

Fukuyama
福山

Kure
呉
Onomichi
尾道

Takah
香川
KAGAWA
高松

Cheju-do
チェジュ島

Iki
壱岐

YAMAGUCHI
山口

Yamaguchi
山口

Tokuyama
徳山

Iwakuni
岩国

Matsuyama
松山

TOKUS
徳

FUKUOKA
福岡

KITAKYŪSHŪ
北九州

Kunisaki Hantō
国東半島

EHIME
愛媛

Kōchi
高知

Chinju
チンジュ

Gotō Rettō
五島列島

FUKUOKA
福岡

SAGA
佐賀

Saga
佐賀

Kurume
久留米

ŌITA
大分

Beppu
別府

KŌCHI
高知

SHIKOK

Fukue-jima
福江島

Sasebo
佐世保

NAGASAKI
長崎

Oita
大分

Ashizuri-misaki
足摺岬

Nagasaki
長崎

Kumamoto
熊本

Aso-san
阿蘇山
1592

KUMAMOTO
熊本

MIYAZAKI
宮崎

Nobeoka
延岡

Amakusa Nada
天草灘

Amakusa Shotō
天草諸島

Danjo Guntō
男女群島

Kirishima-yama
1700 霧島山

Miyazaki
宮崎

KYŪSHŪ 九州

Hyūga Nada
日向灘

EAST CHINA SEA
東シナ海

Koshikijima Rettō
甑島列島

KAGOSHIMA
鹿児島

Kagoshima
鹿児島
Sakurajima
1117 桜島

都井岬
Toi-misaki

Satsuma Hantō
薩摩半島

Ōsumi Hantō
大隅半島

130°
佐多岬
Sata-misaki

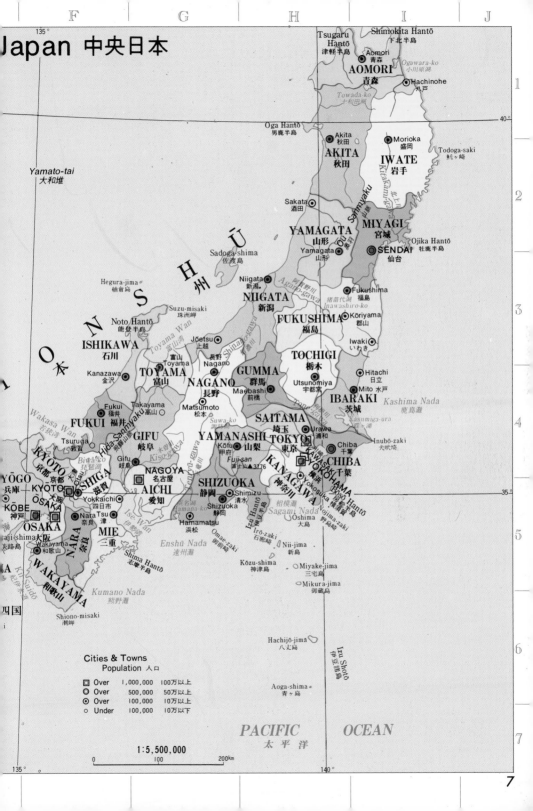

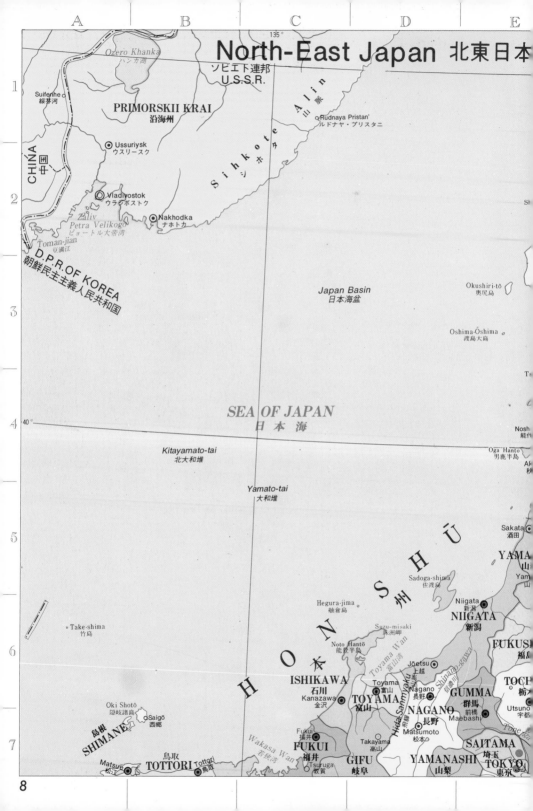

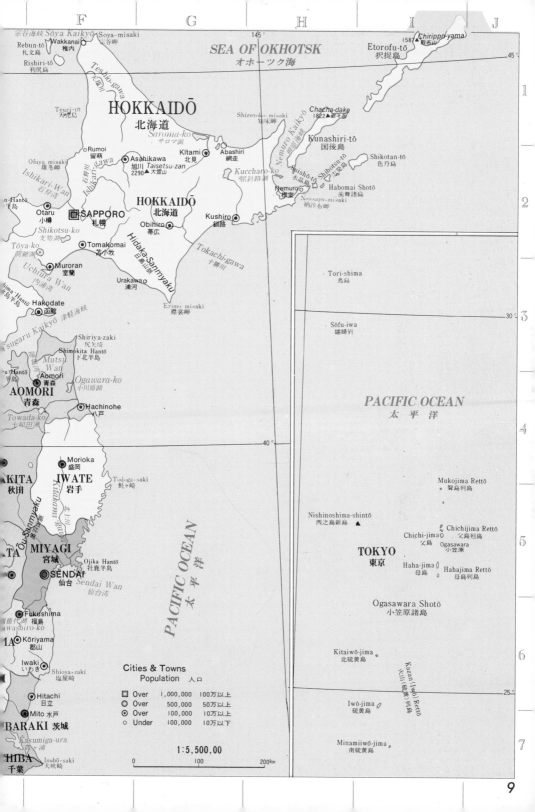

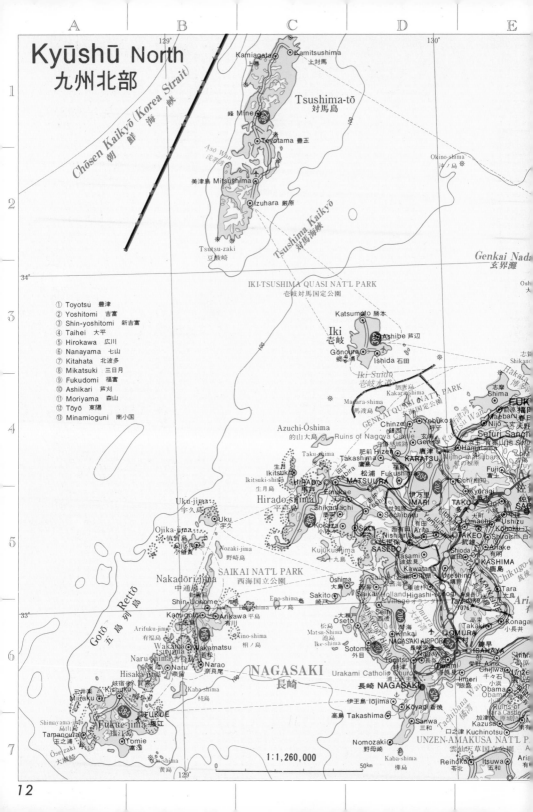

Kyūshū North
九州北部

Chōsen Kaikyō (Korea Strait)
朝鮮海峡

Kamiagata 上県　●Kamitsushima 土対馬

Tsushima-tō
対馬島

峰 Mine

Toyotama 豊玉

Aso Wan
浅海湾

Okino-shima
沖ノ島

美津島 Mitsushima

34°

Izuhara 巌原

Genkai Nada
玄界灘

Tsutsu-zaki
豆酘崎

Tsushima Kaikyō 対馬海峡

① Toyotsu 豊津
② Yoshitomi 吉富
③ Shin-yoshitomi 新吉富
④ Taihei 大平
⑤ Hirokawa 広川
⑥ Nanayama 七山
⑦ Kitahata 北波多
⑧ Mikatsuki 三日月
⑨ Fukudomi 福富
⑩ Ashikari 芦刈
⑪ Moriyama 森山
⑫ Tōyō 東陽
⑬ Minamioguni 南小国

IKI-TSUSHIMA QUASI NAT'L PARK
壱岐対馬国定公園

Katsumoto 勝本

Iki
壱岐

Ashibe 芦辺

Gonoura
郷ノ浦

Ishida 石田

Iki-Suidō
壱岐水道

Shikano-
志賀

Hakata
博多
Shima

FUK

Maebaru
前原

Sefuri Sanchi
脊振山地

Azuchi-Ōshima
的山大島

Chinzei 鎮西

GENKAI QUASI NAT'L PARK

Yobuko 呼子

Genkai 玄海

Nijo 二丈

肥前 Hizen

Ruins of Nagoya Castle

Nijo-matsubara

Hamatama

Fuji
富士

Taku-shima

KARATSU

Furuyu

Takashima 鷹島

IMARI

Ochi 相知

Kyuragi

Hirado-shima
平戸島

MATSUURA
松浦

生月
Ikitsuki
Ikitsuki-shima
生月島

Emukae

Saza

Nishiarita

Arita

Ōmachi

TAKU

SA

Kohoku

Ushiku

Shiroishi 白

Hirado
平戸

Shikamachi

Sechibaru

Uku-jima
宇久島

Kosaki

西有田

TAKEO
武雄

Shioda

KASHIMA
鹿島

Uku
宇久

Hasami
波佐見

Anrake

Ojika-jima
小値賀

Nozaki-jima
野崎島

Kujukushima
九十九島

SASEBO

Chikugo-

Tara
太良

Kawatana

Higashi-sonogi

Ari

Nakadōri-jima
中通島

SAIKAI NAT'L PARK
西海国立公園

Ōshima
大島

Eno-shima

Saikai

Holland
Village

Tara-dake
多良岳
1076

33°

Kamigotō
上五島

Arikawa 有川

Shin-Uonome

Sakito
崎戸

Seihi

OMURA
大村

Takaki

Konaga

Oseto

Matsu-shima
松島

ISAHAYA

小長井

Arifuku-jima
有福島

Aino-shima

NAGASAKI AIRPORT
長崎空港

Unze

Wakamatsu 若松

Ike-shima

Sotome

Togitsu

Imari

Kazusa

Naru-shima

Natu

Kaba-shima

NAGASAKI
長崎

Urakami Catholic Church

NAGASAKI
長崎

Hisaka-jima

Kishuku

Miiraku
三井楽

Tamanoura
玉之浦

Gotō Rettō
五島列島

Kaba-shima

Koyagi 香焼

Sanwa

Fukue-jima
福江島

FUKUE
福江

Koyagi

Iōjima 伊王島

Takashima 高島

Kuchinotsu

Shimayama-jima

Ōsezaki
大瀬崎

Tomie
富江

Nomozaki
野母崎

Kaba-shima

UNZEN-AMAKUSA NAT'L P.
雲仙天草国立公園

Reihoku

Itsuwa

1:1,260,000

0　　　　　　　50km

129°

12

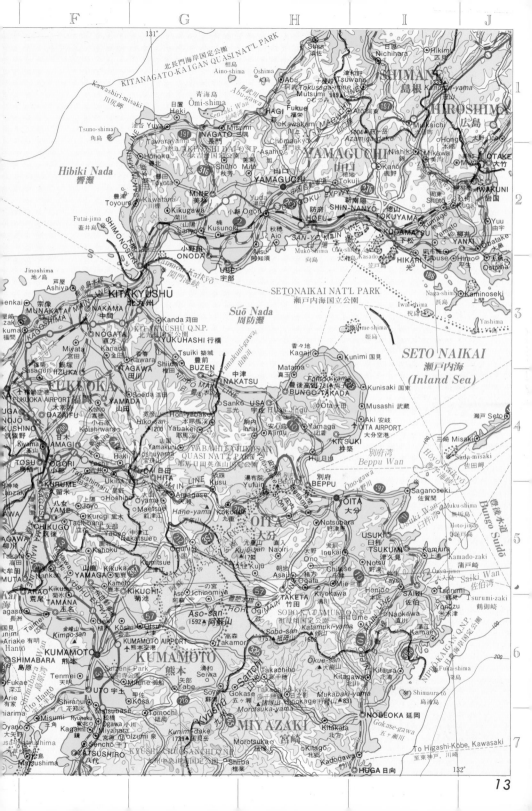

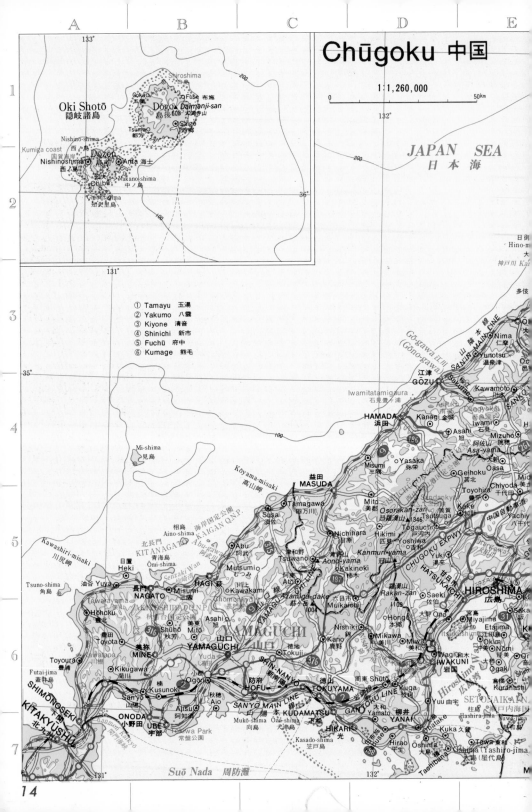

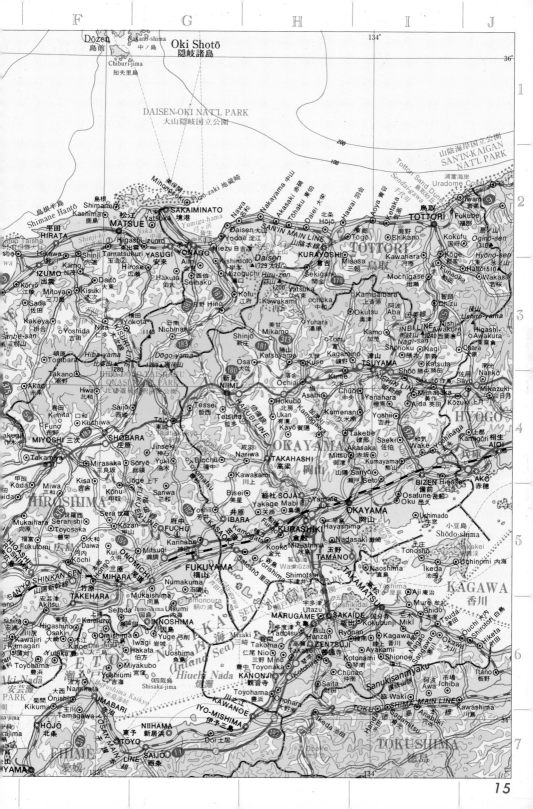

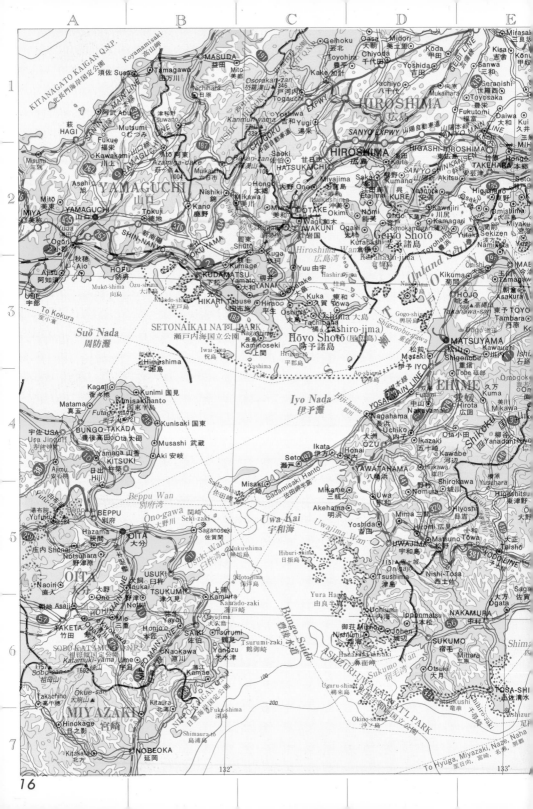

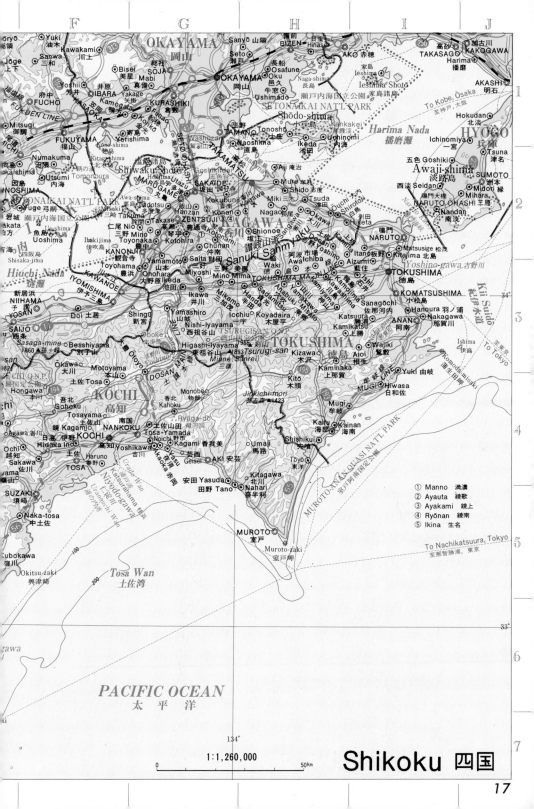

Shikoku 四国

1:1,260,000

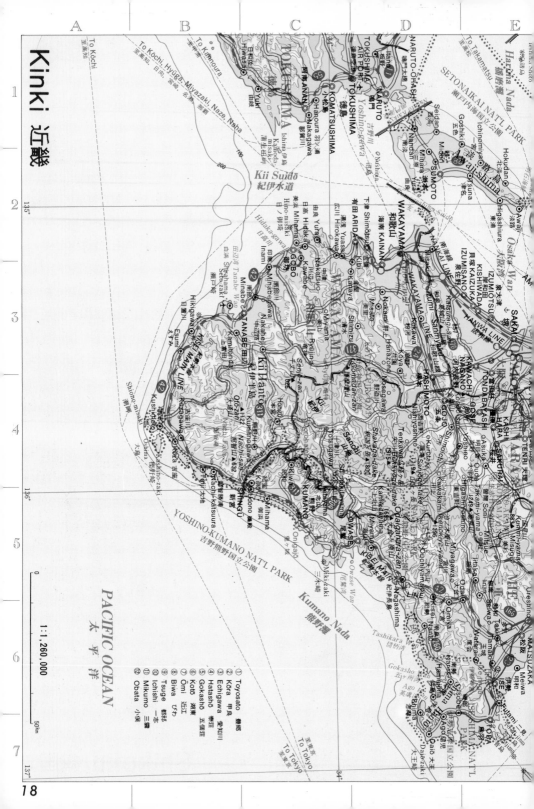

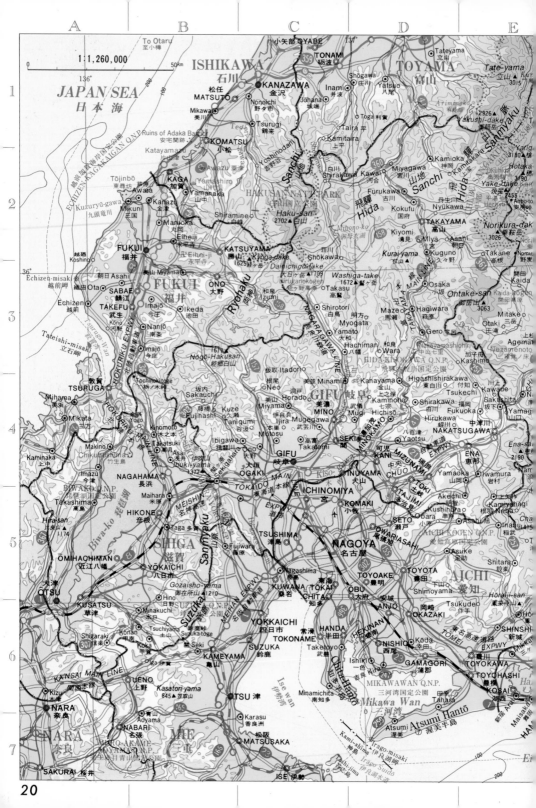

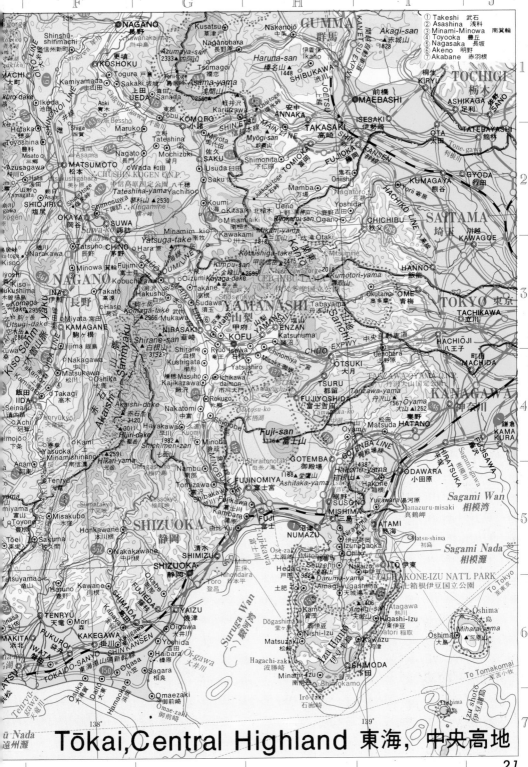

Tōkai, Central Highland 東海，中央高地

Hokuriku 北陸

1:1,260,000

0   50km

① Shimo 下
② Kamishihi 上志比
③ Sakae 栄
④ Takayama 高山
⑤ Horigane 堀金
⑥ Matsukawa 松川

JAPAN SEA
日本海

137°

136°

Hegura-jima
舳倉島

Nanatsu-shima
七ツ島

NOTOHANTŌ QUASI NAT'L PARK
能登半島国定公園

Suzu-misaki
珠洲岬
(Rokkō-zaki)
(禄剛崎)

Sosogi Coast
曽々木海岸

WAJIMA
輪島

Kōshū-zan
高洲山
567

Yanagida
柳田

SUZU
珠洲

Saruyama-misaki
猿山岬

Noto Hantō
能登半島

Uchiura
内浦

Monzen
門前

Anamizu
穴水

Noto
能都

Tsukumo-Wan
九十九湾

Ama-zaki
海士崎

Togi
富来

Nakajima
中島

Noto-jima
能登島

Notojima
能登島

37°

Noto-kongō
能登金剛

七尾湾
Nanao Wan

Wakura
和倉

Tatsuruhama
田鶴浜

Shika
志賀

Tonya
富屋

NANAO
七尾

Rokusei
鹿西

Kashima
鹿島

羽咋 HAKUI
Chirihama 千里浜

Sekido-san
石動山

Toyama Wan
富山湾

Kurobe-gawa
黒部川

Oyashirazu
親不知

千里浜 Chirihama

Shio
志雄

HIMI
氷見

ISHIKAWA
石川

高松 Takamatsu
637

Hōdatsu-san
宝達山

Oshimizu
押水

新湊
SHINMINATO

KUROBE
黒部

Unazuki
宇奈月

七塚 Nanatsuka
宇ノ気 Unoke

Tsubata
津幡

Fukuoka
福岡

TAKAOKA
高岡

Daimon
大門

Kosugi
小杉

UOZU
魚津

NAMERIKAWA
滑川

Shiroma
白馬

Uchinada
内灘

HOKURIKU MAIN LINE

OYABE
小矢部

Fuchū
婦中

TOYAMA
富山

Kamiichi
上市

Kekachi-yama
毛勝山
2414

Sai-gawa
犀川
Kahoku-gata
河北潟

Kenroku-en Garden
兼六園

KANAZAWA
金沢

TONAMI
砺波

Yamada
山田

Oyama
大山

Tateyama
立山

Tate-yama
立山

美川 Mikawa

Nonoichi
野々市

Fukumitsu
福光

Inami
井波

Shōgawa
庄川

Yatsuo
八尾

Hosoiri
細入

TOYAMA
富山

根上 Neagari

Terai
寺井

Kawakita
川北

Yuwaku
湯涌

Johana
城端

Inokuchi
井口

Osawano
大沢野

Tsurugi
鶴来

KOMATSU
小松

Tatsunokuchi
辰口

Kawachi
河内

Tairadate
平館

Toga
利賀

Kamitaira
上平

TOYAMA
富山

Katayamazu
片山津

Torigoe
鳥越

CHŪBUSANGAKU
NAT'L PARK
中部山岳国立公園

Yakushi-dake
薬師岳
2926

subakuro-da

KAGA
加賀

Yamashiro
山代

Yoshinodani
吉野谷

Okuchi
尾口

Shirakawa
白川

Kawai
河合

Miyagawa
宮川

Kamioka
神岡

Yariga-take
槍ヶ岳
3180

Hota

東尋坊
三国 Mikuni

Awazu
粟津

Yamanaka
山中

Hotaka-dake
穂高岳
3190

Toyoshi

Kuzuryū-gawa
九頭竜川

Kanazu
金津

Maruoka
丸岡

Okuni
尾口

Kokufu
国府

Kamitakara
上宝

Yake-dake
焼岳

越廼
Koshino

坂井 Sakai

Matsuoka
松岡

Shiramine
白峰

Haku-san
白山 2702

白川
Shirakawa

Furukawa
古川

Kamikochi
上高地

Mi

Shimizu
清水

FUKUI
福井

Eiheiji
永平寺

Asahi
朝日

GIFU
岐阜

Kokufu
国府

TAKAYAMA
高山

Norikura-dake
乗鞍岳
3026

Azusagawa

織田 Ota

Miyama
美山

KATSUYAMA
勝山

Kyōga-take
経ヶ岳
1625

Hida
飛騨

Kiyomi
清見

Miya

Asahi
朝日

Miyazaki
宮崎

SABAE
鯖江

ONO
大野

Shokawa
荘川

Shimo

Nyukawa
丹生川

Kamioka

SHIO
塩尻

22

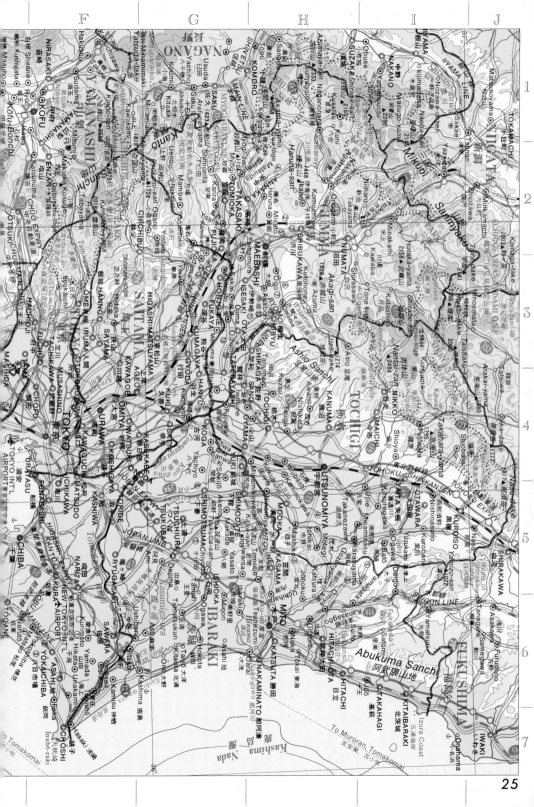

Tōhoku South 東北南部

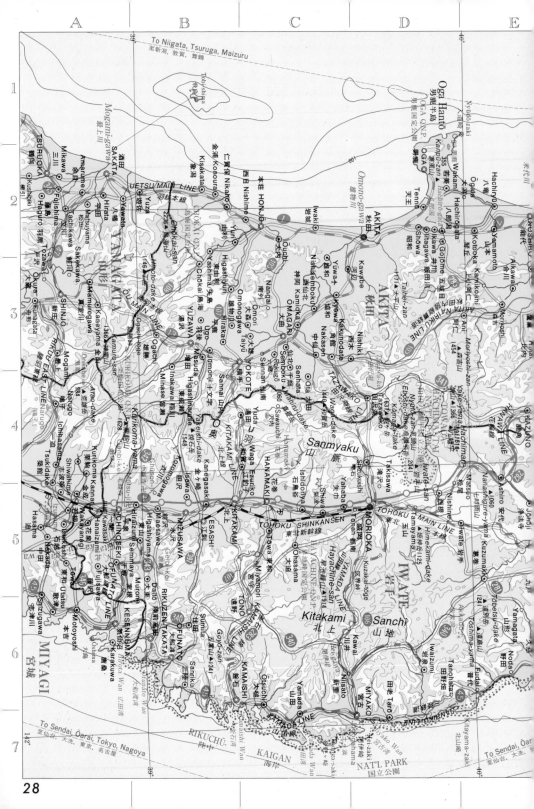

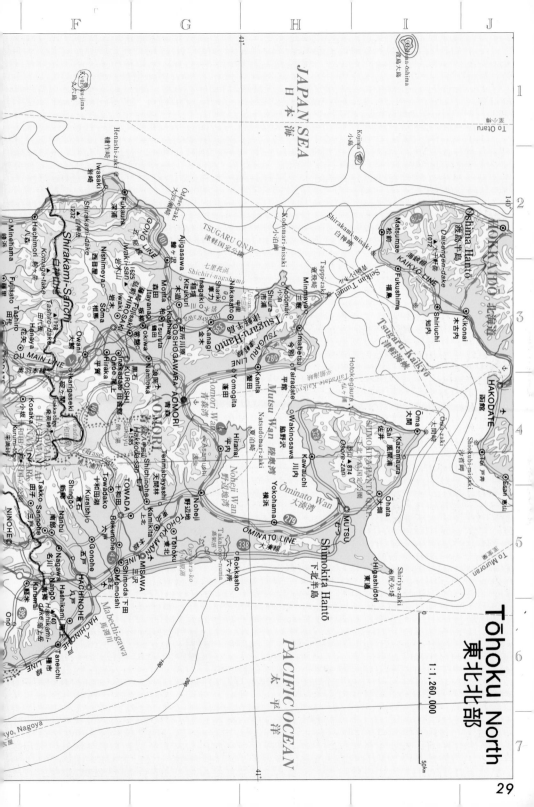

140°

141°

To Rishiri, Rebun
至利尻, 礼文

Ishikari Wan
石狩湾

Atsuta
厚田

石狩川
Ishikari-gawa

JAPAN SEA
日 本 海

Shakotan-misaki
積丹岬

Kamui-misaki
神威岬

Shakotan 積丹
Furubira 古平

Takashima-misaki
高島岬

Ishikari
石狩

OKADAMA

Yobetsu-dake
余別岳
1298

Kamoenai
神恵内

Yoichi
余市

Niki
仁木

一木

OTARU
小樽

SASSON EXPWY
札幌自動車道

SAPPORO
札幌

Tomari
泊

NISEKO-SHAKOTAN-OTARUKAIGAN
QUASI NAT'L PARK
ニセコ積丹小樽海岸国定公園

Akaigawa
赤井川

Yoichi-dake
余市岳
1488

Jozanke
定山渓

43°

Iwanai
岩内

Kyowa
共和

SHIRIBESHI
後志

Kutchan
倶知安

Muine-zan
無意根山
1461

Sapporo-dake
札幌岳
1294

Nisekoan-nupuri
ニセコアンヌプリ
雷雷山 1309
Raiden-yama

Niseko
ニセコ

Kyōgoku
京極

Kimobetsu
喜茂別

Eniwa-dake
恵庭岳
1320

IBURI
胆振

Benkei-misaki
弁慶岬

Rankoshi
蘭越

Yotei-zan
羊蹄山
1893

Kimobetsu

SHIKOTSU-TOYA
NAT'L PARK
支笏洞爺国立公園

Shikotsu-ko
支笏湖

Tacumae
樽前

Suttsu
寿都

Makkario
真狩

Rusutsu
留寿都

Otaki 大滝
1038

Fuppesi
Fupushi

To Naoetsu
至直江津

Shimamaki
島牧

Konbu-dake
昆布岳
1045

Toya
洞爺

Tōya-ko
洞爺湖

Orofure-yama
オロフレ山
1231

Kariba-yama
狩場山
1520

Kuromatsunai
黒松内

Rebunge-tōge
礼文華峠

Toyoura
豊浦

Usu-zan
有珠山

Motsuta-misaki
茂津多岬

Oshamanbe
長万部

Abuta
虻田

Sobetsu
壮瞥

Showa Shizan
昭和新山

Noboribetsu
登別

DOO EXPWY
道央自動車道

NOBORIBETSU
登別

MAIN LINE

Setana
瀬棚

Imagane
今金

DATE
伊達

Uchiura Wan
内浦湾

MURORAN
室蘭

Kitahiyama
北桧山

Chikyū-misaki
チキウ岬

Inaho-misaki
稲穂岬

Taisei
大成

Yurappu-dake
遊楽部岳
1276

Yakumo
八雲

Okushiri
奥尻

Okushi-tō
奥尻島

Kumaishi
熊石

Mori
森

Sawara 砂原

Shikabe
鹿部

42°

Aonae-misaki
青苗岬

OSHIMA
渡島

Komaga-take
133A 駒ヶ岳

Minamikayabe
南茅部

Otobe
乙部

ONUMA Q.N.P.
大沼国定公園

Yokotsu-dake
横津岳
1167

Kameda Hantō
亀田半島

Esashi
江差

Assabu
厚沢部

Ōno
大野

Nanae
七飯

Todohokke
椴法華

Kaminokuni
上ノ国

Kamiiso
上磯

HAKODATE AIRPORT
函館空港

Esan
恵山

Esan-misaki
恵山岬

Toi 戸井

HAKODATE
函館

Kikonai
木古内

Shirakubi-misaki
汐首岬

Daisengen-dake
大千軒岳
1072

Shiriuchi
知内

Ōma-zaki
大間崎

Oshima-ōshima
渡島大島

Fukushima
福島

Matsumae
松前

Shirakami-misaki
白神岬

Ōma
大間

To Aomori
至青森

AOMORI
青森

Kojima
小島

Tsugaru Kaikyo
津軽海峡

30

Hokkaidō South-West 北海道南西部

31

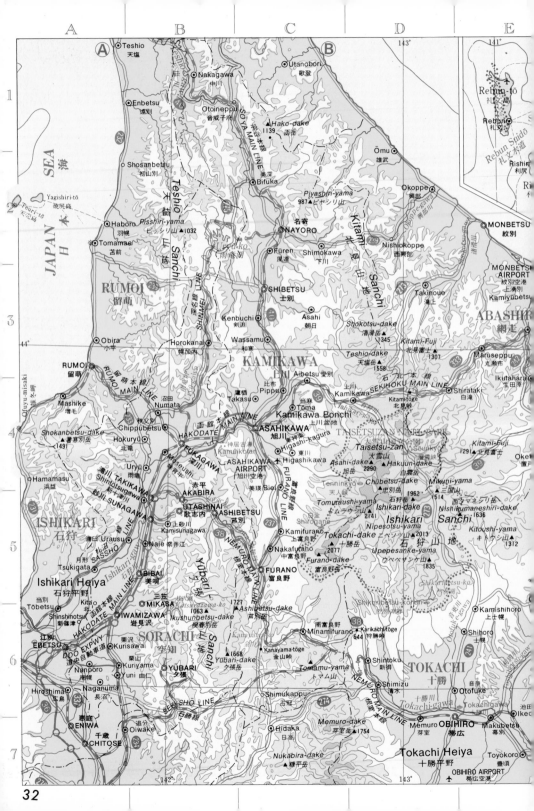

Hokkaidō North-East
北海道北東部

SEA OF OKHOTSK
オホーツク海

F G H I J

Soya-misaki
宗谷岬

Noshappu-misaki
野寒布岬

WAKKANAI
稚内

WAKKANAI AIRPORT
稚内空港

Sarufutsu
猿払

RISHIRI-REBUN-
BETSU NAT'L PARK
利尻礼文サロベツ国立公園

Higashi-Rishiri
東利尻
Rishiri-san
利尻山

Sarobetsu
サロベツ

SŌYA
宗谷

Poroshiri-yama
427▲ポロシリ山

Kucchauro-ko
クッチャロ湖

Hamatonbetsu
浜頓別

Toyotomi 豊富

Horonobe
幌延

Nakatonbetsu
中頓別

A   142°   **B**

Panke-nui
パンケ沼

ABASHIRI Q.N.P.
網走国定公園

Shiretoko-misaki
知床岬

Saroma-ko
サロマ湖

Notoro-misaki
能取岬

Shiretoko-dake
▲知床岳

SHIRETOKO NAT'L PARK
知床国立公園

Iwo-yama
▲1563 硫黄山

Tokoro
常呂

Notoro-ko
能取湖

200

Utoro
ウトロ

Rausu-dake
▲1661 羅臼岳

Rausu
羅臼

Nemuro Kaikyō
根室海峡

Kunashiri-tō
国後島

佐呂間
Saroma
238

ABASHIRI
網走

Abashiri-ko
網走湖

Gensei Kaen
原生花園

100

Onnebetsu-dake
▲遠音別岳
1331

Tentosan
天都山

MEMANBETSU
AIRPORT
女満別空港

Tōfutsu-ko
濤沸湖

Shari
斜里

端野 Tanno
Memanbetsu
女満別

Higashimokoto
東藻琴

Koshimizu 小清水

Kiyosato
清里

Unabetsu-dake
▲海別岳
1419

Keramui-zaki
ケラムイ崎

Nokke Suidō
野付水道

Shibetsu
標津

KITAMI
北見
241

Bihoro
美幌

Shari-dake
斜里岳▲1545

Mokoto-yama
藻琴山
1000

Kawayu
川湯

Shibetsu-dake
▲標津岳
1061

NAKASHIBETSU AIRPORT
中標津空港

Nokke-saki
野付崎

Kunneppu
訓子府

Tsubetsu
津別

Bihoro-toge
美幌峠

Masshū-ko
摩周湖

Nakashibetsu
中標津

Nossapu-misaki
納沙布岬

Atosa Nupuri
アトサヌプリ

KamuiNupuri
カムイヌプリ

Teshikaga

AKAN NAT'L PARK
阿寒国立公園

Oakan-dake
▲雄阿寒岳
1371

Teshikaga
弟子屈

NEMURO
根室

Nemuro Wan
根室湾

Nemuro Hanto
根室半島

Rikubetsu
陸別

Meakan-dake
▲1499 雌阿寒岳

Nishibetsu-gawa
西別川

Betsukai
別海

NEMURO
根室

Akan-Fuji
阿寒富士

241

KUSHIRO
釧路

Shibecha
標茶

Konsen Daichi
根釧台地

Furen-ko
風蓮湖

Fure-gawa
風蓮川

Ochiishi-misaki
落石岬

KUSHIRO-SHITSUGEN
NAT'L PARK
釧路湿原国立公園

Akan
阿寒

Hamanaka Wan
浜中湾

本別

KUSHIRO AIRPORT
釧路空港

Shiranuka
白糠

Kushiro
釧路

NEMURO MAIN LINE
根室本線

Akkeshi-ko
厚岸湖

Hamanaka
浜中

Tōbutsu-misaki
湯沸岬

KUSHIRO
釧路

Shiranuka Kyūryō
白糠丘陵

Onbetsu
音別

Akkeshi
厚岸

Shirira-misaki
尻羽岬

Akkeshi Wan
厚岸湾

43°

Urahoro
浦幌

*To TOKYO
東京へ*

144°

145°

PACIFIC OCEAN
太平洋

1:1,260,000

0   50km

33

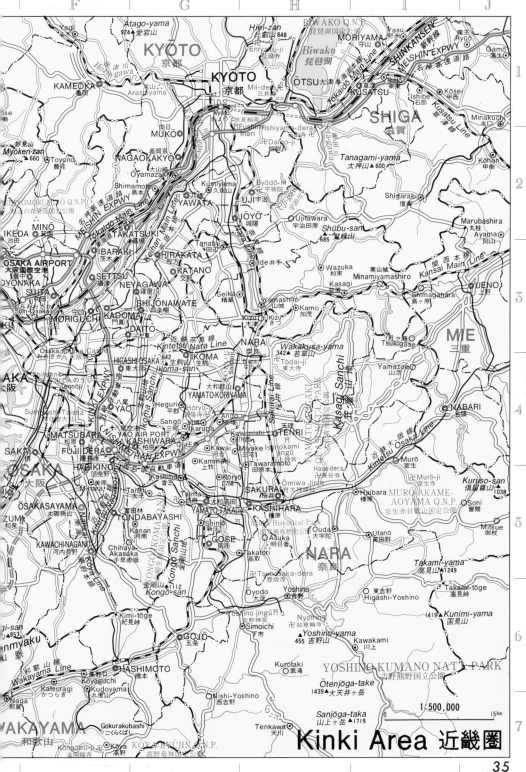

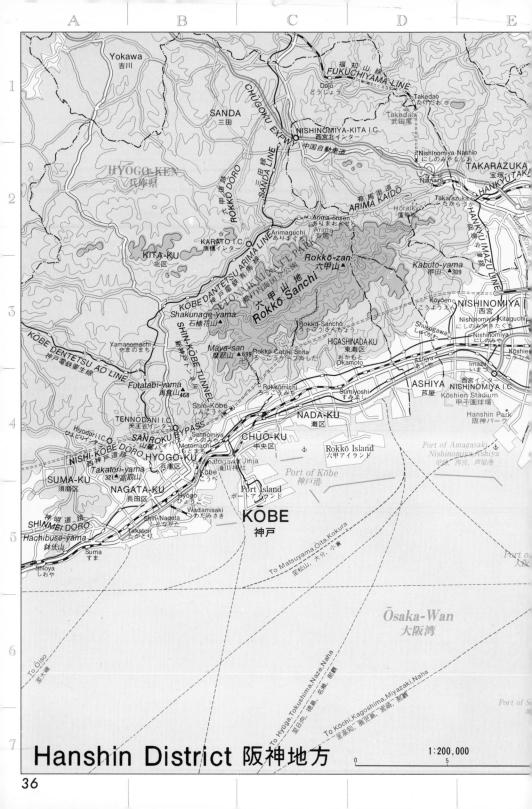

Hanshin District 阪神地方

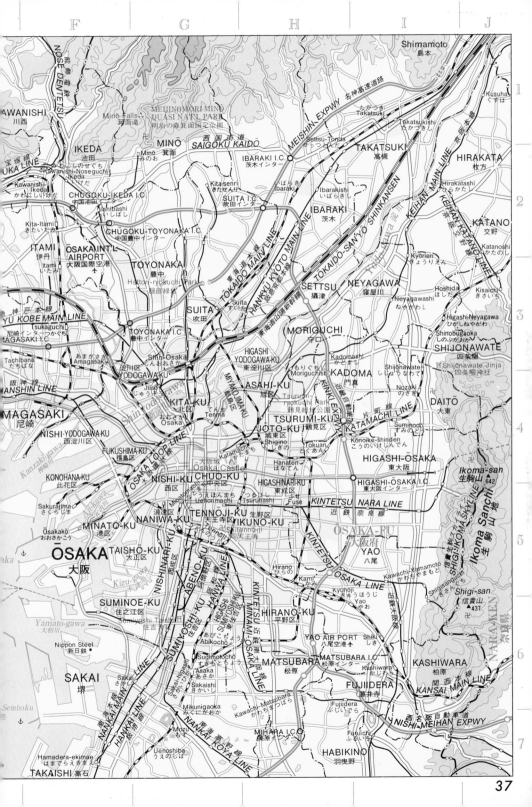

Chūkyō (Nagoya) Area 中京（名古屋）圏

38

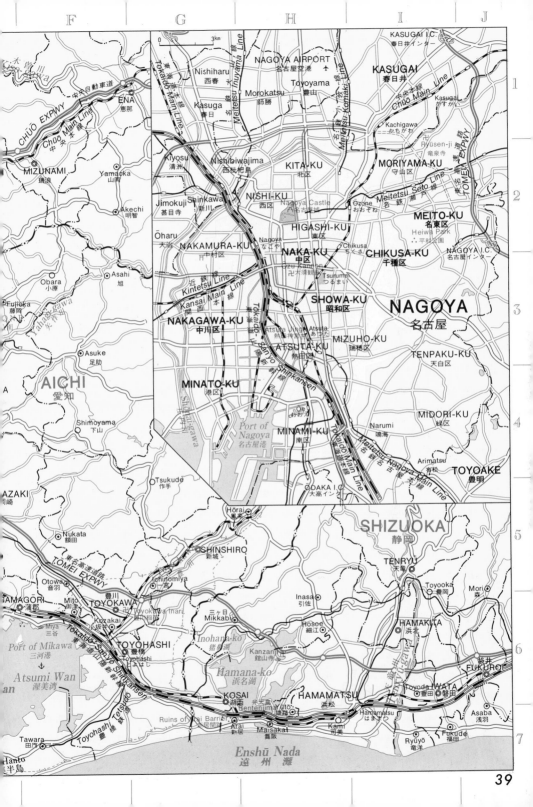

1 : 500 000

0 5 10 15Km

C

Nagatoro 長瀞
Yori 寄居
GYODA 行田
KAZO 加須
Kisai 騎西
Shōbu 菖蒲

Nagatoro 長瀞
Minano 皆野
Higashi-chichibu 東秩父
Ogawa 小川
Namegawa 滑川
Fukiage 吹上
KŌNOSU 鴻巣
KITAMOTO 北本
Ina 伊奈

Yoshida 吉田
HIGASHI-MATSUYAMA 東松山

Ryōkami 両神
Ogano 小鹿野
Yokoze 横瀬
Tokigawa 都幾川
Ranzan 嵐山
Tamagawa 玉川
Hatoyama 鳩山
OKEGAWA 桶川
AGEO 上尾

CHICHIBU 秩父
Mitsumineguchi 三峰口
SAITAMA-KEN 埼玉県
Kawajima 川島
Omiya 大宮

Ōtaki 大滝
Shōmaru-tōge 正丸峠
Ogose 越生
SAKADO 坂戸
Kawagoe 川越

Mitsumine-san 三峰山
Bukō-san 武甲山
Moroyama 毛呂山
Tsurugashima 鶴ヶ島
KAWAGOE 川越
KANETSU EXPWY
KAMI-FUKUOKA 上福岡
YONO 与野

CHICHIBU-TAMA NAT'L PARK 秩父多摩国立公園
Naguri 名栗
Hidaka 日高
SAYAMA 狭山
FUJIMI 富士見
SHIKI 志木

Kumotori-yama 雲取山 2017
Seibu Chichibu Line 西武秩父線
HANNO 飯能
IRUMA 入間
Miyoshi 三芳

Tabayama 丹波山
Ōme Line 青梅線
Mizuho 瑞穂
MUSASHI-MURAYAMA 武蔵村山
TOKOROZAWA 所沢
NIIZA 新座
ASAKA 朝霞

Kosuge 小菅
Okutama 奥多摩
ŌME 青梅
Hamura 羽村
HIGASHI-YAMATO 東大和
KIYOSE 清瀬
HIGASHI-KURUME 東久留米
WAKŌ 和光

Ōtake-san 大岳山 1266
Hinode 日の出
AKIGAWA 秋川
FUSSA 福生
YOKOTA 横田
HIGASHI-MURAYAMA 東村山
HŌYA 保谷

Hinohara 檜原
Itsukaichi 五日市
AKISHIMA 昭島
KODAIRA 小平
MUSASHINO 武蔵野

MEIJI-NO-MORI-TAKAO QUASI-NAT'L PARK 明治の森高尾国定公園
HACHIŌJI 八王子
TACHIKAWA 立川
KUNITACHI 国立
KOKUBUNJI 国分寺
KOGANEI 小金井
MITAKA 三鷹

YAMANASHI-KEN 山梨県
Ogiyama 扇山 1138
Uenohara 上野原
Sagamiko 相模湖
CHŪŌ EXPWY
FUCHŪ 府中
CHŌFU 調布

Chūō Honsen 中央本線
Fujino 藤野
Takao-san 高尾山 599
TAMA 多摩
INAGI 稲城
Odakyū Line 小田急線
KOMAE 狛江

ŌTSUKI 大月
Sagami-ko 相模湖
Shiroyama 城山
TAMA NEW TOWN 多摩ニュータウン
CHŌFU 調布

Akiyama 秋山
Tsukui 津久井
Shiroyama 城山
MACHIDA 町田
KOHOKU NEW TOWN 港北ニュータウン

TSURU 都留
Dōshi 道志
Aikawa 愛川
SAGAMIHARA 相模原
Yokohama Line 横浜線
Shin-Yokohama 新横浜

Tanzawa-yama 丹沢山 1567
Kiyokawa 清川
ZAMA 座間
YAMATO 大和
Nampu Line

TANZAWA-ŌYAMA QUASI-NAT'L PARK 丹沢大山国定公園
Oyama 大山 1252
ATSUGI 厚木
AYASE 綾瀬
Tōkaidō Shinkansen 東海道新幹線

KANAGAWA-KEN 神奈川県
ISEHARA 伊勢原
EBINA 海老名
KŌMEI EXPWY

FUJI-HAKONE-IZU NAT'L PARK 富士箱根伊豆国立公園
Oyama 小山
HADANO 秦野
Samukawa 寒川
FUJISAWA 藤沢

GOTENBA 御殿場
Matsuda 松田
Odakyū Line 小田急線
HIRATSUKA 平塚
Ōfuna 大船

Gotenba Line 御殿場線
Yamakita 山北
Kaisei 開成
Nakai 中井
Ōi 大井
CHIGASAKI 茅ヶ崎
KAMAKURA 鎌倉

MINAMI-ASHIGARA 南足柄
Nakai 中井
HIRATSUKA 平塚
Enoshima 江ノ島

Oyama 小山
Ninomiya 二宮
Ōiso 大磯
ZUSHI 逗子

Hakone-yama 箱根山 1438
Kōzu 国府津
ODAWARA 小田原
Sagami Wan (Bay) 相模湾
Hayama 葉山

Hakone 箱根

40

Miura

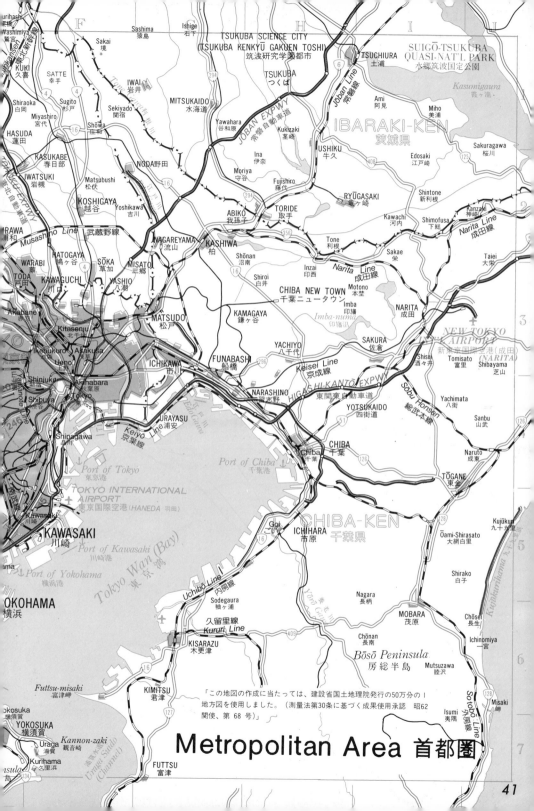

Metropolitan Area 首都圏

41

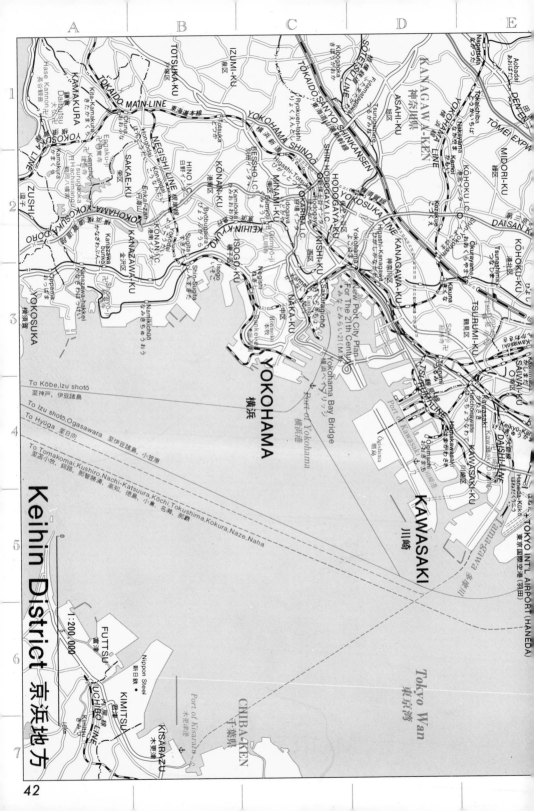

Keihin District 京浜地方

YOKOHAMA 横浜

KAWASAKI 川崎

KANAGAWA-KEN 神奈川県

CHIBA-KEN 千葉県

Tokyo Wan 東京湾

Port of Yokohama 横浜港

Port of Kawasaki 川崎港

Port of Kisarazu 木更津港

New Port City Plan For The 21th Century みなとみらい21 (M.M.)

Yokohama Bay Bridge 横浜ベイブリッジ

TOKYO INT'L AIRPORT (HANEDA) 東京国際空港 (羽田)

TOKAIDO MAIN LINE 東海道本線

TOKAIDO SANYO SHINKANSEN 東海道・山陽新幹線

YOKOHAMA SHINDO 横浜新道

SOTETSU LINE 相鉄線

YOKOSUKA LINE 横須賀線

NEGISHI LINE 根岸線

KEIHIN-KYŪKŌ 京浜急行

YOKOHAMA-YOKOSUKA DŌRO 横浜横須賀道路

HODOGAYA I.C. 保土ヶ谷

To Kōbe,Izu shotō 至神戸、伊豆諸島

To Izu shotō,Ogasawara 至伊豆諸島、小笠原

To Hyūga 至日向

To Tomakomai,Kushiro,Nachi-Katsuura,Kōchi,Tokushima,Kokura,Naze,Naha
至苫小牧、釧路、那智勝浦、高知、徳島、小倉、名瀬、那覇

1:200,000

TOTSUKA-KU 戸塚区

IZUMI-KU 泉区

ASAHI-KU 旭区

KŌHOKU-KU 港北区

MIDORI-KU 緑区

TSURUMI-KU 鶴見区

SAIWAI-KU 幸区

KAWASAKI-KU 川崎区

SAKAE-KU 栄区

KŌNAN-KU 港南区

KANAZAWA-KU 金沢区

ISOGO-KU 磯子区

NAKA-KU 中区

MINAMI-KU 南区

NISHI-KU 西区

KAMAKURA 鎌倉

ZUSHI 逗子

YOKOSUKA 横須賀

FUTTSU 富津

KIMITSU 君津

KISARAZU 木更津

UCHIBO LINE 内房線

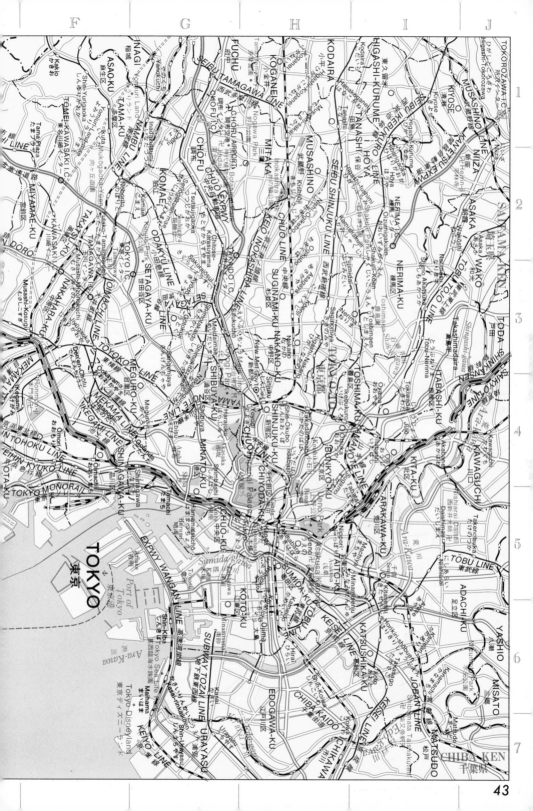

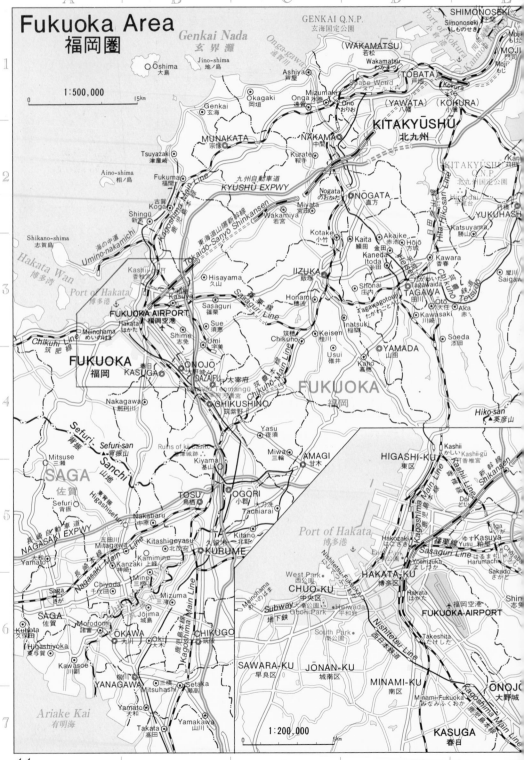

Fukuoka Area
福岡圏

1:500,000

0　　　　　　　　15km

City Maps

市街図

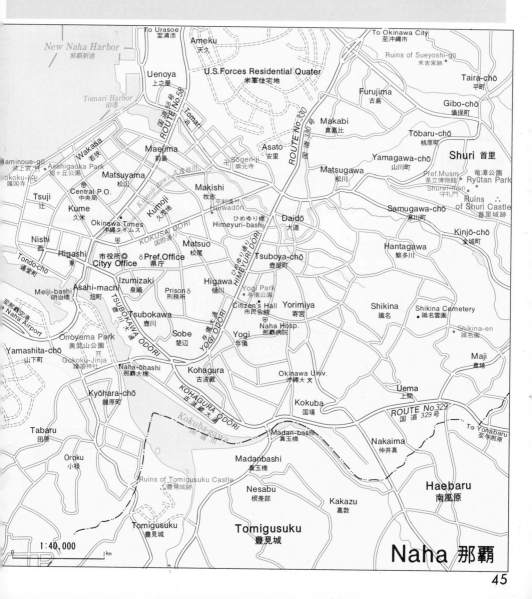

New Naha Harbor
那覇新港

To Urasoe
至浦添

Ameku
天久

To Okinawa City
至沖縄市

Ruins of Sueyoshi-gū
末吉宮跡

Tomari Harbor
泊港

Uenoya
上之屋

U.S.Forces Residential Quater
米軍住宅地

Taira-chō
平町

Furujima
古島

Gibo-chō
儀保町

Wakasa
若狭

Maejima
前島

Makabi
真嘉比

Tōbaru-chō
桃原町

Yamagawa-chō
山川町

Shuri 首里

aminoue-gū
ongū

Asato
安里

Matsugawa
松川

Pref.Musm
県立博物館

竜潭公園
Ryūtan Park

oku-gū
護国寺

Asahigaoka Park
旭ヶ丘公園

Matsuyama
松山

Sōgen-ji
崇元寺

Shurei-mon
守礼門

Ruins
of Shuri Castle
首里城跡

Tsuji
辻

Central P.O.
中央局

Makishi
牧志

平和通り
Hanwadōri

Samugawa-chō
寒川町

Kinjō-chō
金城町

Kume
久米

Kumoji
久茂地

Himeyuri-bashi
ひめゆり橋
Himeyuri-bashi

Daidō
大道

Hantagawa
繁多川

Okinawa Times
沖縄タイムス

KOKUSAI DORI
国際通り

Nishi
西

Higashi
東

Matsuo
松尾

Tsuboya-chō
壺屋町

Shikina
識名

Shikina Cemetery
識名霊園

Tondo-chō
通堂町

市役所
Cityy Office
市役所

Pref.Office
県庁

HIMEYURI DORI

Izumizaki
泉崎

Higawa
樋川

Yorimiya
寄宮

Meiji-bashi
明治橋

Asahi-machi
旭町

Prison
刑務所

Citizen's Hall
市民会館

Shikina-en
識名園

至那覇空港
Naha Airport

TSUBOKAWA ODORI

Tsubokawa
壺川

Naha Hosp.
那覇病院

Maji
真地

Onoyama Park
奥武山公園

Sobe
楚辺

Yogi
与儀

YOGI ODORI

Gokoku-Jinja
護国神社

Yamashita-chō
山下町

Naha-ōhashi
那覇大橋

Kohagura
古波蔵

Okinawa Univ.
沖縄大

Uema
上間

ROUTE No.329
国道329号

Kokuba
国場

Nakaima
仲井真

To Yonabaru
至与那原

Kyōhara-chō
鏡原町

KOHAGURA ODORI
古波蔵大通

Kokuba-kawa
国場川

Tabaru
田原

Madan-bashi
真玉橋

Haebaru
南風原

Oroku
小禄

Madanbashi
真玉橋

Ruins of Tomigusuku Castle
豊見城跡

Nesabu
根差部

Kakazu
嘉数

1:40,000

Tomigusuku
豊見城

Tomigusuku
豊見城

Naha 那覇

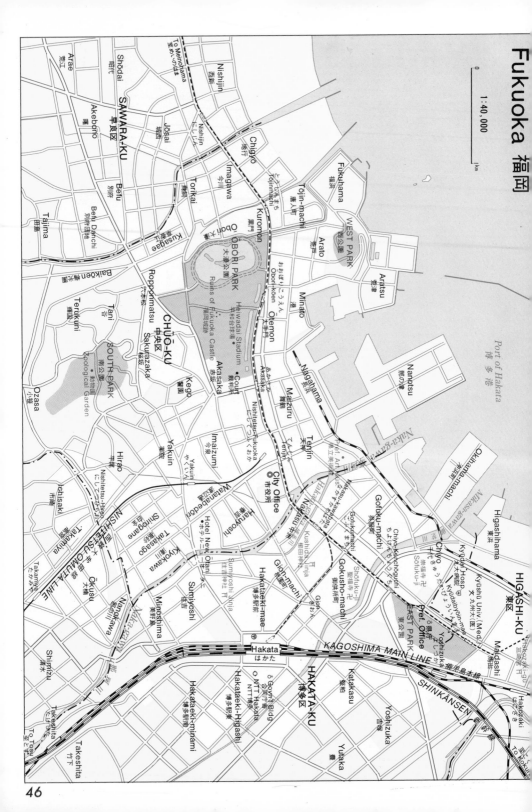

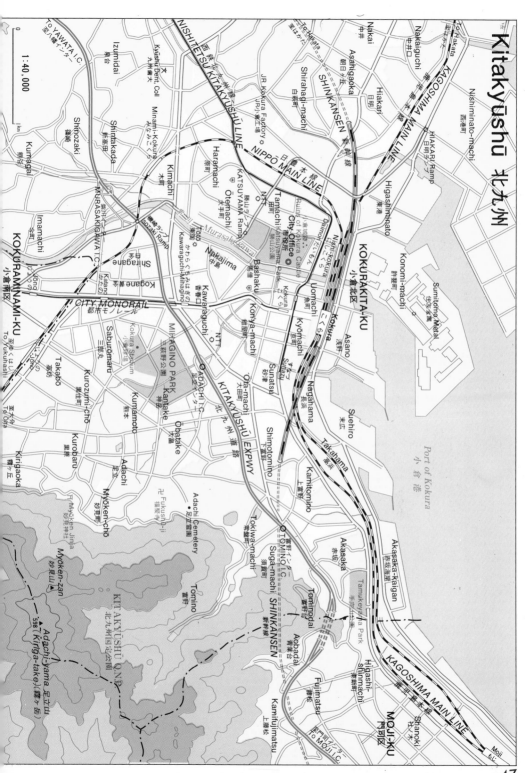

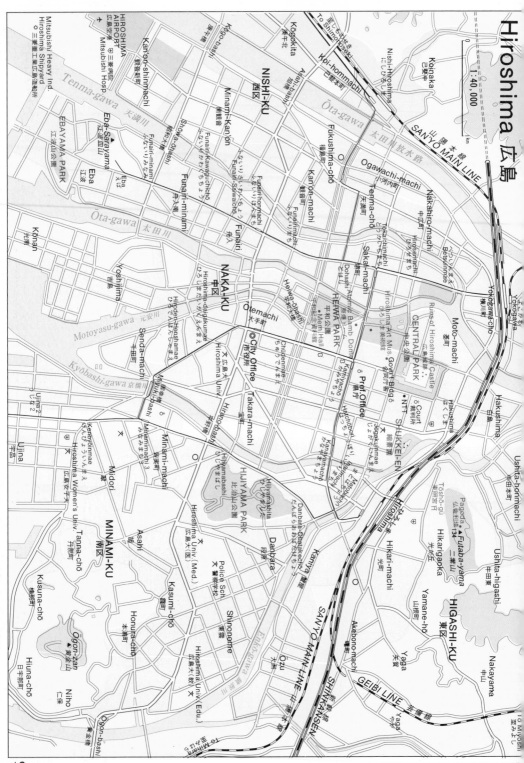

Hiroshima 広島

1:40,000

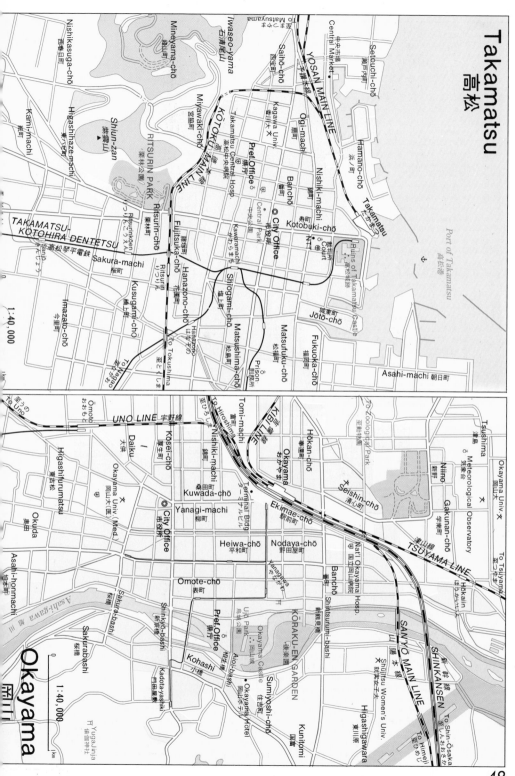

Takamatsu 高松

- Setouchi-chō 瀬戸内町
- Central Market 中央市場前
- To Matsuyama 至まつやま
- YOSAN MAIN LINE 予讃本線
- Hamano-chō 浜ノ町
- Takamatsu 高松
- Saihō-chō 西宝町
- Ogi-machi 扇町
- Nishiki-machi 錦町
- Kagawa Univ. 香川大
- Miyawaki-chō 宮脇町
- Takamatsu Central Hosp. 高松中央病院
- Pref. Office 県庁
- Banchō 番町
- Kotobuki-chō 寿町
- Kotobuki-chō
- Central Park 中央公園
- Iwaseo-yama 石清尾山
- Mineyama-chō 峰山町
- KŌTOKU MAIN LINE 高徳本線
- Shun-zan 紫雲山
- RITSURIN PARK 栗林公園
- Nishikasuga-chō 西春日町
- Kami-machi 上町
- Higashihaze-machi 東ハゼ町
- Ritsurinkōen 栗林公園
- Ritsurin-chō 栗林町
- City Office 市役所
- Court 裁判所
- Ruins of Takamatsu Castle 高松城跡
- Port of Takamatsu 高松港
- TAKAMATSU-KOTOHIRA DENTETSU 高松琴平電鉄
- Sakura-machi 桜町
- Sanjō さんじょう
- Fujitsuka-chō 藤塚町
- Hanazono-chō 花園町
- Kawaramachi かわらまち
- Shiogami-chō 塩上町
- Kusugami-chō 楠上町
- Imazato-chō 今里町
- Matsushima-chō 松島町
- Hanazono はなぞの
- Matsufuku-chō 福岡町
- Fukuoka-chō 福岡町
- To Wagō 至わご
- To Tokushima 至とくしま
- Prison 刑務所
- Jōtō-chō 城東町
- Asahi-machi 朝日町
- 1:40,000
- 0 ... 1 Km

Okayama 岡山

- To Uno 至うの
- UNO LINE 宇野線
- Ōmoto おおもと
- Daiku 大供
- Tomi-machi 富町
- Nishiki-machi 錦町
- Kōsei-chō 厚生町
- Okayama Univ. (Med.) 岡山大(医)
- Kuwada-chō 桑田町
- Yanagi-machi 柳町
- Higashifurumatsu 東古松
- Okuda 奥田
- Asahi-honmachi 旭本町
- City Office 市役所
- Heiwa-chō 平和町
- Nodaya-chō 野田屋町
- Omote-chō 表町
- Sakura-bashi 桜橋
- Shinkyō-bashi 新京橋
- Kohashi 小橋
- Kadotayashiki 門田屋敷
- Sakurabashi 桜橋
- Yūgaunja 有隣社
- 1:40,000
- 0 ... 1 Km
- To Hiroshima 至ひろしま
- KB LINE K市線
- Hōkan-chō 奉還町
- Okayama おかやま
- Ekimae-chō 駅前町
- Seishin-chō 清心町
- Banchō 番町
- Shintsurumi-bashi 新鶴見橋
- Uno Park 宇野公園
- KŌRAKU-EN GARDEN 後楽園
- Okayama Castle 岡山城
- Aioi-bashi 相生橋
- Sumiyoshi-chō 住吉町
- Kunitomi 国富
- N'at'l Okayama Hosp. 国立岡山病院
- Okayama Hotel 岡山ホテル
- Higashigawara 東川原
- Tsushima 津島
- Niino 新野
- Okayama Univ. 岡山大
- Meteorological Observatory 気象台
- Gakunan-chō 学南町
- Hōkain ほうかいん
- To Tsuyama 至つやま
- TSUYAMA LINE 津山線
- Shujitsu Women's Univ. 就実女子大
- SAN'YŌ MAIN LINE 山陽本線
- SHINKANSEN 新幹線
- To Shin-Ōsaka 至しんおおさか
- To Himeji 至ひめじ
- To Zoological Park 至動物園
- Asahi-gawa 旭川

49

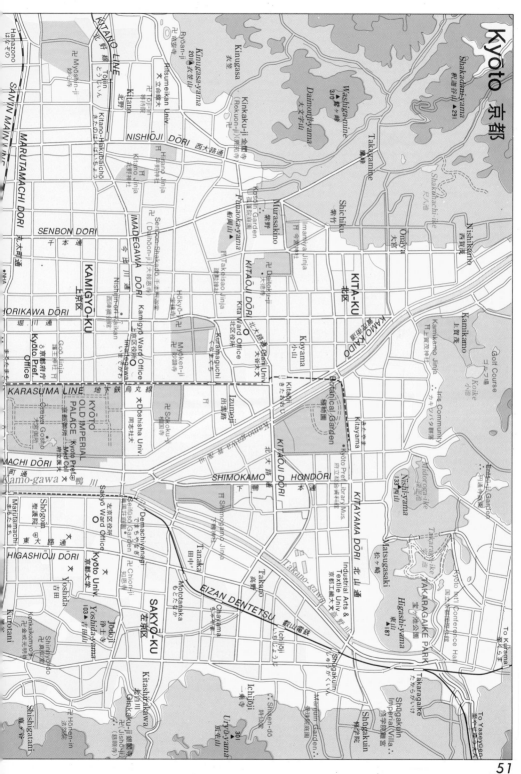

Kyōto 京都

Shakadani-yama 釈迦谷山 ▲291

Washizu-mine 鷲ヶ峰 ▲310

Daimonji-yama 大文字山

Takazamine 鷹峯

Shakahachi-ike 釈迦八池

SANIN MAIN LINE

KITANO LINE

Hanazono はなぞの

Myōshin-ji 妙心寺 卍

Tōjin とうじん 卍

Ryōan-ji 龍安寺 卍

Ritsumeikan Univ. 立命館大学

Kinugasa-yama 衣笠山 ▲201

Kinugasa 衣笠

Kinkaku-ji 金閣寺 卍 (Rokuon-ji) (鹿苑寺)

MARUTAMACHI DORI 丸太町通

NISHIOJI DORI 西大路通

Hirano Jinja 平野神社 卍

Kitano 北野

Kitano-Hakubaichō 北野白梅町

Koike 小池

Nishikamo 西賀茂

Ōmiya 大宮

Kamikamo 上賀茂

Golf Course ゴルフ場

Kamikamo Jinja 卍 上賀茂神社

Iris Community カキツバタ群落

KITA-KU 北区

SENBON DORI 千本通

Murasakino 紫野

Imamiya Jinja 卍 今宮神社

Shichiku 紫竹

Kōsin Garden 紫野

Daitoku-ji 卍 大徳寺

KAMO KAIDO 加茂街道

卍 NHA

KAMIGYO-KU 上京区

Senbon-Shakadō 千本釈迦堂 (Daihōon-ji) 大報恩寺

NISHIJIN-ori-kaikan 西陣織会館

KITAOJI DORI 北大路通

Funaoka-yama 船岡山 ▲

Takeisao Jinja 建勲神社 卍

Kita Ward Office 北区役所

Kita Ōtani Univ. 大谷大

Koyama 小山

Kitaōji きたおおじ

KITAYAMA 北山

Botanical Garden 植物園

Kyōto Pref. Library Mus. 府立総合資料館

HORIKAWA DORI 堀川通

Goō Jinja 護王神社 卍

Kyōto Pref. Office 京都府庁

Kamigyō Ward Office 上京区役所

Myōken-ji 妙顕寺 卍

Kuramaguchi 鞍馬口

Izumoji 出雲路

KARASUMA LINE 地下鉄

KYŌTO OLD IMPERIAL PALACE 京都御所

Kyōto Gosho 京都御所

Ōmiya Gosho 大宮御所

Dōshisha Univ. 同志社大学

Sōkoku-ji 相国寺 卍

Izumoji 出雲路

KITAOJI HONDORI 北大路本通

Kitayama 北山

KITAYAMA DORI 北山通

Nishi-yama 133西山

Midoroga-ike 深泥池

Takaragaike 宝ヶ池

Matsugasaki 松ヶ崎

TAKARAGAIKE PARK 宝ヶ池公園

Kyōto Int'l Conference Hall 国立京都国際会館

Higashi-yama ▲187 東山

Kamo-gawa 鴨川

MACHI DORI 町通

SHIMOKAMO 下鴨

Shimogamo Jinja 卍 下鴨神社

Tanaka 田中

Demachiyanagi でまちやなぎ

Sakyō Ward Office 左京区役所

Seifūsō (Garden) 清風荘

Takano 高野

EIZAN DENTETSU 叡山電鉄

Takano-gawa 高野川

Industrial Arts & Textile Univ. 京都工芸繊維大学

Shūgakuin 修学院

Shūgakuin Imperial Villa 修学院離宮

HIGASHIOJI DORI 東大路通

Shōgoin 聖護院

Kyōto Univ. 京都大学

Chion-ji 知恩寺 卍

Mototanaka もとたなか

Ōyama 大山

Shigakuin 詩仙堂

Ichijōji 一乗寺

SAKYO-KU 左京区

Yoshida 吉田

Jōdo-ji 浄土寺 卍

Yoshida-yama 103▲吉田山

Ichijōji 一乗寺

Manju-in 曼殊院

Kitashirakawa 北白川

Ginkaku-ji 銀閣寺 卍 (Jishō-ji) 慈照寺 ▲301

Uryū-yama 瓜生山

Shishigatani 鹿ヶ谷

Kurotani 黒谷

Shinnyo-dō 真如堂 卍

Konkaikōmyō-ji 卍 金戒光明寺

Hōnen-in 法然院 卍

To Kurama 鞍馬 へ至る

To Yaseyūen 八瀬遊園 へ至る

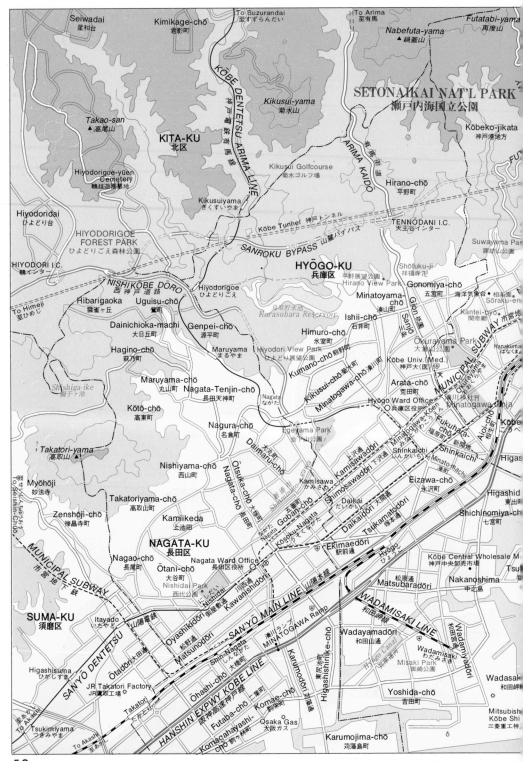

Seiwadai
星和台

Kimikage-chō
君影町

To Suzurandai
至すずらんだい

To Arima
至有馬

Nabefuta-yama
鍋蓋山

Futatabi-yama
再度山

SETONAIKAI NAT'L PARK
瀬戸内海国立公園

Kikusui-yama
菊水山

Takao-san
▲高尾山

KITA-KU
北区

Kōbeko-jikata
神戸港地方

Hiyodorigoe-yūen
Cemetery
鶴越遊園墓地

Kikusui Golfcourse
菊水ゴルフ場

Hirano-chō
平野町

Kikusuiyama
きくすいやま

ARIMA KAIDŌ

有馬街道

Hiyodoridai
ひよどり台

Kōbe Tunnel 神戸トンネル

TENNŌDANI I.C.
天王谷インター

Suwayama Pa
諏訪山公園

HIYODORIGOE
FOREST PARK
ひよどりごえ森林公園

SANROKU BYPASS 山麓バイパス

HIYODORI I.C.
鶴インター

HYŌGO-KU
兵庫区

Shōfuku-ji
祥福寺卍

NISHIKŌBE DŌRO
西神戸道路

Hiyodorigoe
ひよどりごえ

Hirano View Park
平野展望公園

Gonomiya-chō
五宮町

To Himeji
至ひめじ

Hibarigaoka
雲雀ヶ丘

Uguisu-chō
鶯町

Minatoyama-chō
湊山町

海洋気象台▲ 相楽園
Sōraku-en

Kantei-byō
関帝廟

Dainichioka-machi
大日丘町

Genpei-chō
源平町

Himuro-chō
氷室町

Ishii-chō
石井町

Gion 祇
園

三
宮

Sanjo

市
民

Hagino-chō
萩乃町

Maruyama
まるやま

Hiyodori View Park
ひよどり展望公園

Kumano-chō 熊野町

Kōbe Univ. (Med.)
神戸大(医)

Okurayama Park
大倉山公園

Okurayama
Hanakuma
はなくま

Maruyama-chō
丸山町

Nagata-Tenjin-chō
長田天神町

Kōtō-chō
高東町

Nagata
なかた

Kikusui-chō菊水町

Minatogawa-chō湊川町

Arata-chō
荒田町

Hyōgo Ward Office
兵庫区役所

湊
川
神
社

Minatogawa Jinja

Shishiga-ike
獅子ヶ池

Nagura-chō
名倉町

Egeyama Park
会下山公園

Fukuhara-
chō
福原町

Aioi通

Kōbe
こうべ

Higas

Takatori-yama
▲高取山

Nishiyama-chō
西山町

Ōtsuka-chō 大塚町

Daimaru-chō
大丸町

Kamisawadōri
上沢通

Shinkaichi
しんかいち

Shinkaichi
新開地

Minato-machi
湊町

Myōhōji
妙法寺

To Seishin-Chō

Takatoriyama-chō
高取山町

Kamisawa
かみさわ

Shimosawadōri
下沢通

Eizawa-chō
永沢町

Higashid
東出

Nagata-chō 長田町

Shimonsawadōri

Daikai
だいかい

Daikaidōri 大開通

Higashid

Zenshōji-chō
禅昌寺町

Kamiikeda
上池田

Goban-chō
五番町

Kōsoku-Nagata
こうそくながた

Tsukamotodōri
塚本通

Shichinomiya-chō
七宮町

NAGATA-KU
長田区

Nagao-chō
長尾町

Nagata Ward Office
長田区役所

Ekimaedōri
駅前通

Hyōgo
兵庫

MUNICIPAL SUBWAY
市営地下鉄

Ōtani-chō
大谷町

Kōbe Central Wholesale M
神戸中央卸売市場

SUMA-KU
須磨区

Nishidai Park
西代公園

Nishidai
にしだい

Kawanishidōri
川西通

Matsubaradōri
松原通

Nakanoshima
中之島

Tsu

SANYO DENTETSU

Itayado
いたやど

Oyashikidōri
御屋敷通

Matsunodōri
松野通

SAN'YO MAIN LINE 山陽本線

MINATOGAWA Ramp
湊川ランプ

WADAMISAKI LINE
和田岬線

Wadayamadōri
和田山通

Wadamisaki
わだみさき

Wadamiyadōri
和田宮通

Higashisuma
ひがしすま

Ōtadōri大田通

Shin-Nagata
しんながた

HANSHIN EXPWY KOBE LINE
阪神高速神戸線

Higashishirike-chō
東尻池町

Hyōgo Canal
兵庫運河

Misaki Park
御崎公園

Wadasak
和田岬

JR Takatori Factory
JR鷹取工場

Takatori
たかとり

Ōhashi-chō
大橋町

Karumodōri 苅藻通

Yoshida-chō
吉田町

Mitsubish
Kōbe Shi
三菱重工神

Tsukimiyama
つきみやま

To Akashi
至あかし

Komae-chō
駒栄町

Futaba-chō
二葉町

Osaka Gas
大阪ガス

Mitsubishi
Kōbe Shi

Komacahayashi-
chō 駒ヶ林町

Karumojima-chō
苅藻島町

Wadasak

Yotsugi-yama
世継山

HOKUSHIN KYUKO LINE 北神急行線
SHIN KOBE TUNNEL No.2 第2新神戸トンネル
SHIN KOBE TUNNEL 新神戸トンネル

Fukiai-chō
葺合町

Shinsenjidōri
神仙寺通

Shironoshitadōri
城の下通

Uenodōri 上野通

To Shin-Osaka 至新大阪

Nada Ward Office
灘区役所

NADA-KU
灘区

Rokkōmichi 六甲道 To Osaka 至大阪

Nunobiki Reservoir
布引貯水池

Nunobiki Falls
布引の滝

NUNOBIKI PARK
布引公園

TOKAIDO-SAN'YO SHINKANSEN 東海道・山陽新幹線

Nobiki Tunnel 布引トンネル

Shin-Kōbe Oriental Hotel
新神戸オリエンタルホテル

Shin-Kobe
しんこうべ

Kagoikedōri
籠池通

Nozakidōri 野崎通

大日通

Dainichidōri

HANKYU KOBE MAIN LINE 阪急神戸本線

Ojikōen
おうじこうえん

Oji-Park
王子公園

Suidōsuji 水道筋

Nadakitadōri 灘北通

Nada
なだ

HANSHIN MAIN LINE 阪神本線

TOKAIDO MAIN LINE 東海道本線

Nishinada
西灘

Ōishi
おおいし

Ōishi
大石

Shinzaike
しんざいけ

Shinzaike-minamichō
新在家南町

Kōbe Steel
神戸製鋼

JŌ-KU
央区

Kitano-chō
北野町

Kasuganomichi
かすがのみち

Tsutsui-chō
筒井町

Iwaya
いわや

Kōbe Steel
神戸製鋼

MAYA Ramp
摩耶ランプ

Nadahama-chō
灘浜町

Ikuta-chō
生田町

Kanō-chō 加納町

Maya-Ōhashi
摩耶大橋

Maya-Futō
摩耶埠頭

Yamamotodōri 山本通

amatedōri 中山手通

amated Yamatedōri 下山手通

Kumoidōri
雲井通

Sannomiya
さんのみや

Kawasaki Steel
川崎製鉄

IKUTA Ramp
生田ランプ

Ikuta Jinja
生田神社

Ikuta 生田

Pref.Office
県庁

Motomach
元町

Hachimandōri
八幡通

HARBOR HIGHWAY ハーバーハイウェイ

Port of Kōbe
神戸港

Chūō Ward Office
中央区役所

Sannomiya
三宮

Motomachidōri
元町通

City Office
市役所

Kyōmachi
京町

Onohama-chō
小野浜町

Trade Center Bldg
貿易センタービル

algandōri 海岸通

aigandōri 海岸通

KYŌBASHI P.A.
京橋パーキング

Kōbe Customhouse
神戸税関

KYŌBASHI P.A.

Port Tower
ポートタワー

Meriken Hatoba
メリケン波止場

Shinkō-chō
新港町

Port Terminal
ポートターミナル

Port of Kōbe
神戸港

awasaki-chō
崎町

Kawasaki Heavy Ind.
川崎重工

Kōbe-ōhashi
神戸大橋

Minatojima
港島

Customhouse
税関

Port Iland Bldg
ポートアイランドビル

Nakakōen
なかこうえん

Customhouse
税関

Kitafutō
きたふとう

PORT ISLAND
ポートアイランド

Nakafutō
なかふとう

Shimin-byōinmae
しみんびょういんまえ

Minatojima-
Nakamachi
港島中町

World Mem.Hall
ワールド記念ホール

Minamikōen
みなみこうえん

Kōbe Portpier Land
神戸ポートピアランド

Port of Kōbe
神戸港

Wada-misaki
和田岬

vy Ind.

Ōsaka Wan
大阪湾

1:40,000

km

Kōbe 神戸

53

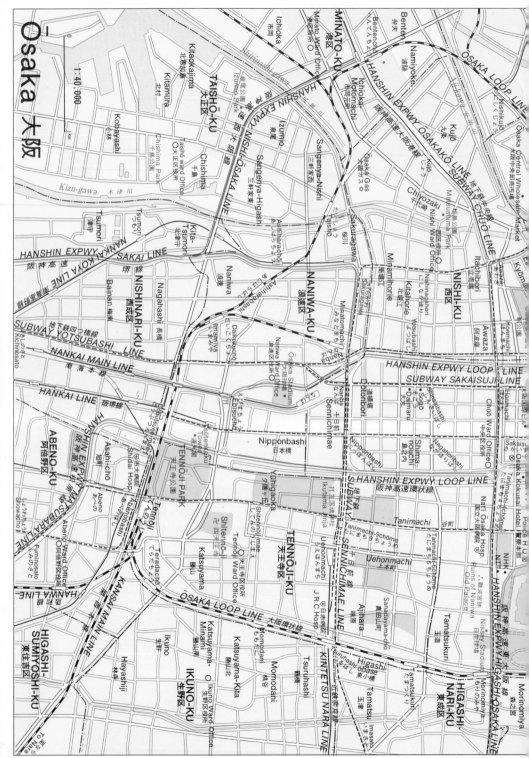

Osaka 大阪

1:40,000

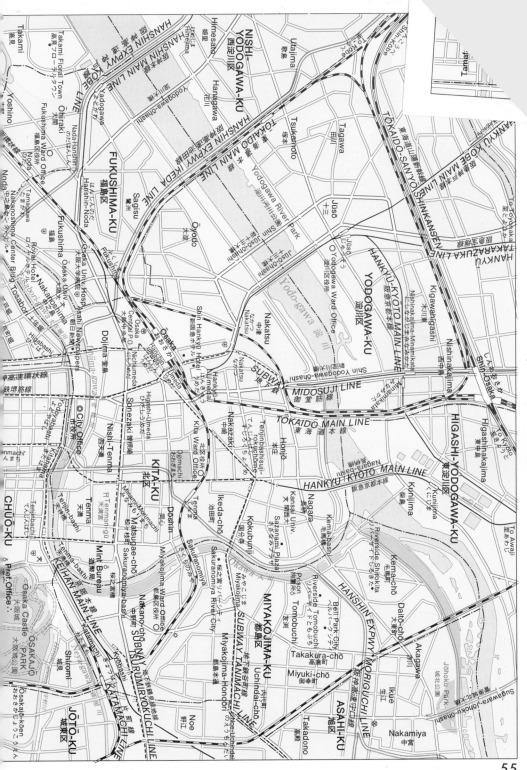

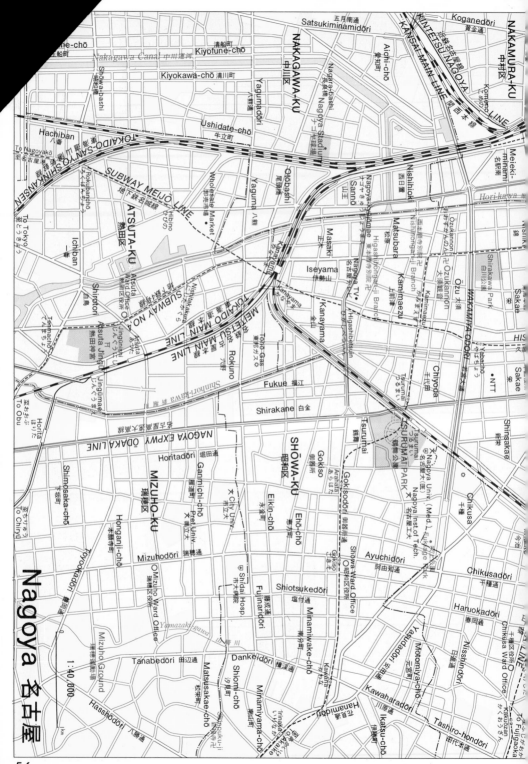

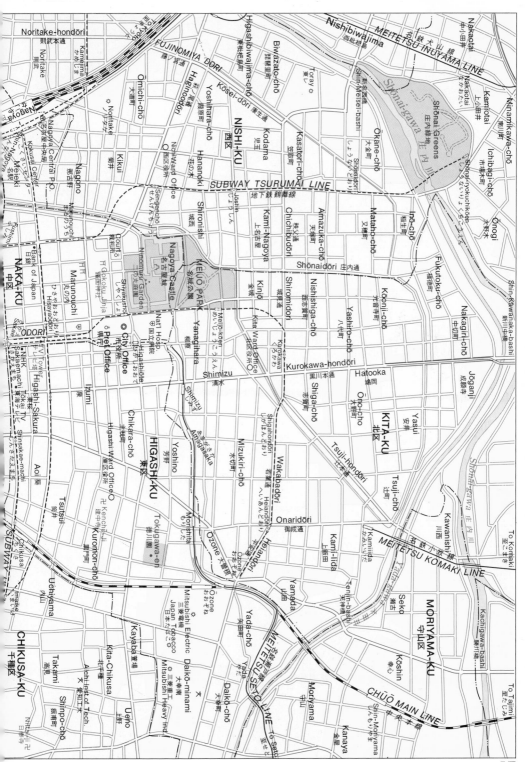

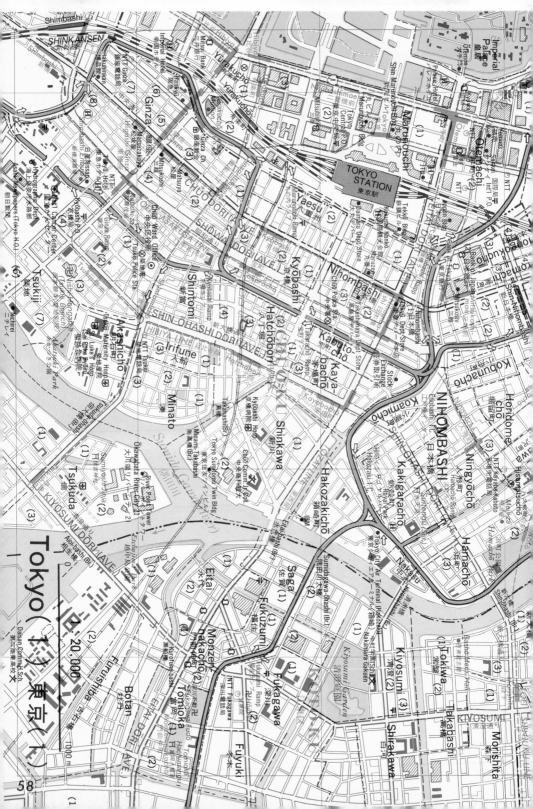

Yokohama 横浜

① Bronze Statue of Naosuke Ii　井伊直弼像
② Prefectural Concert Hall　県立音楽堂
③ Prefectural Library　県立図書館
④ Science Museum　文化資料館
⑤ Kanagawa Youth Hostel　神奈川ユースホステル
⑥ Opening Port Mem. Hall　開港記念会館
⑦ Yokohama Archives of History　横浜開港資料館
⑧ Silk Museum　シルク博物館
⑨ Yokohama Doll Museum　横浜人形の家
⑩ Yokohama Marine Science Mus.　横浜海洋科学博物館
⑪ Yamate Museum　山手資料館
⑫ Iwasaki Museum　岩崎博物館
⑬ Jirō Osaragi Mem. Museum　大仏次郎記念館
⑭ Kanagawa Mus. of Modern Literature　神奈川近代文学館

Mizuho Futō (wharf) 瑞穂ふ頭

Port of Yokohama
横浜港

City Plan
entury
らい 21

Shinkō Futō (wharf)
新港ふ頭

Grand Pier
(Ōsanbashi Futō)
大さん橋ふ頭

Shinkōchō
新港町

Bank
Shinkō-bashi (Br.)
新港橋

International
Passenger Terminal
国際船客ターミナルビル

Yokohama Custom house
横浜税関

Marine Police Sta.
水上署

Yamashita Futō (wharf)
山下ふ頭

Hikawa-maru
氷川丸

Yamashita Park
山下公園

Hotel Yokohama
Hotel New Grand
Star Hotel
Holiday Inn

Marine Tower
Yamashitachō Ramp
山下町ランプ

Shin-Yamashita Ramp
ランプ

Bund Hotel

Meteorological Observatory

Minato-no-mieruoka Park
港の見える丘公園

Shin-Yamashita
新山下

Motomachi 元町

Foreigners' Cemetery
外国人墓地

Suwa-
chō

Yamatechō 山手町

Yamate Park
山手公園

Chiyozakichō
千代崎町

1 : 20,000

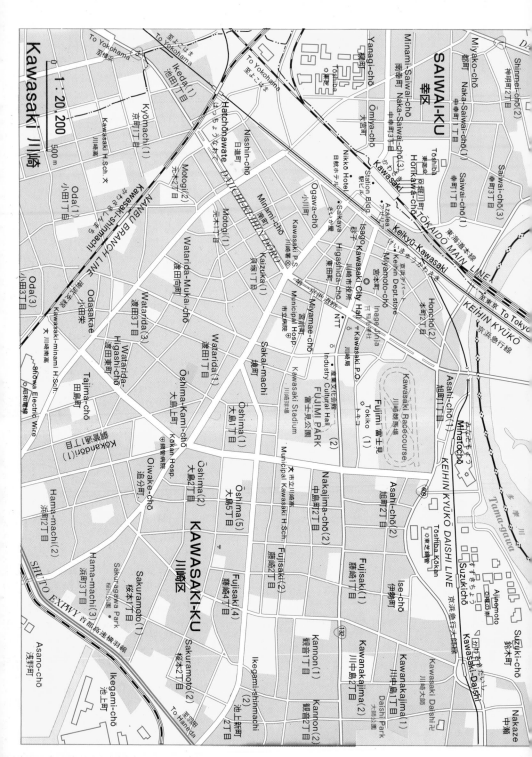

Kawasaki 川崎

1:20.200

0   500 m

SAIWAI-KU 幸区

KAWASAKI-KU 川崎区

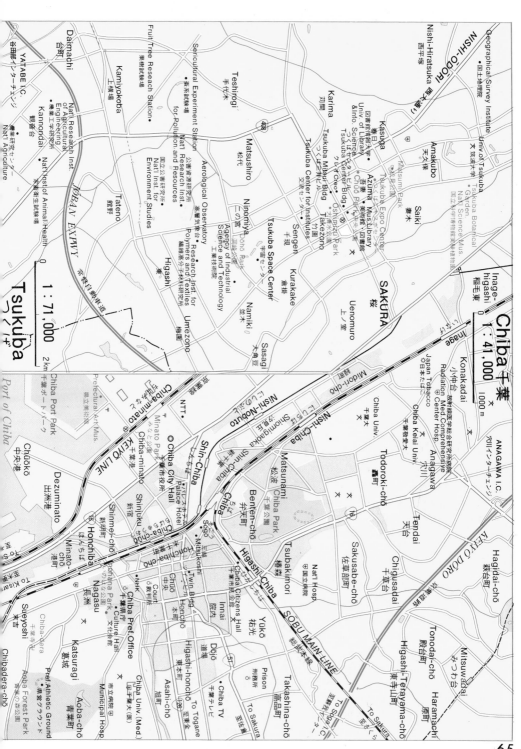

Chiba 千葉
1:41,000
0   1000 m

Tsukuba つくば
1:71,000
0   1   2km

Inage-higashi 稲毛東

Konakadai 小仲台
Japan Tobacco
Radiation Med.Comprehensive
Research Center Hosp.
日本たばこ
放射線医学総合研究所病院
附属病院

Chiba Keiai Univ. 千葉敬愛大学

Chiba Univ. 千葉大

Todoroki-chō 轟町

Tendai 天台

Anagawa 穴川

ANAGAWA I.C. アナガワインターチェンジ

KEIYO DORO 京葉道路

Hagidai-chō 萩台町

Mitsuwadai みつわ台

Haramachi 原町

Tonodai-chō 殿台町

Higashi-Terayama-chō 東寺山町

Takashina-chō 高品町

Sakusabe-chō 作草部町

Chigusadai 千草台

Matsunami 松波

Chiba Park 千葉公園

Benten-chō 弁天町

Tsubakimori 椿森

Nat'l Hosp. 国立病院

Yūkō 祐光

Dōjō 道場

Prison 刑務所

Chiba TV 千葉テレビ

Asahi-chō 旭町

Higashi-honchō 東本町

Chiba Univ.(Med.) 千葉大学(医)

Municipal Hosp. 市立病院

Nagasu 長洲

To Sakura 至佐倉

SOBU MAIN LINE 総武本線

Higashi-Chiba 東千葉

Chiba Citizens Hall 千葉市民会館

Court 千葉地方裁判所

Twin Bldg. ツインビル

NHK

Chō 中央

Honcho 本町

Mitsukoshi 三越

Sogo そごう

Chiba City Hall 千葉市役所

Chiba-minato 千葉みなと

Shin-Chiba 新千葉

KEIYO LINE 京葉線

Minato Park みなと公園

Chiba Palace Hotel 千葉パレスホテル

Shin-Chiba 新千葉

Nishi-Nobuto 西登戸

Nishi-Chiba 西千葉

Shin-Chiba 新千葉

Shiomigaoka 汐見丘

Midori-chō 緑町

NTT

Chiba-minato 千葉みなと

Port of Chiba 千葉港

Chiba Port Park 千葉ポートパーク

Chuoko 中央港

Dezuminato 出洲港

Prefectural Art.Mus. 県立美術館

Minato-chō 港町

Shinmei-chō 神明町

Shinjuku 新宿

Honchiba 本千葉

Chiba Pref.Office 千葉県庁

Chiba Pref.Office 千葉県庁

Culture Hall 文化会館

Inai 院内

Chūō Park 中央公園

Hanamigawa Park 花見川公園

Chiba-dera 千葉寺

Sueyoshi 末吉

Katsuragi 葛城

Aoba-chō 青葉町

Chibadera-chō 千葉寺町

Aoba Forest Park 青葉の森公園

Pref.Athletic Ground 県営総合グラウンド

To Kisarazu 至木更津

YATABE I.C. 谷田部インターチェンジ

Daimachi 台町

Nishi-Hiratsuka 西平塚

NISHI-ODORI 西大通り

Geographical Survey Institute 国土地理院

Univ.of Tsukuba 筑波大学

Kasuga 春日

Amakubo 天久保

Saiki 妻木

Karima 苅間

Univ.of Library &Info. Science 図書館情報大学

Tsukuba Center for Institutes つくば研究支援センター

Tsukuba Mitsui Bldg つくば三井ビル

Tsukuba Center Bldg. つくばセンタービル

Azuma Mus.Library 吾妻 美術館・図書館

Oshima Park 大島公園

Tsukuba Expo Center つくばエキスポセンター

Tsukuba Botanical Garden Nat'l Science Mus. 筑波実験植物園 国立科学博物館

Takezono 竹園

Matsushiro 松代

Teshirogi 手代木

Nat'l Research Inst. of Agricultural Engineering 農業工学研究所

Nat'l Research Inst. for Pollution and Resources 公害資源研究所

Sericultural Experiment Station 蚕糸試験場

Aerological Observatory 高層気象台

Research Inst. for Polymers and Textiles 繊維高分子材料研究所

Agency of Industrial Science and Technology 工業技術院

Nipponiya 二の宮

Sengen 千現

Kurakake 鞍掛

Higashi 東

Tateno 館野

Namiki 並木

Uenomuro 上ノ室

Sasagi 篠木

Umezono 梅園

Dōno Park 洞峰公園

Tsukuba Space Center 宇宙センター

SAKURA 桜

Nat'l Research Inst. of Agricultural 農業研究センター

Kannondai 観音台

Nat'l Inst.of Animal Health 家畜衛生試験場

Nat'l Institute for Environment Studies 国立環境研究所

Fruit/Tree Reseach Station 果樹試験場

Kamiyokoba 上横場

JOBAN EXPWY 常磐自動車道

Matsum Park 松見公園

Chuo Park 中央公園

Inage-higashi 稲毛東

SAKURA 桜

Nishi-Nobuto 西登戸

0   1:71,000   2km

65

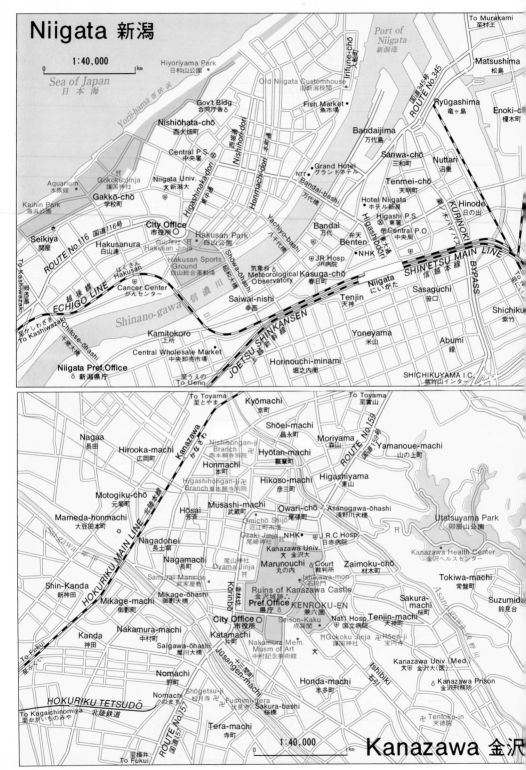

Niigata 新潟

1:40,000

Sea of Japan
日本海

Yori-hama 寄居浜

Hiyoriyama Park
日和山公園

Old Niigata Customhouse
旧新潟税関

Port of Niigata
新潟港

Irifune-cho
入船町

To Murakami
至村上

Route No.345
国道345号

Matsushima
松島

Gov't Bldg
合同庁舎

Fish Market
魚市場

Ryūgashima
竜ヶ島

Enoki-c
榎木町

Nishiōhata-cho
西大畑町

Bandaijima
万代島

Sanwa-cho
三和町

Nuttari
沼垂

Central P.S.
中央警

Gokoku Jinja
護国神社

Niigata Univ.
文 新潟大

Grand Hotel
グランドホテル

NTT

Tenmei-cho
天明町

Hinode
日の出

Aquarium
水族館

Gakkō-cho
学校町

Niigata Univ.
文 新潟大

Bandai-bashi
万代橋

Hotel Niigata
ホテル新潟

Higashi P.S.
東署

KURINOKI
栗ノ木バイパス

Kaihin Park
海浜公園

City Office
市役所

Hakusan Park
白山公園

Yachiyo-bashi
八千代橋

Bandai
万代

Central P.O.
中央局

Seikiya
関屋

Hakusanura
白山浦

Hakusan Jinja
白山神社

Showa-ōhashi
昭和大橋

Benten
弁天

NHK

Hakusan Sports Ground
白山総合運動場

Hakusan
はくさん

Meteorological Observatory
気象台

JR Hosp.
JR病院

Higashidōri
東大通

SHIN·ETSU MAIN LINE
信越本線

ECHIGO LINE
越後線

Cancer Center
がんセンター

Kasuga-cho
春日町

Niigata
にいがた

Sasaguchi
笹口

Shichiku
紫竹

To Kashiwazaki
至かしわざき

Chitose-ōhashi
千歳大橋

Saiwai-nishi
幸西

Tenjin
天神

BYPASS
バイパス

Shinano-gawa 信濃川

Kamitokoro
上所

Yoneyama
米山

Abumi
鐙

To Kashiwazaki
至かしわざき

Central Wholesale Market
中央卸売市場

Horinouchi-minami
堀之内南

JOETSU SHINKANSEN
上越新幹線

SHICHIKUYAMA I.C.
紫竹山インター

Niigata Pref.Office
新潟県庁

うちの
To Ueno
至上野

Kanazawa 金沢

To Toyama
至とやま

Kyōmachi
京町

To Toyama
至富山

Nagaa
長田

Hirooka-machi
広岡町

Nishihongan-ji Branch
西本願寺別院

Shōei-machi
昌永町

Hyōtan-machi
瓢箪町

Moriyama
森山

ROUTE No.159
国道159号

Yamanoue-machi
山の上町

Honmachi
本町

Higashihongan-ji Branch
東本願寺別院

Hikoso-machi
彦三町

Higashiyama
東山

Motogiku-cho
元菊町

Hōsai
芳斉

Musashi-machi
武蔵町

Owari-cho
尾張町

Asanogawa-ōhashi
浅野川大橋

Utatsuyama Park
卯辰山公園

Mameda-honmachi
大豆田本町

Nagadohei
長土塀

Ōmichō Shijō
近江町市場

NHK

J.R.C.Hosp.
日赤病院

Kanazawa Health Center
金沢ヘルスセンター

Sai-gawa 犀川

Nagamachi
長町

Ozaki Jinja
尾崎神社

Kanazawa Univ.
文 金沢大

Shin-Kanda
新神田

Oyama Jinja
尾山神社

Marunouchi
丸の内

Court
裁判所

Zaimoku-cho
材木町

Tokiwa-machi
常盤町

Suzumida
鈴見田

Mikage-machi
御影町

Samurai Mansion
武家屋敷

Mikage-ōhashi
御影大橋

Ishikawa-mon
石川門

KENROKU-EN
兼六園

Kōrinbō
香林坊

Ruins of Kanazawa Castle
金沢城跡

Asano-gawa 浅野川

Kanda
神田

Nakamura-machi
中村町

Saigawa-ōhashi
犀川大橋

City Office
市役所

Katamachi
片町

Pref.Office
県庁

Seison-Kaku
成巽閣

Nat'l Hosp.
国立病院

Gokoku Jinja
護国神社

Hōen-ji
宝円寺

Sakura-machi
桜町

Tenjin-machi
天神町

Nomachi
野町

Nomachi のまち

Shōgetsu-ji
松月寺

Jūsangen-machi
十三間町

Nakamura Mem. Musm of Art
中村記念美術館

Fushimi-dera
伏見寺

Honda-machi
本多町

Kanazawa Univ.(Med.)
文 金沢大(医)

Ishibiki
石引

HOKURIKU TETSUDŌ
北陸鉄道

To Kagaichinomiya
至かがいちのみや

Nomachi のまち

Sakura-bashi
桜橋

Kanazawa Prison
金沢刑務所

ROUTE No.157
国道157号

Tera-machi
寺町

Tentoku-in
天徳院

To Fukui
至福井

1:40,000

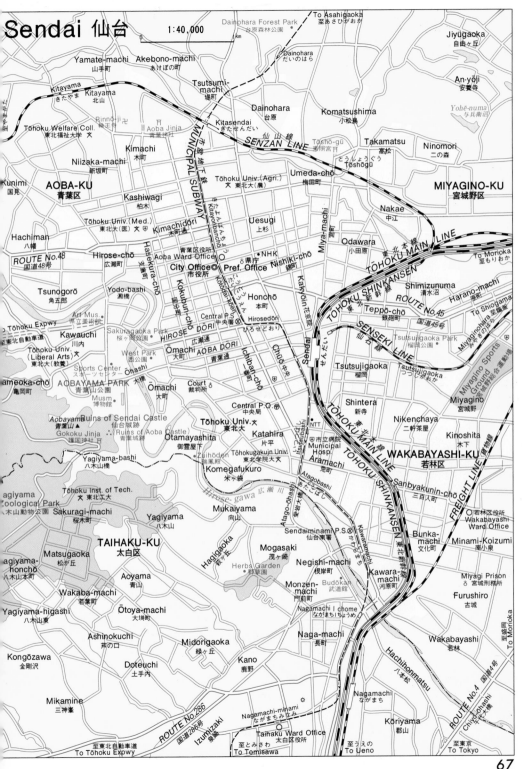

Sendai 仙台

1:40,000

To Asahigaoka / 至あさひがおか

Dainohara Forest Park / 台原森林公園
1 km

Jiyūgaoka / 自由ヶ丘

Dainohara / だいのはら

An-yōji / 安養寺

Yohē-numa / 与兵衛沼

Yamate-machi / 山手町　Akebono-machi / あけぼの町

Tsutsumi-machi / 堤町

Kitayama / きたやま　Kitayama / 北山

Rinnō-ji / 輪王寺

Aoba Jinja / 青葉神社

Kitasendai / きたせんだい

Dainohara / 台原

Komatsushima / 小松島

仙山線　SENZAN LINE

Takamatsu / 高松

Ninomori / 二の森

Tōhoku Welfare Coll. / 東北福祉大学

Kimachi / 木町

Tōhoku Univ. (Agri.) / 東北大 (農)

Umeda-chō / 梅田町

Tōshō-gū / 東照宮　どうしょうぐう

Tōshōgū / 東照宮

MIYAGINO-KU / 宮城野区

Niizaka-machi / 新坂町

AOBA-KU / 青葉区

Kashiwagi / 柏木

Uesugi / 上杉

Nakae / 中江

Kunimi / 国見

Tōhoku Univ. (Med.) / 東北大 (医)

Kimachidōri / 木町通

NHK

Odawara / 小田原

TŌHOKU MAIN LINE / 東北本線

To Morioka / 至もりおか

Hachiman / 八幡

Hirose-chō / 広瀬町

Aoba Ward Office / 青葉区役所

Pref. Office / 県庁

Nishiki-chō / 錦町

ROUTE No.48 / 国道48号

Hasekura-chō / 支倉町

City Office / 市役所

TŌHOKU SHINKANSEN / 東北新幹線

Shimizunuma / 清水沼

Harano-machi / 原ノ町

Tsunogorō / 角五郎

Yodo-bashi / 澱橋

Kokubun-chō / 国分町

Honchō / 本町

Kakyōin / 花京院

Teppō-chō / 鉄砲町

ROUTE No.45 / 国道45号

To Shiogama / 至塩釜

Tōhoku Expwy / 東北自動車道

Art Mus. / 県立美術館

Sakuragaoka Park / 桜ヶ岡公園

HIROSE DŌRI / 広瀬通

Hirosedōri / ひろせどおり

Tsutsujigaoka Park / 榴岡公園

Miyaginohara / みやぎのはら

SENSEKI LINE / 仙石線

Kawauchi / 川内

West Park / 西公園

ŌMACHI / 大町

AOBA DŌRI / 青葉通

Ichiban-chō / 一番町

Tsutsujigaoka / 榴岡

Tsutsujigaoka / つつじがおか

Miyagino Sports Ground / 宮城野総合運動場

Tōhoku Univ. (Liberal Arts) / 東北大 (教養)

Sports Center / スポーツセンター

Ōhashi / 大橋

Ōmachi / 大町

Court / 裁判所

Chūō / 中央

Sendai / せんだい

Shintera / 新寺

Miyagino / 宮城野

ameoka-chō / 亀岡町

AOBAYAMA PARK / 青葉山公園

Musm / 博物館

Central P.O. / 中央局

Nikenchaya / 二軒茶屋

Kinoshita / 木下

Aobayama / 青葉山

Ruins of Sendai Castle

Tōhoku Univ. / 東北大

NTT

Aobayama / 青葉山　Gokoku Jinja / 護国神社

Ruins of Aoba Castle / 仙台城跡

Katahira / 片平

Municipal Hosp. / 市立病院

TŌHOKU MAIN LINE / 東北本線

WAKABAYASHI-KU / 若林区

Otamayashita / 御霊屋下

Zuihōden / 瑞鳳殿

Tōhokugakuin Univ. / 東北学院大

TŌHOKU SHINKANSEN / 東北新幹線

Yagiyama-bashi / 八木山橋

Komegafukuro / 米ヶ袋

Aramachi / 荒町

Sanbyakunin-chō / 三百人町

FREIGHT LINE / 貨物線

Tōhoku Inst. of Tech. / 東北工大

Atagobashi / あたごばし

agiyama Zoological Park / 八木山動物公園

Sakuragi-machi / 桜木町

Yagiyama / 八木山

Hirose-gawa / 広瀬川

Atago-ōhashi / 愛宕大橋

Bunka-machi / 文化町

Minami-Koizumi / 南小泉

Wakabayashi Ward Office / 若林区役所

Mukaiyama / 向山

Mogasaki / 茂ヶ崎

Wakabayashi Ward Office

TAIHAKU-KU / 太白区

Hagigaoka / 萩ヶ丘

Sendaiminami P.S. / 仙台南署

Kawaramachi / かわらまち

Miyagi Prison / 宮城刑務所

Matsugaoka / 松ヶ丘

Herbs Garden / 野草園

Negishi-machi / 根岸町

Kawara-machi / 河原町

Furushiro / 古城

Aoyama / 青山

Monzen-machi / 門前町

Budōkan / 武道館

agiyama-honchō / 八木山本町

Wakaba-machi / 若葉町

Ōtoya-machi / 大堀町

Nagamachi 1 chome / ながまち1ちょうめ

Naga-machi / 長町

Wakabayashi / 若林

Yagiyama-higashi / 八木山東

Ashinokuchi / 芦の口

Midorigaoka / 緑ヶ丘

Kano / 鹿野

Hachihonmatsu / 八本松

Kongōzawa / 金剛沢

Doteuchi / 土手内

ROUTE No.4 / 国道4号

To Morioka / 至盛岡

Mikamine / 三神峯

Nagamachi / ながまち

Kōriyama / 郡山

ROUTE No.286 / 国道286号

Nagamachi-minami / ながまちみなみ

Chūō-ōhashi / 中央大橋

To Tōhoku Expwy / 至東北自動車道

Izumizaki / 泉崎

Taihaku Ward Office / 太白区役所

To Tomisawa / 至とみさわ

To Ueno / 至うえの

To Tokyo / 至東京

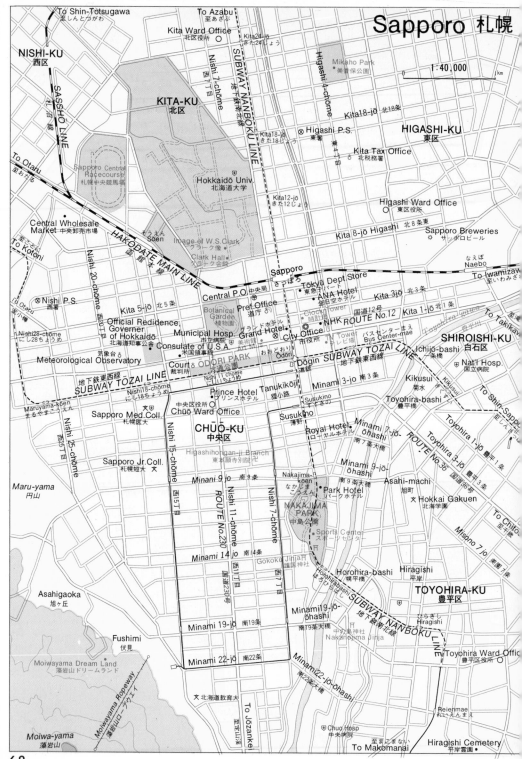

Sapporo 札幌

1:40,000

To Shin-Totsugawa
至しんとつがわ

To Azabu
至あざぶ

Kita Ward Office
北区役所

Kita24-jo
きた24じょう

Higashi 4-chome
東4丁目

Mikaho Park
美香保公園

Kita18-jo 北18条

KITA-KU
北区

Nishi 7-chome
西7丁目

SUBWAY NANBOKU LINE
地下鉄南北線

Higashi P.S.
東署

HIGASHI-KU
東区

Kita18-jo
きた18じょう

Kita Tax Office
北税務署

To Otaru
至おたる

SASSHŌ LINE
札沼線

Sapporo Central Racecourse
札幌中央競馬場

Hokkaidō Univ.
北海道大学

Kita12-jo
きた12じょう

Higashi Ward Office
東区役所

HAKODATE MAIN LINE
函館本線

Central Wholesale Market 中央卸売市場

Soen
そうえん

Image of W.S. Clark
クラーク像

Kita 8-jo Higashi 北8条東

Sapporo Breweries
サッポロビール

To Kotoni
至ことに

Clark Hall
クラーク会館

Naebo
なえぼ

To Iwamizaw
至いわみざ

Sapporo
さっぽろ

Nishi 20-chome
西20丁目

Nishi P.S.
西署

Kita 5-jo 北5条

Central P.O
中央局

Tokyū Dept Store
東急デパート

Kita 3-jo 北3条

Kita 1-jo 北1条

To Takikawa
至たきかわ

Nishi28-chome
にし28ちょうめ

Official Redidence, Governer of Hokkaido
北海道知事公舎

Botanical Garden
植物園

Pref. Office
道庁

ANA Hotel
全日空ホテル

国道12号

ROUTE No.12

SHIROISHI-KU
白石区

Municipal Hosp.
市立病院

Grand Hotel
グランドホテル

Clock Tower
時計台

NHK

Kita 1-jo 北1条

Ichijo-bashi
一条橋

Meteorological Observatory
気象台

Consulate of U.S.A.
米国領事館

City Office
市役所

Tower
テレビ塔

Bus Center-mae
バスセンターまえ

Nat'l Hosp.
国立病院

Court
裁判所

ODŌRI PARK
大通公園

Odori
おおどおり

SUBWAY TOZAI LINE
地下鉄東西線

Dōgin
道銀

Kikusui
菊水

Nishi 11-chome
西11ちょうめ

SUBWAY TOZAI LINE
地下鉄東西線

Minami 3-jo 南3条

Toyohira-bashi
豊平橋

Nishi18-chome
にし18ちょうめ

Prince Hotel
プリンスホテル

Tanukikōji
狸小路

Susukino
すすきの

Toyohira 1-jo 豊平1条

To Shin-Sappo
至しん

Nishi 25-chome
西25丁目

Sapporo Med.Coll.
札幌医大

Chūō Ward Office
中央区役所

Susukino
薄野

Royal Hotel
ロイヤルホテル

Minami 7-jō-ōhashi
南7条大橋

Toyohira 3-jo 豊平3条

国道36号

ROUTE No.36

Maruyama-koen
まるやまこうえん

CHŪO-KU
中央区

Nishi 15-chome
西15ちょうめ

Asahi-machi
旭町

Hokkai Gakuen
北海学園

Maru-yama
円山

Higashihongan-ji Branch
東本願寺別院

Minami 9-jō-ōhashi
南9条大橋

ROUTE No.230
国道230号

Sapporo Jr.Coll.
札幌短大

Minani 9 jo 南9条

Nakajima-koen
なかじまこうえん

Park Hotel
パークホテル

Misono 7 jo 美園7条

To Chito
至ち

Minami 14 jo 南14条

Nishi 11-chome
西11ちょうめ

Nishi 7-chome
西7ちょうめ

NAKAJIMA PARK
中島公園

Sports Center
スポーツセンター

TOYOHIRA-KU
豊平区

Asahigaoka
旭ヶ丘

Gokoku Jinja
護国神社

Horohira-bashi
幌平橋

Hiragishi
平岸

Fushimi
伏見

Minami 19-jo 南19条

Minami 9-jō-ōhashi
南9条大橋

Hiragishi
平岸

SUBWAY NANBOKU LINE
地下鉄南北線

Moiwayama Dream Land
藻岩山ドリームランド

Minami 22-jo 南22条

Nakanoshima Jinja
中の島神社

Toyohira Ward Office
豊平区役所

Moiwa-yama
藻岩山

Moiwayama Ropeway
藻岩山ロープウエイ

北海道教育大

Minami22-jō-ōhashi
南22条大橋

Reienmae
れいえんまえ

Chuo Hosp
中央病院

To Jōzankei
至じょうざんけい

To Makomanai
至まこまない

Hiragishi Cemetery
平岸霊園

Sight-seeing Maps
観光図

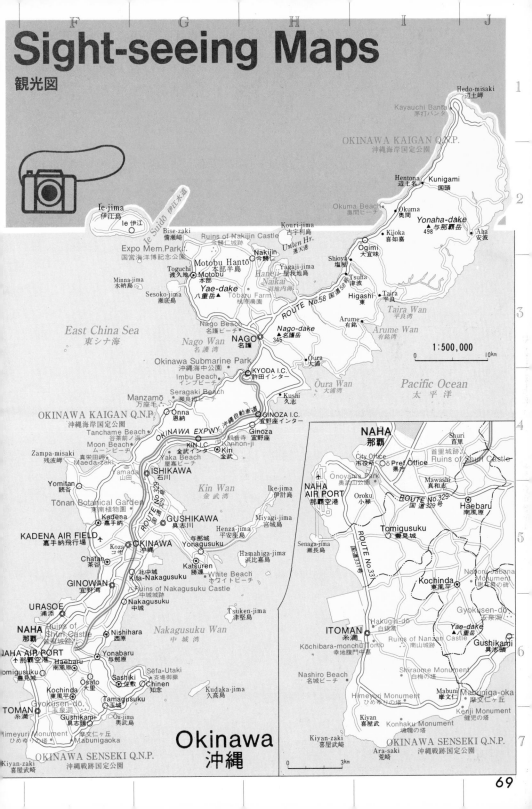

Okinawa
沖縄

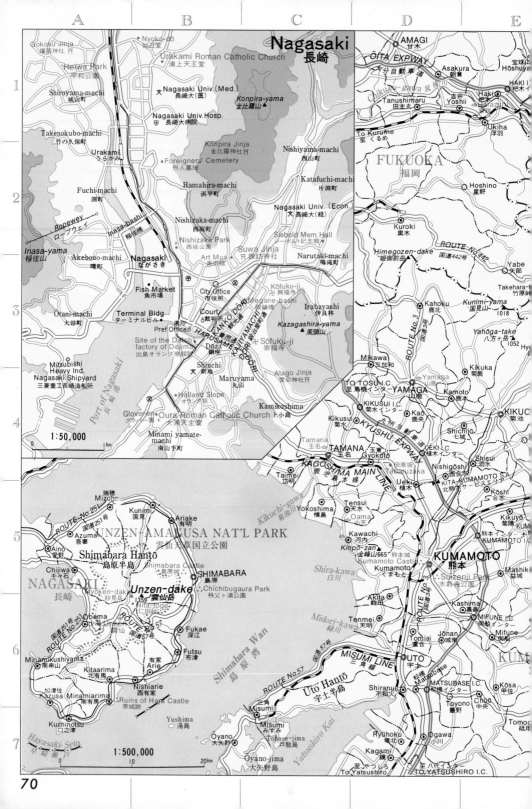

Nagasaki
長崎

1:50,000

1:500,000

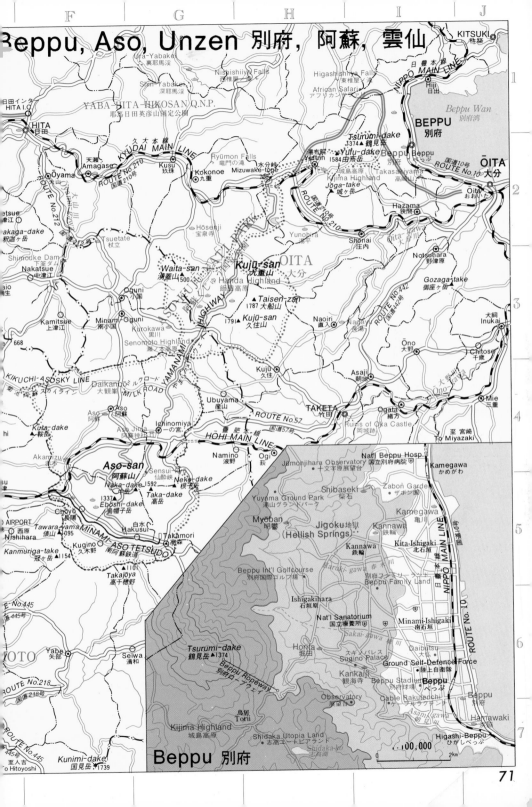

KITSUKI
杵築

日豊本線
NIPPO MAIN LINE

Ura-Yabakei
裏耶馬渓

Nishishiiya Falls
西椎屋ノ滝

Higashishiiya Falls
東椎屋ノ滝

African Safari
アフリカンサファリ

Hiji
日出

BEPPU
別府

Beppu Wan
別府湾

Shin-Yabakei
深耶馬渓

YABA-HITA-HIKOSAN Q.N.P.
耶馬日田英彦山国定公園

HITA I.C.
日田インタ

Tsurumi-dake
鶴見岳
1374▲

Beppu
別府 Beppu
べっぷ

HITA
日田

KYUDAI MAIN LINE
久大本線

Ryūmon Falls
竜門の滝

Yufuin
湯布院

Yufu-dake
1584▲由布岳

別府 ŌITA
国道10号 大分
ROUTE No.10

ŌITA
大分

Amagase
天瀬

Kusu
玖珠

Kokonoe
九重

Mizuwake-tōge
水分峠

Kijima Highland
城島高原

Takasakiyama
高崎山

Oyama
大山

ROUTE No.210
国道210号

Oita
おおいた

Oita
大分

大山川

ROUTE No.212
国道212号

Jōga-take
城ヶ岳

Hazama
狭間

Otetsue
乙鶴

Shakaga-dake
釈迦ヶ岳

Tsuetate
杖立

Hōsenji
宝泉寺

Yunohira
湯平

Shonai
庄内

Oita-gawa
大分川

Notsuhara
野津原

Shimouoke Dam
下筌ダム

Nakatsue
中津江

Waita-san
涌蓋山
500▲

Kujū-san
九重山

ŌITA
大分

Handa Highland
飯田高原

ROUTE No.142
国道442号

Gozaga-take
御座ヶ岳

Kamitsue
上津江

Minami-Oguni
南小国

Oguni
小国

SOYU-QUASI NAT'L PARK / YAMANAMI HIGHWAY
阻蘇くじゅう国立公園 やまなみハイウェイ

Taisen-zan
1787▲大船山

Naoiri
直入

Nagayu
長湯

Inukai
大飼

Kurokawa
黒川

668

Kujū-san
1791▲久住山

Ōno
大野

Chitose
千歳

Senomoto Highland
瀬ノ本高原

Kujū
久住

Asaji
朝治

Mie
三重

KIKUCHI-ASOSKY LINE
菊池阿蘇スカイライン

Daikanbō
大観峰

MILK ROAD
ミルクロード スカイライン

Ubuyama
産山

ROUTE No.57
国道57号

TAKETA
竹田

Ogata
緒方

Aso
阿蘇

Aso
阿蘇

Ichinomiya
一の宮

Aso Jinja
阿蘇神社

HOHI MAIN LINE
豊肥本線

Ruins of Oka Castle
岡城跡

至 宮崎
To Miyazaki

Kita-dake
鞍岳

Akamizu
赤水

Aso-san
阿蘇山

Naka-dake 1592
中岳

Neko-dake
根子岳

Namino
波野

Ogi
荻

Sensui
仙酔峡

1337▲
Eboshi-dake
烏帽子岳

Taka-dake
高岳

Hakusui
白水

AIRPORT

Nishihara
西原

Tawara-yama
俵山
1095▲

Choyō
長陽

Kugino
久木野

Takamori
高森

MINAMI-ASO TETSUDO
南阿蘇鉄道

Kanmuriga-take
冠ヶ岳
1154▲

Takachihoya
高千穂野
1101▲

ROUTE No.445
国道445号

ROUTE No.218
国道218号

Yabe
矢部

Seiwa
清和

Kunimi-dake
国見岳
1739▲

Takajōya
高城野

至 人吉
To Hitoyoshi

Beppu 別府

Nat'l Beppu Hosp.
国立別府病院

Jūmonjihara Observatory
十文字原展望所

Kamegawa
かめがわ

Kamegawa
亀川

Shibaseki
柴石

Zabon Garden
ザボン園

Yuyama Ground Park
湯山グランドパーク

Myōban
明礬

Jigoku 地獄
(Hellish Springs)

Kannawa
鉄輪

Kita-Ishigaki
北石垣

Kannawa
鉄輪

Beppu Int'l Golfcourse
別府国際ゴルフ場

Beppu Family Land
別府ファミリーランド

Ishigakihara
石垣原

Maruki-gawa 春木川

Nat'l Sanatorium
国立療養所

Minami-Ishigaki
南石垣

Sakai-gawa 境川

Tsurumi-dake
鶴見岳
▲1374

Beppu Ropeway
別府ロープウェイ

Honta
堀田

Sugino Palace
スギノパレス

Daibutsu
大仏

Ground Self-Defence Force
陸上自衛隊

Observatory
展望台

Kankaiji
観海寺

Beppu Stadium
別府野球場

Beppu
別府
べっぷ

Kijima Highland
城島高原

Torii
鳥居

Cable Rakutenchi
ラクテンチケーブル

Beppu
別府

Shidaka Utopia Land
志高ユートピアランド

Asami-gawa 朝見川

Higashi-Beppu
ひがしべっぷ

Hamawaki
浜脇

100,000

0   1   2km

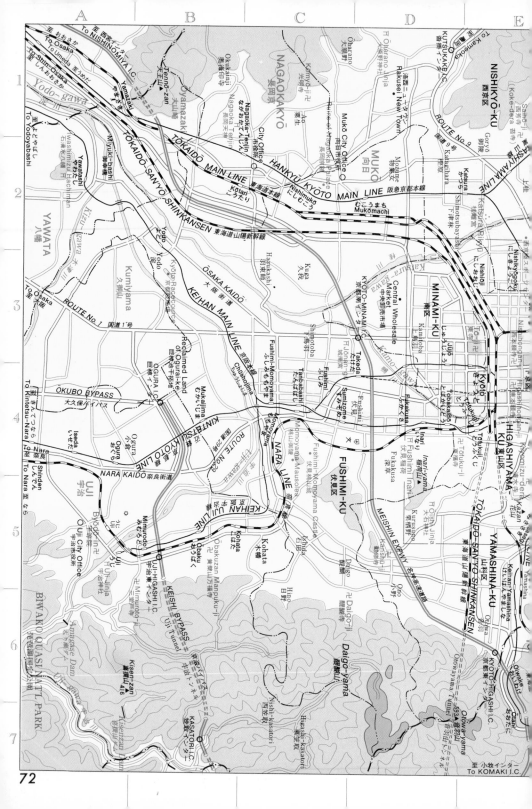

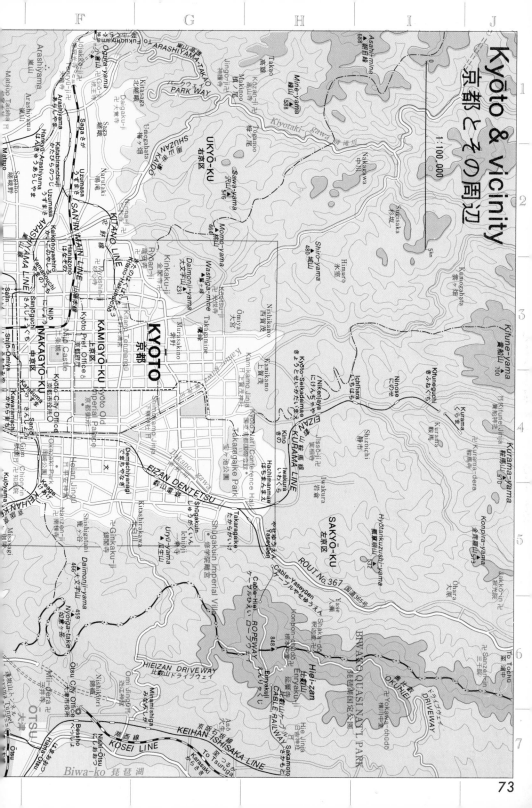

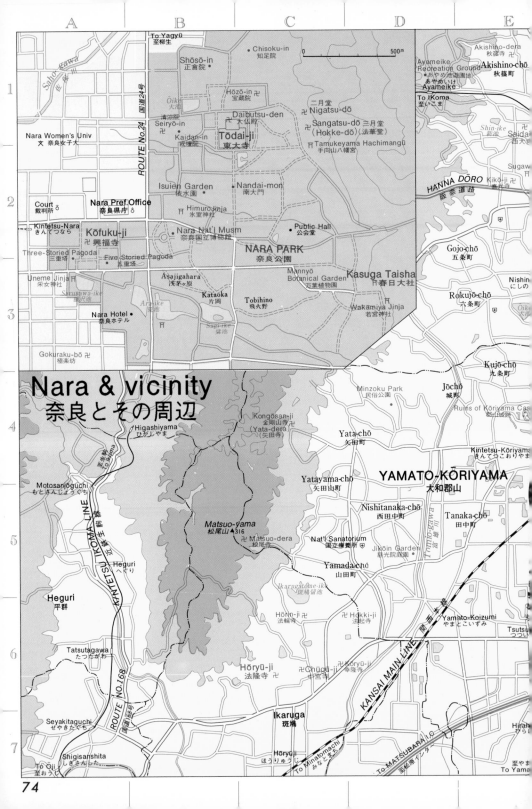

Nara & vicinity
奈良とその周辺

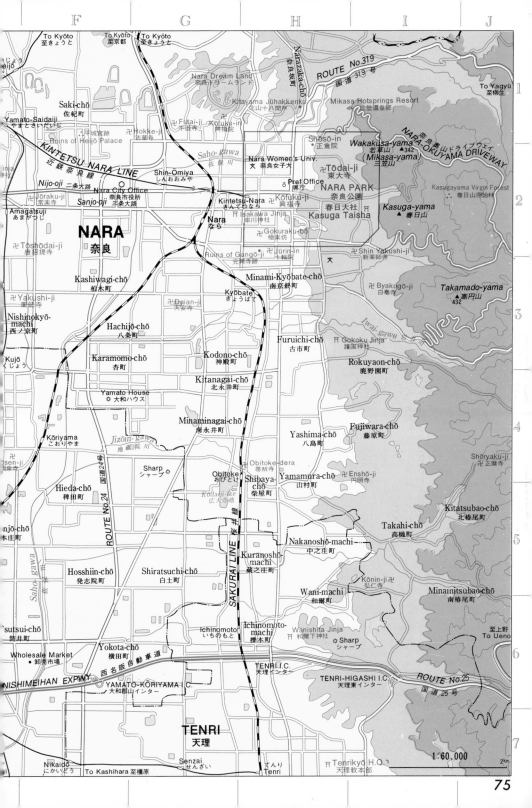

To Kyōto
至きょうと
To Kyōto
至京都
To Kyōto
至きょうと

奈良坂町
Narazaka-chō

ROUTE No.319
国道 319 号

To Yagyū
至柳生

Nara Dream Land
奈良ドリームランド

Kitayama Jūhakkenko
北山十八間戸

Mikasa Hotsprings Resort
笠原泉郷

NARA-OKUYAMA DRIVEWAY
奈良奥山ドライブウェイ

Saki-chō
佐紀町

卍 Hokke-ji
法華寺

卍 Futai-ji
不退寺

Kōfuku-in
興福院

Shōsō-in
正倉院

Wakakusa-yama
若草山
(Mikasa-yama)
三笠山
▲342

Kasugayama Virgin Forest
春日山原始林

Yamato-Saidaiji
やまとさいだいじ

Ruins of Heijō Palace

KINTETSU-NARA LINE
近鉄奈良線

Saho-gawa
佐保川

Nara Women's Univ.
文 奈良女子大

Tōdai-ji
東大寺

卍 Jōraku-ji
常楽寺

Shin-Ōmiya
しんおおみや

Nara City Office
奈良市役所

NARA PARK
奈良公園

Kasuga-yama
▲ 春日山

Nijo-oji
二条大路

Sanjo-oji
三条大路

Kintetsu-Nara
きんてつなら

Kōfuku-ji
興福寺

春日大社
Kasuga Taisha

Amagatsuji
あまがつじ

卍 Tōshōdai-ji
唐招提寺

Nara
なら

卍 Gokuraku-bō
極楽坊

卍 Shin Yakushi-ji
新薬師寺

NARA
奈良

Ruins of Gangō-ji
元興寺跡

卍 Jūrin-in
十輪院

文

Takamado-yama
高円山
▲432

Kashiwagi-chō
柏木町

Minami-Kyōbate-chō
南京終町

卍 Byakugō-ji
白毫寺

Nishinokyō-machi
西ノ京町

卍 Yakushi-ji
薬師寺

卍 Daian-ji
大安寺

Kyōbate
きょうばて

Hachijō-chō
八条町

Furuichi-chō
古市町

Gokoku Jinja
護国神社

Iwai-gawa
岩井川

Rokuyaon-chō
鹿野園町

Karamomo-chō
杏町

Kodono-chō
神殿町

Yamato House
✿ 大和ハウス

Kitanagai-chō
北永井町

Fujiwara-chō
藤原町

Shōryaku-ji
卍 正暦寺

Kōriyama
こおりやま

Jizōin-gawa
地蔵院川

Minaminagai-chō
南永井町

Yashima-chō
八島町

Yamamura-chō
山村町

卍 Enshō-ji
円照寺

Sharp
シャープ

Obitoke-dera
帯解寺

Kitatsubao-chō
北椿尾町

Hieda-chō
稗田町

Obitoke
おびとけ

Shibaya-chō
柴屋町

Kōdai-ike
広大寺池

Takahi-chō
高樋町

njō-chō
本庄町

Hosshiin-chō
発志院町

Shiratsuchi-chō
白土町

SAKURAI LINE
桜井線

Nakanoshō-machi
中之庄町

Kōnin-ji 卍
弘仁寺

Minamitsubao-chō
南椿尾町

Kuranoshō-machi
蔵之庄町

Wani-machi
和爾町

sutsui-chō
筒井町

Ichinomoto
いちのもと

Ichinomoto-machi
櫟本町

Wanishita Jinja
卍 和爾下神社

至上野
To Ueno

卍 Sharp
シャープ

Wholesale Market
● 卸売市場

Yokota-chō
横田町

NISHIMEIHAN EXPWY
西名阪自動車道

YAMATO-KŌRIYAMA I.C.
大和郡山インター

TENRI I.C.
天理インター

TENRI-HIGASHI I.C.
天理東インター

ROUTE No.25
国道 25 号

TENRI
天理

Nikaidō
にかいどう

To Kashihara 至橿原

Senzai
せんざい

Tenri
てんり

Tenrikyō H.Q.
天理教本部

1:60,000

2km

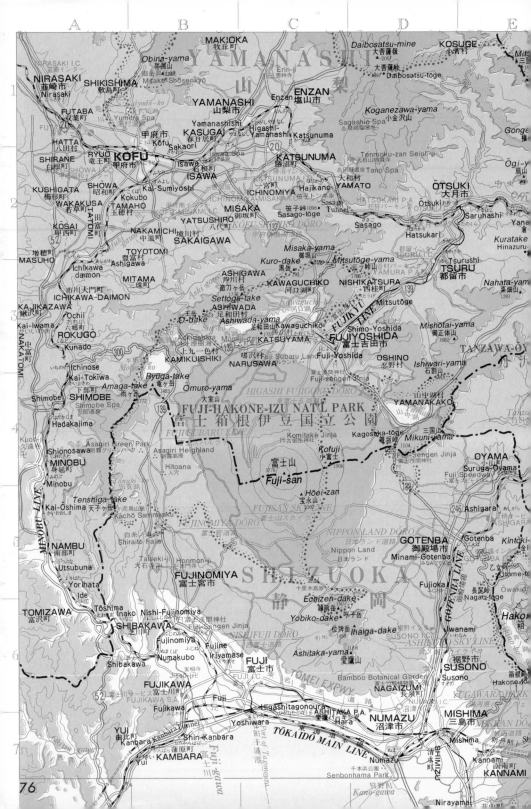

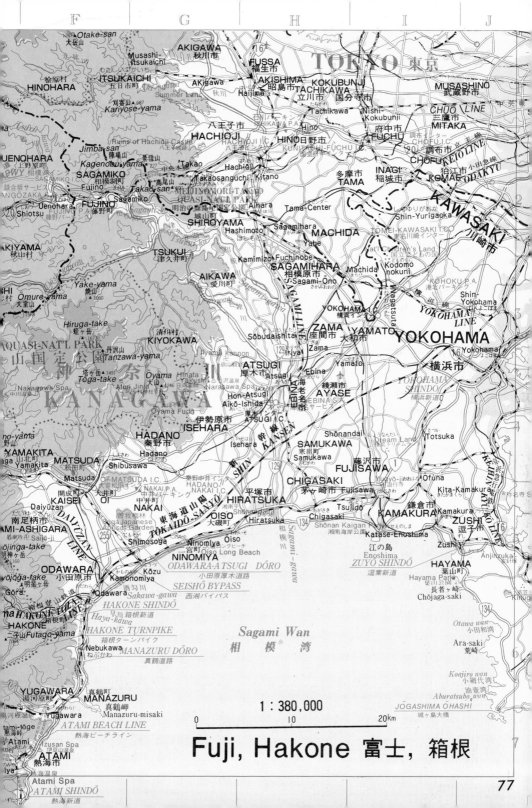

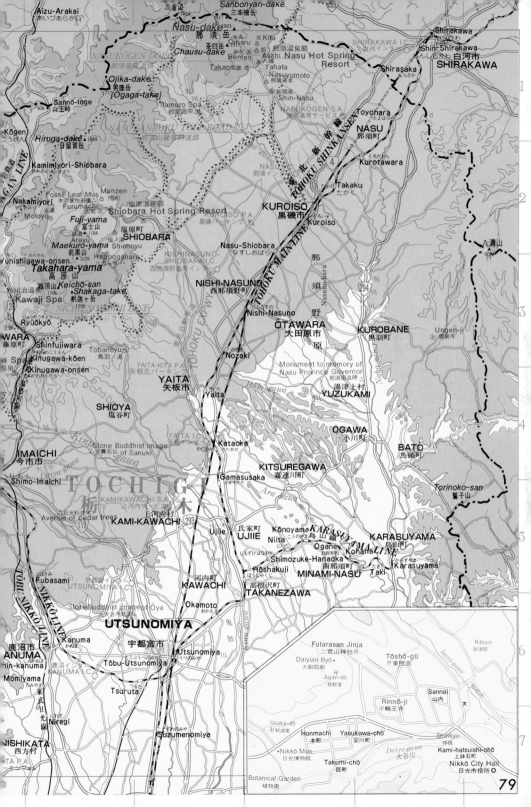

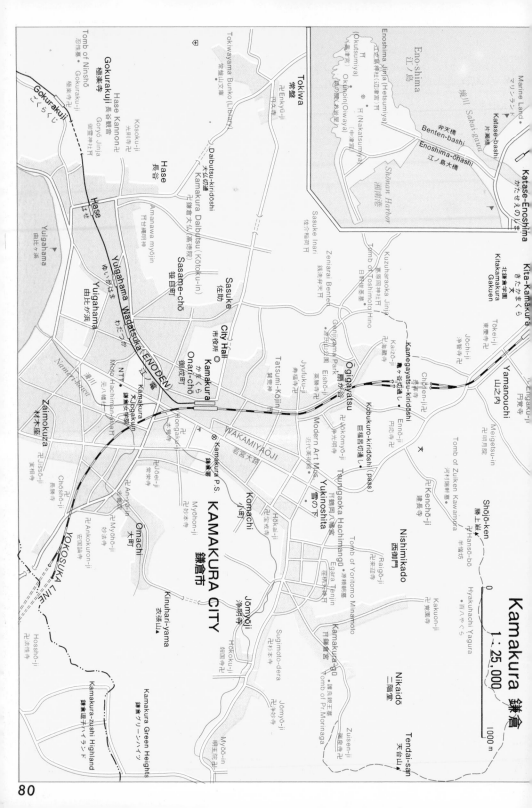

Transportation Maps

交通図

Metropolitan Hiking path 首都圏自然歩道

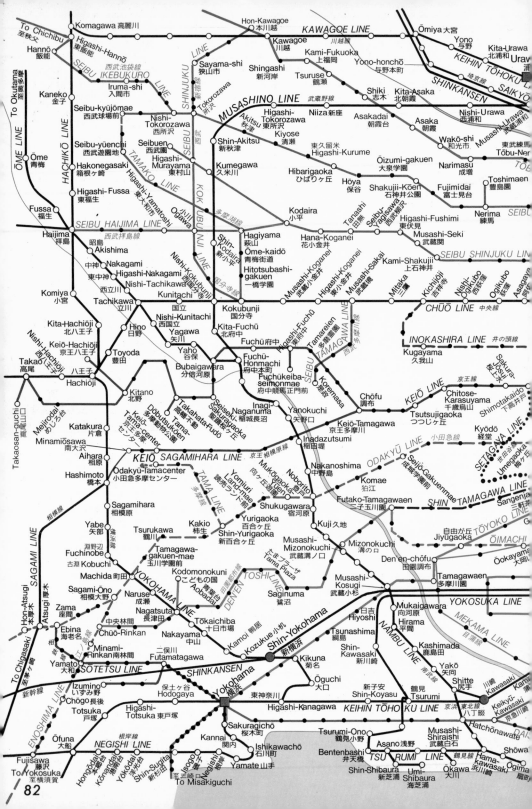

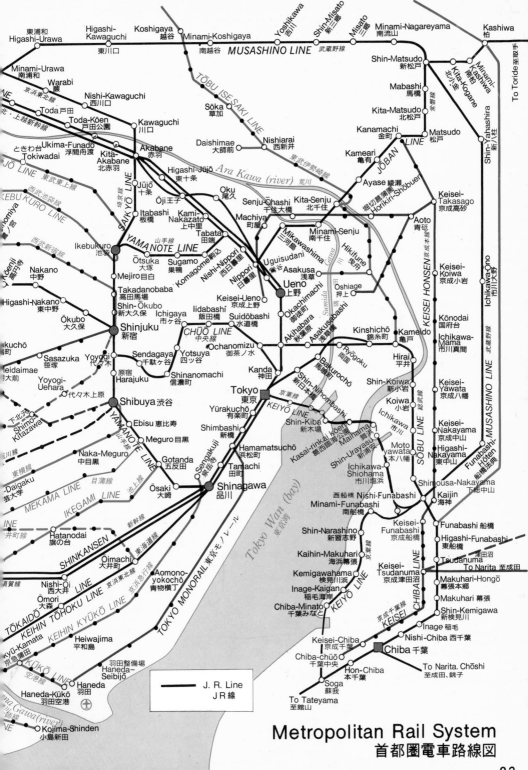

Metropolitan Rail System
首都圏電車路線図

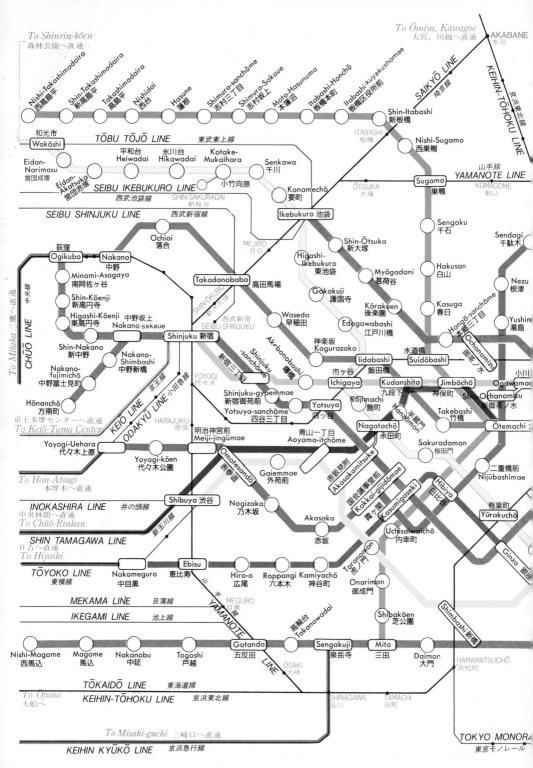

Tokyo Subway System
東京地下鉄路線図

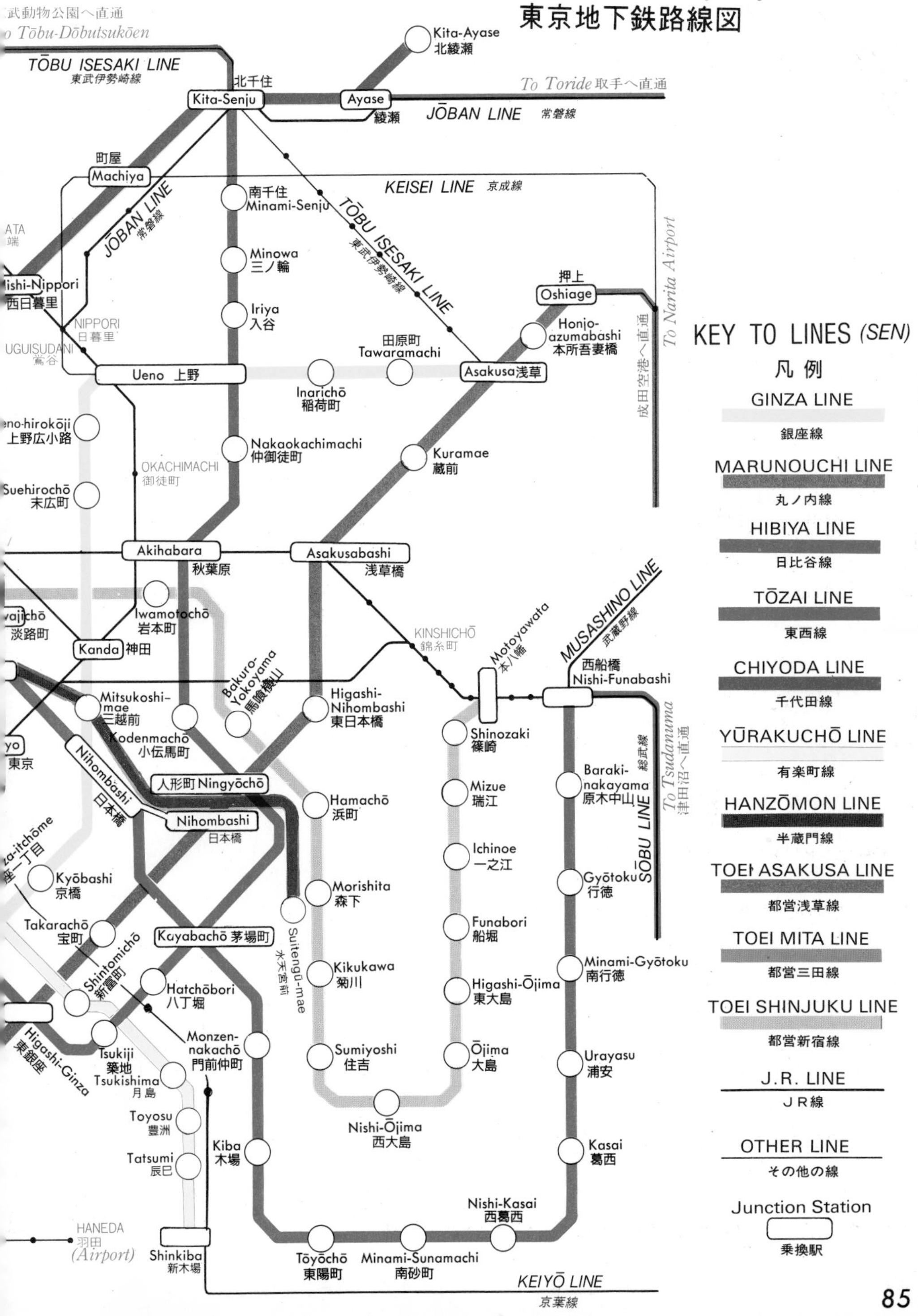

武動物公園へ直通
o Tōbu-Dōbutsukōen

Kita-Ayase
北綾瀬

TŌBU ISESAKI LINE
東武伊勢崎線

北千住
Kita-Senju

Ayase
綾瀬

To Toride 取手へ直通

JŌBAN LINE 常磐線

町屋
Machiya

KEISEI LINE 京成線

南千住
Minami-Senju

JŌBAN LINE 常磐線

ATA
端

TŌBU ISESAKI LINE
東武伊勢崎線

Minowa
三ノ輪

押上
Oshiage

ishi-Nippori
西日暮里

Iriya
入谷

Honjo-
azumabashi
本所吾妻橋

To Narita Airport 成田空港へ直通

NIPPORI
日暮里

UGUISUDANI
鴬谷

Ueno 上野

田原町
Tawaramachi

Asakusa 浅草

Inarichō
稲荷町

no-hirokōji
上野広小路

Nakaokachimachi
仲御徒町

Kuramae
蔵前

OKACHIMACHI
御徒町

Suehirochō
末広町

Akihabara
秋葉原

Asakusabashi
浅草橋

MUSASHINO LINE 武蔵野線

wajichō
淡路町

Iwamotochō
岩本町

Kanda 神田

Motoyawata
本八幡

KINSHICHŌ
錦糸町

西船橋
Nishi-Funabashi

Mitsukoshi-
mae
三越前

Bakuro-
Yokoyama
馬喰横山

Higashi-
Nihombashi
東日本橋

Shinozaki
篠崎

yo
東京

Kodenmachō
小伝馬町

Nihombashi
日本橋

Mizue
瑞江

Baraki-
nakayama
原木中山

人形町 Ningyōchō
日本橋

Hamachō
浜町

Ichinoe
一之江

Gyōtoku
行徳

Nihombashi
日本橋

za-itchōme
座一丁目

Morishita
森下

Funabori
船堀

SŌBU LINE 総武線

To Tsudanuma 津田沼へ直通

Kyōbashi
京橋

Kayabachō 茅場町

Kikukawa
菊川

Higashi-Ōjima
東大島

Minami-Gyōtoku
南行徳

Takarachō
宝町

Suitengū-mae 水天宮前

Shintomichō
新富町

Hatchōbori
八丁堀

Sumiyoshi
住吉

Ōjima
大島

Urayasu
浦安

Higashi-Ginza
東銀座

Tsukiji
築地

Monzen-
nakachō
門前仲町

Tsukishima
月島

Nishi-Ōjima
西大島

Kasai
葛西

Toyosu
豊洲

Kiba
木場

Tatsumi
辰巳

Nishi-Kasai
西葛西

HANEDA
羽田
(Airport)

Shinkiba
新木場

Tōyōchō
東陽町

Minami-Sunamachi
南砂町

KEIYŌ LINE
京葉線

KEY TO LINES (SEN)
凡 例

GINZA LINE
銀座線

MARUNOUCHI LINE
丸ノ内線

HIBIYA LINE
日比谷線

TŌZAI LINE
東西線

CHIYODA LINE
千代田線

YŪRAKUCHŌ LINE
有楽町線

HANZŌMON LINE
半蔵門線

TOEI ASAKUSA LINE
都営浅草線

TOEI MITA LINE
都営三田線

TOEI SHINJUKU LINE
都営新宿線

J. R. LINE
JR線

OTHER LINE
その他の線

Junction Station
乗換駅

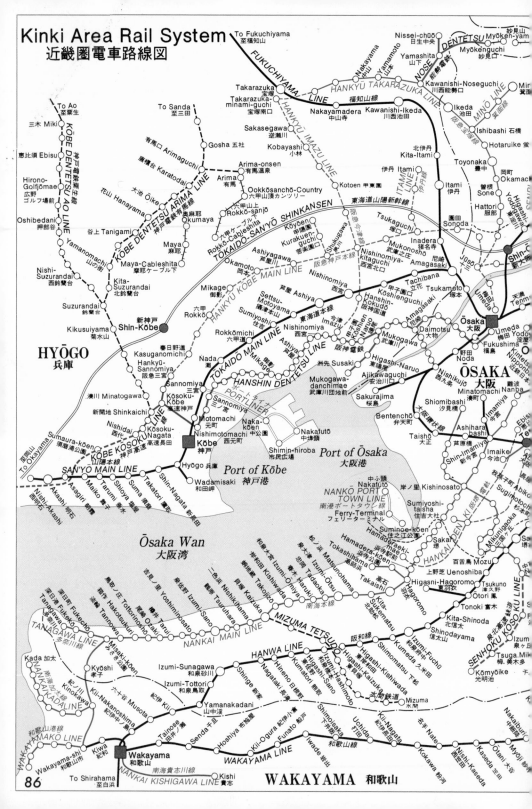

Kinki Area Rail System
近畿圏電車路線図

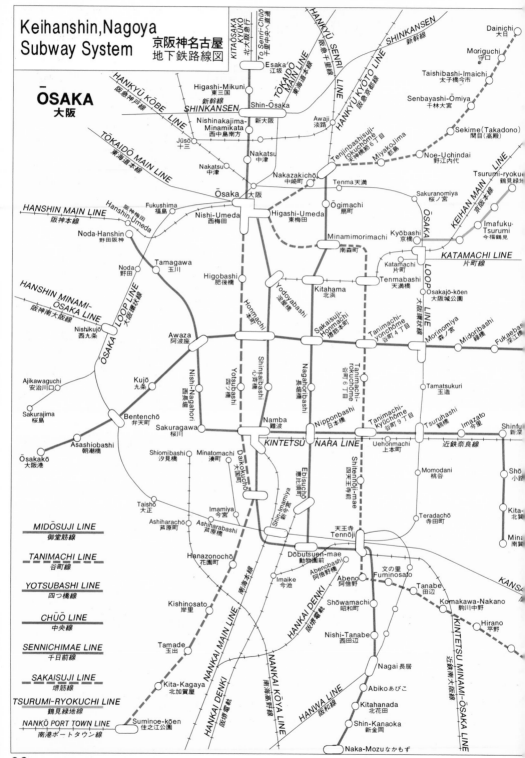

Keihanshin,Nagoya Subway System

京阪神名古屋
地下鉄路線図

ŌSAKA
大阪

HANKYŪ KŌBE LINE 阪急神戸線

TŌKAIDŌ MAIN LINE 東海道本線

HANSHIN MAIN LINE 阪神本線

HANSHIN MINAMI-ŌSAKA LINE 阪神南大阪線

KITAOSAKA KYŪKŌ 北大阪急行
To Senri-Chūō 千里中央方面行
Esaka 江坂

HANKYŪ SENRI LINE 阪急千里線

SHINKANSEN 新幹線

HANKYŪ KYOTO LINE 阪急京都線

KEIHAN MAIN LINE 京阪本線

Higashi-Mikuni 東三国
Shin-Ōsaka 新大阪
SHINKANSEN 新幹線
Nishinakajima-Minamikata 西中島南方
Awaji 淡路
Jūsō 十三
Nakatsu 中津
Nakatsu 中津
Nakazakichō 中崎町
Tenma 天満
Tenjinbashisuji-rokuchōme 天神橋筋6丁目
Miyakojima 都島
Ōsaka 大阪
Dainichi 大日
Moriguchi 守口
Taishibashi-Imaichi 太子橋今市
Senbayashi-Ōmiya 千林大宮
Sekime (Takadono) 関目(高殿)
Noe-Uchindai 野江内代
Tsurumi-ryoku 鶴見緑地
Imafuku-Tsurumi 今福鶴見

Fukushima 福島
Nishi-Umeda 西梅田
Noda-Hanshin 野田阪神
Tamagawa 玉川
Noda 野田
Higashi-Umeda 東梅田
Ōgimachi 扇町
Sakuranomiya 桜ノ宮
Minamimorimachi 南森町
Kyōbashi 京橋
ŌSAKA LOOP LINE 大阪環状線
KATAMACHI LINE 片町線
Katamachi 片町
Tenmabashi 天満橋
Ōsakajō-kōen 大阪城公園
Higobashi 肥後橋
Kitahama 北浜
Yodoyabashi 淀屋橋
Hommachi 本町
Sakaisuji-Hommachi 堺筋本町
Tanimachi-Yonchōme 谷町4丁目
Morinomiya 森ノ宮
Midoribashi 緑橋
Fukaebas 深江橋
Awaza 阿波座
Nishi-Nagahori 西長堀
Shinsaibashi 心斎橋
Nagahoribashi 長堀橋
Tanimachi-rokuchōme 谷町6丁目
Tamatsukuri 玉造
Tsuruhashi 鶴橋
Imazato 今里
Shinful 新深
Sho 小路
Kita 北蒲
Mina 南蒲
Ajikawaguchi 安治川口
Kujō 九条
Yotsubashi 四ツ橋
Namba 難波
Nipponbashi 日本橋
Tanimachi-kyuchōme 谷町9丁目
Uehonmachi 上本町
KINTETSU NARA LINE 近鉄奈良線
Sakurajima 桜島
Bentenchō 弁天町
Sakuragawa 桜川
Asashiobashi 朝潮橋
Ōsakakō 大阪港
Shiomibashi 汐見橋
Minatomachi 湊町
Daikokuchō 大国町
Ebisuchō 恵美須町
Shin-Imamiya 新今宮
Shitennōji-mae 四天王寺前
Momodani 桃谷
Teradachō 寺田町
Taishō 大正
Imamiya 今宮
Ashiharachō 芦原町
Ashiharabashi 芦原橋
Tennōji 天王寺
Hanazonochō 花園町
Dōbutsuen-mae 動物園前
Abenobashi 阿倍野橋
Abeno 阿倍野
Fuminosato 文の里
Tanabe 田辺
Komakawa-Nakano 駒川中野
Imaike 今池
Shōwamachi 昭和町
Hirano 平野
Kishinosato 岸里
Nishi-Tanabe 西田辺
HANKAI DENKI 阪堺電気
HANWA LINE 阪和線
KINTETSU MINAMI-ŌSAKA LINE 近鉄南大阪線
KANSAI
Tamade 玉出
Nagai 長居
Kita-Kagaya 北加賀屋
Abiko あびこ
Kitahanada 北花田
Shin-Kanaoka 新金岡
Suminoe-kōen 住之江公園
Naka-Mozu なかもず

MIDŌSUJI LINE 御堂筋線

TANIMACHI LINE 谷町線

YOTSUBASHI LINE 四つ橋線

CHŪŌ LINE 中央線

SENNICHIMAE LINE 千日前線

SAKAISUJI LINE 堺筋線

TSURUMI-RYOKUCHI LINE 鶴見緑地線

NANKŌ PORT TOWN LINE 南港ポートタウン線

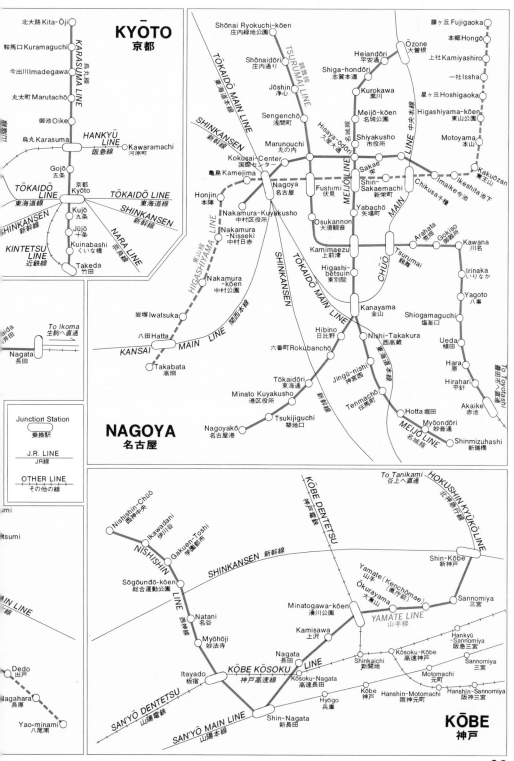

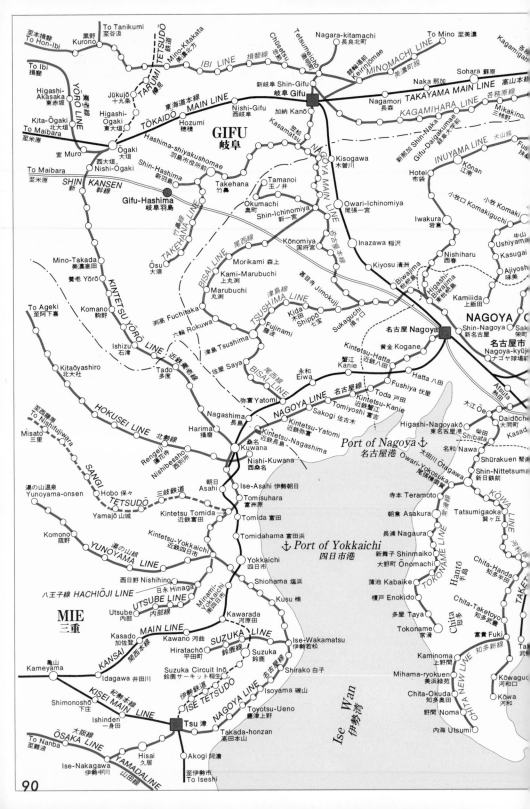

Chūkyō (Nagoya) Area Rail System
中京圏電車路線図

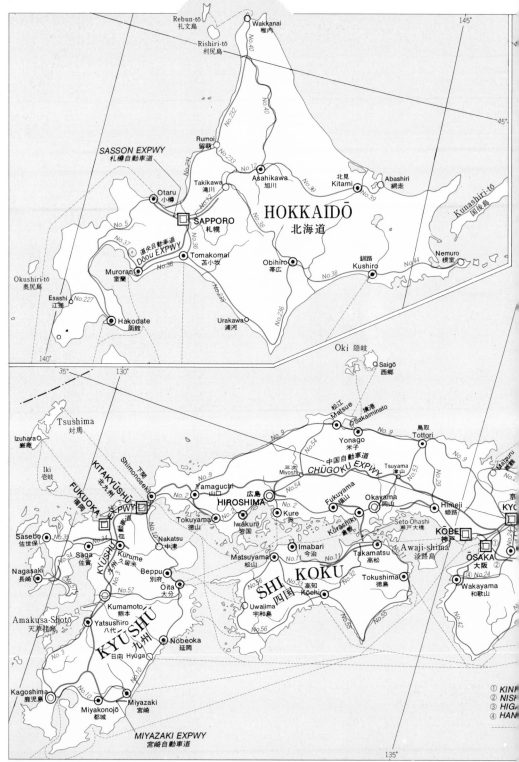

Rebun-tō
礼文島
Wakkanai
稚内
Rishiri-tō
利尻島

No.40

No.232

No.40

45°

Rumoi
留萌
No.231
No.233

SASSON EXPWY
札幌自動車道

Takikawa
滝川
No.12
Asahikawa
旭川
No.39
北見
Kitami
Abashiri
網走

Otaru
小樽

No.12

No.36

Kunashiri-tō
国後島

Okushiri-tō
奥尻島

No.5

SAPPORO
札幌

HOKKAIDŌ
北海道

No.37
道央自動車道
Dōou EXPWY

No.38

Tomakomai
苫小牧

Muroran
室蘭

No.36

No.36

Obihiro
帯広

Kushiro
釧路

No.44

Nemuro
根室

Esashi
江差
No.227

No.235

No.236

No.38

Hakodate
函館

Urakawa
浦河

140°

35°

130°

Oki 隠岐

Saigō
西郷

Tsushima
対馬

Matsue
松江
Sakaiminato
境港
Yonago
米子

No.9

Tottori
鳥取

No.9

Izuhara
厳原

No.9

三次
Miyoshi
No.54

中国自動車道
CHŪGOKU EXPWY

Tsuyama
津山
No.53

Maizuru
No.29

Iki
壱岐

KITAKYŪSHŪ
北九州
Shimonoseki
下関

No.9

Yamaguchi
山口

広島
HIROSHIMA

No.54

Fukuyama
福山

福山
Okayama
岡山

Himeji
姫路

KYO

FUKUOKA
福岡

PWY
九州自動車道

No.2

Tokuyama
徳山

No.2

Kure
呉

Kurashiki
倉敷

Seto-Ōhashi
瀬戸大橋

KŌBE
神戸

Sasebo
佐世保
No.35

No.34

Nakatsu
中津

Iwakuni
岩国

Imabari
今治

Takamatsu
高松

Awaji-shima
淡路島

OSAKA
大阪

Saga
佐賀

Kurume
久留米

Matsuyama
松山

No.11

No.32

No.24

Nagasaki
長崎

No.34

Beppu
別府

No.57

Ōita
大分

SHI KOKU
四国

高知
Kōchi

Tokushima
徳島

Wakayama
和歌山

Amakusa-Shotō
天草諸島

Kumamoto
熊本

Uwajima
宇和島

No.56

No.55

No.42

Yatsushiro
八代

KYŪSHU
九州

日向 Hyūga

Nobeoka
延岡

No.3

No.10

Kagoshima
鹿児島
No.10

Miyazaki
宮崎

Miyakonojō
都城

MIYAZAKI EXPWY
宮崎自動車道

135°

① KIN
② NISH
③ HIGA
④ HAN

Major Roads 主要道路

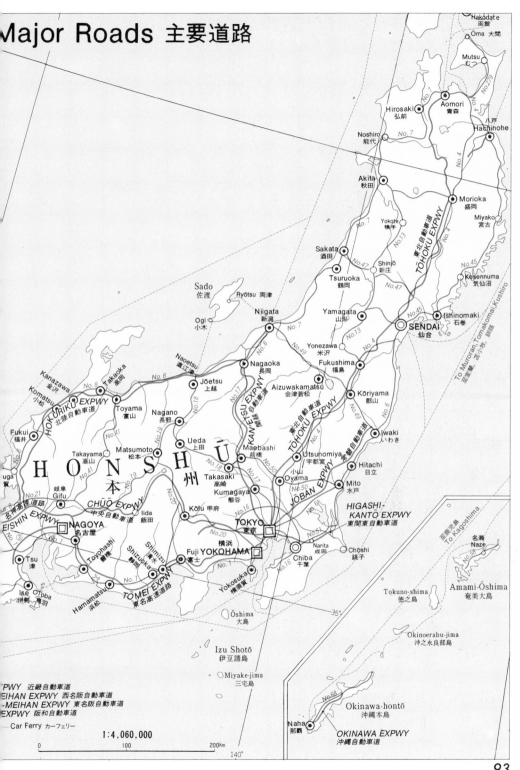

Hakodate 函館
Oma 大間
Mutsu むつ
Aomori 青森
Hirosaki 弘前
Hachinohe 八戸
Noshiro 能代
Akita 秋田
Morioka 盛岡
Miyako 宮古
Yokote 横手
Sakata 酒田
Shinjō 新庄
Kesennuma 気仙沼
Tsuruoka 鶴岡
Yamagata 山形
Ishinomaki 石巻
Niigata 新潟
Yonezawa 米沢
SENDAI 仙台
Sado 佐渡
Ryōtsu 両津
Fukushima 福島
Ogi 小木
Nagaoka 長岡
Aizuwakamatsu 会津若松
Kōriyama 郡山
Naoetsu 直江津
Jōetsu 上越
Kanazawa 金沢
Takaoka 高岡
Iwaki いわき
Komatsu 小松
Toyama 富山
Nagano 長野
Ueda 上田
Utsunomiya 宇都宮
Hitachi 日立
Fukui 福井
Maebashi 前橋
Mito 水戸
Takayama 高山
Matsumoto 松本
Oyama 小山
HONSHŪ 本州
Gifu 岐阜
Takasaki 高崎
Iida 飯田
Kumagaya 熊谷
NAGOYA 名古屋
Kōfu 甲府
TOKYO 東京
Narita 成田
Chōshi 銚子
Tsu 津
Toyohashi 豊橋
Shimizu 清水
Fuji 富士
YOKOHAMA 横浜
Chiba 千葉
Ise 伊勢
Ōbata 鳥羽
Shizuoka 静岡
Yokosuka 横須賀
Hamamatsu 浜松
Ōshima 大島

Naze 名瀬
Amami-Ōshima 奄美大島
Tokuno-shima 徳之島
Okinoerabu-jima 沖之永良部島

Izu Shotō 伊豆諸島
Miyake-jima 三宅島

Okinawa-hontō 沖縄本島
Naha 那覇
OKINAWA EXPWY 沖縄自動車道

HOKURIKU EXPWY 北陸自動車道
CHŪŌ EXPWY 中央自動車道
TŌMEI EXPWY 東名高速道路
KAN'ETSU EXPWY 関越自動車道
TŌHOKU EXPWY 東北自動車道
JŌBAN EXPWY 常磐自動車道
HIGASHI-KANTŌ EXPWY 東関東自動車道
EISHIN EXPWY 名神高速道路

To Muroran,Tomakomai,Kushiro
室蘭，苫小牧，釧路
To Kagoshima 鹿児島

…PWY 近畿自動車道
…EIHAN EXPWY 西名阪自動車道
…-MEIHAN EXPWY 東名阪自動車道
…EXPWY 阪和自動車道

Car Ferry カーフェリー

1:4,060,000
0   100   200km

93

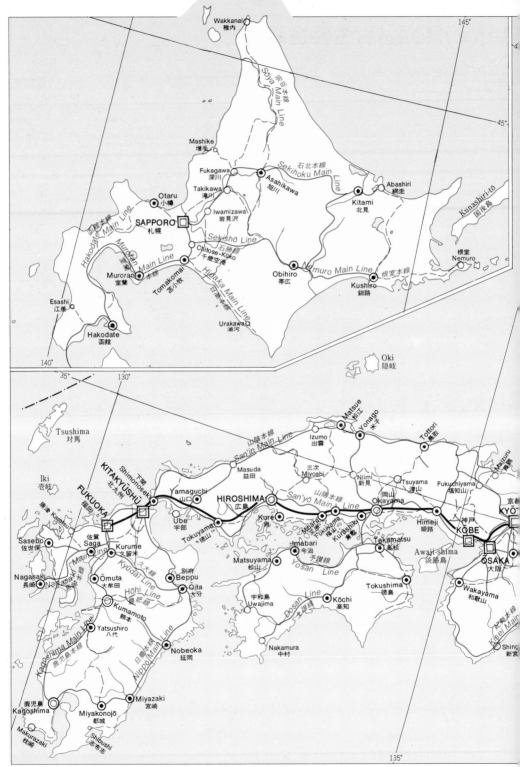

Wakkanai
稚内

Soya Main Line
宗谷本線

Mashike
増毛

Sekihoku Main Line
石北本線

Fukagawa
深川

Abashiri
網走

Asahikawa
旭川

Takikawa
滝川

Iwamizawa
岩見沢

Kitami
北見

Otaru
小樽

SAPPORO
札幌

Hakodate Main Line
函館本線

Chitose-Kūkō
千歳空港

Sekishō Line
石勝線

Muroran Main Line
室蘭本線

Tomakomai
苫小牧

Obihiro
帯広

Nemuro Main Line
根室本線

Kushiro
釧路

根室本線

Muroran
室蘭

Hidaka Main Line
日高本線

Urakawa
浦河

Kunashiri-tō
国後島

Nemuro
根室

Esashi
江差

Hakodate
函館

Oki
隠岐

Tsushima
対馬

San'in Main Line
山陰本線

Matsue
松江

Izumo
出雲

Yonago
米子

Tottori
鳥取

Iki
壱岐

KITAKYŪSHŪ
北九州

Shimonoseki
下関

Masuda
益田

Miyoshi
三次

Niimi
新見

Tsuyama
津山

Fukuchiyama
福知山

Maizuru
舞鶴

FUKUOKA
福岡

Yamaguchi
山口

HIROSHIMA
広島

San'yō Main Line
山陽本線

Okayama
岡山

京都
KYŌTO

Karatsu
唐津

Ube
宇部

Kure
呉

Mihara
三原

Fukuyama
福山

神戸
KOBE

Sasebo
佐世保

Saga
佐賀

Tokuyama
徳山

Kurashiki
倉敷

Himeji
姫路

Nagasaki Main Line
長崎本線

Kurume
久留米

Kyūdai Line
久大線

Imabari
今治

Takamatsu
高松

Awaji-shima
淡路島

OSAKA
大阪

Nagasaki
長崎

Beppu
別府

Matsuyama
松山

Yosan Line
予讃線

Ōmuta
大牟田

Ōita
大分

Wakayama
和歌山

Hōhi Line
豊肥線

Uwajima
宇和島

Tokushima
徳島

Kumamoto
熊本

Dosan Line
土讃線

Kōchi
高知

Kisei Main Line
紀勢本線

Kagoshima Main Line
鹿児島本線

Yatsushiro
八代

Nippo Main Line
日豊本線

Nakamura
中村

Shingū
新宮

Nobeoka
延岡

Kagoshima
鹿児島

Miyazaki
宮崎

Miyakonojō
都城

Makurazaki
枕崎

Shibushi
志布志

145°

45°

140°

35°

130°

135°

94

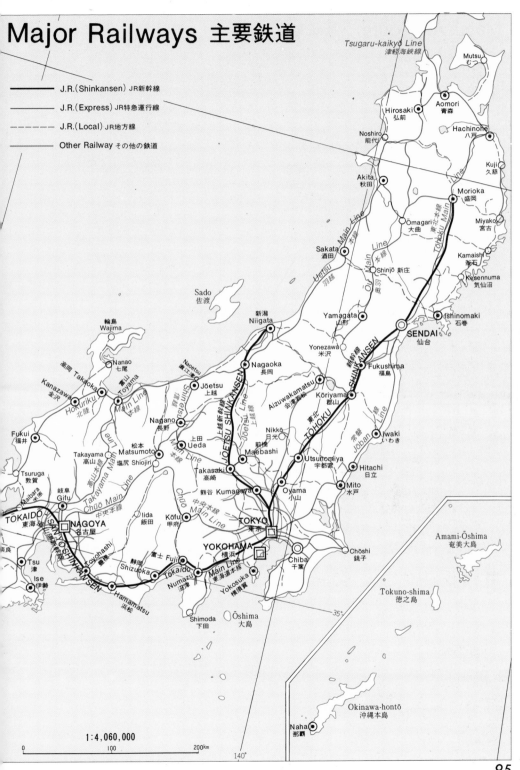

Major Railways 主要鉄道

J.R.(Shinkansen) JR新幹線
J.R.(Express) JR特急運行線
J.R.(Local) JR地方線
Other Railway その他の鉄道

Mutsu
むつ

Hirosaki
弘前

Aomori
青森

Hachinohe
八戸

Noshiro
能代

Kuji
久慈

Akita
秋田

Morioka
盛岡

Ōmagari
大曲

Miyako
宮古

Sado
佐渡

Sakata
酒田

Shinjō 新庄

Kamaishi
釜石

Wajima
輪島

新潟
Niigata

Yamagata
山形

Kesennuma
気仙沼

高岡 Takaoka

Nanao
七尾

Nagaoka
長岡

Yonezawa
米沢

Ishinomaki
石巻

Kanazawa
金沢

Toyama
富山

Jōetsu
上越

SENDAI
仙台

Hokuriku
北陸

Naoetsu
直江津

Aizuwakamatsu
会津若松

Fukushima
福島

Fukui
福井

Nagano
長野

Nikkō
日光

Kōriyama
郡山

Takayama
高山

Matsumoto
松本

Ueda
上田

Maebashi
前橋

Iwaki
いわき

Tsuruga
敦賀

塩尻 Shiojiri

Takasaki
高崎

Utsunomiya
宇都宮

Hitachi
日立

Maibara
米原

岐阜
Gifu

Kumagaya
熊谷

Oyama
小山

Mito
水戸

TOKAIDŌ
東海道

NAGOYA
名古屋

Iida
飯田

Kōfu
甲府

TOKYO
東京

浜松 Tsu
津

Toyohashi
豊橋

富士 Fuji

YOKOHAMA
横浜

Chōshi
銚子

Amami-Ōshima
奄美大島

Ise
伊勢

Shizuoka
静岡

Tōkaidō

Numazu
沼津

Chiba
千葉

Hamamatsu
浜松

Yokosuka
横須賀

Tokuno-shima
徳之島

Shimoda
下田

Ōshima
大島

Okinawa-hontō
沖縄本島

Naha
那覇

1:4,060,000

0   100   200km

95

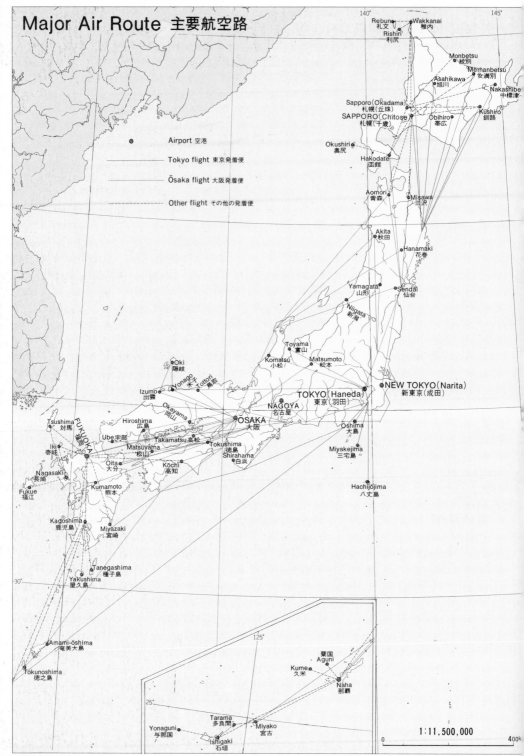

Major Air Route 主要航空路

Rebun 礼文
Rishiri 利尻
Wakkanai 稚内
Monbetsu 紋別
Memanbetsu 女満別
Asahikawa 旭川
Nakashibe 中標津
Sapporo(Okadama) 札幌(丘珠)
SAPPORO(Chitose) 札幌(千歳)
Obihiro 帯広
Kushiro 釧路
Okushiri 奥尻
Hakodate 函館
Aomori 青森
Misawa 三沢
Akita 秋田
Hanamaki 花巻
Yamagata 山形
Sendai 仙台
Niigata 新潟
Toyama 富山
Komatsu 小松
Matsumoto 松本
Oki 隠岐
Yonago 米子
Tottori 鳥取
Izumo 出雲
Okayama 岡山
TOKYO(Haneda) 東京(羽田)
NEW TOKYO(Narita) 新東京(成田)
NAGOYA 名古屋
OSAKA 大阪
Tsushima 対馬
FUKUOKA 福岡
Hiroshima 広島
Ube 宇部
Matsuyama 松山
Takamatsu 高松
Tokushima 徳島
Shirahama 白浜
Ōshima 大島
Iki 壱岐
Oita 大分
Kochi 高知
Miyakejima 三宅島
Nagasaki 長崎
Kumamoto 熊本
Fukue 福江
Kagoshima 鹿児島
Miyazaki 宮崎
Hachijōjima 八丈島
Tanegashima 種子島
Yakushima 屋久島
Amami-ōshima 奄美大島
Tokunoshima 徳之島

Aguni 粟国
Kume 久米
Naha 那覇
Tarama 多良間
Yonaguni 与那国
Miyako 宮古
Ishigaki 石垣

1:11,500,000

0   400k

96

Thematic Maps

テーマ図

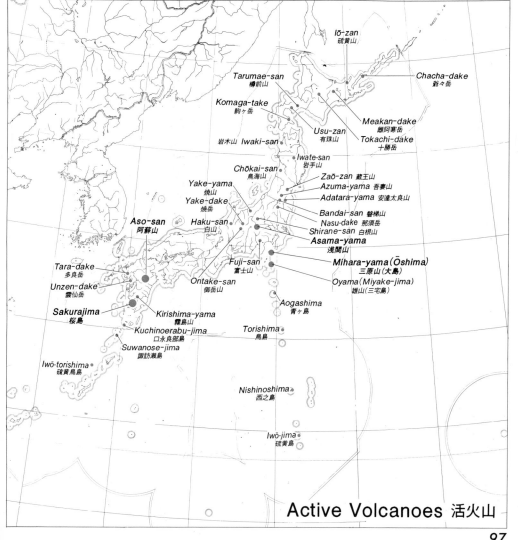

Active Volcanoes 活火山

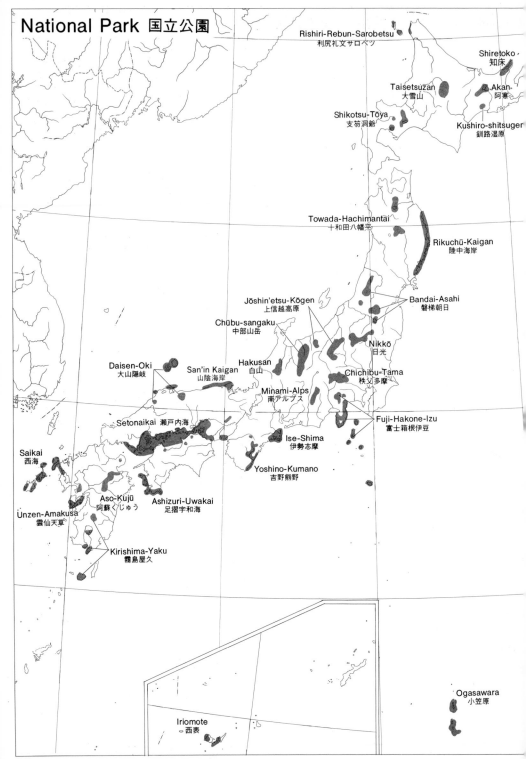

National Park 国立公園

Rishiri-Rebun-Sarobetsu
利尻礼文サロベツ

Shiretoko
知床

Taisetsuzan
大雪山

Akan
阿寒

Shikotsu-Tōya
支笏洞爺

Kushiro-shitsuger
釧路湿原

Towada-Hachimantai
十和田八幡平

Rikuchū-Kaigan
陸中海岸

Jōshin'etsu-Kōgen
上信越高原

Bandai-Asahi
磐梯朝日

Chūbu-sangaku
中部山岳

Nikkō
日光

Daisen-Oki
大山隠岐

San'in Kaigan
山陰海岸

Hakusan
白山

Chichibu-Tama
秩父多摩

Minami-Alps
南アルプス

Fuji-Hakone-Izu
富士箱根伊豆

Setonaikai 瀬戸内海

Saikai
西海

Ise-Shima
伊勢志摩

Aso-Kujū
阿蘇くじゅう

Ashizuri-Uwakai
足摺宇和海

Yoshino-Kumano
吉野熊野

Unzen-Amakusa
雲仙天草

Kirishima-Yaku
霧島屋久

Ogasawara
小笠原

Iriomote
西表

Quasi National Park 国定公園

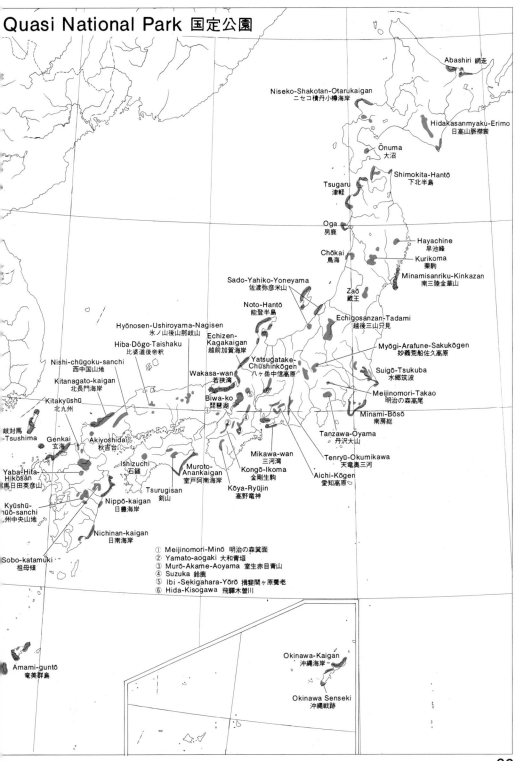

Abashiri 網走

Niseko-Shakotan-Otarukaigan
ニセコ積丹小樽海岸

Hidakasanmyaku-Erimo
日高山脈襟裳

Ōnuma
大沼

Shimokita-Hantō
下北半島

Tsugaru
津軽

Oga
男鹿

Hayachine
早池峰

Chōkai
鳥海

Kurikoma
栗駒

Minamisanriku-Kinkazan
南三陸金華山

Sado-Yahiko-Yoneyama
佐渡弥彦米山

Zaō
蔵王

Noto-Hantō
能登半島

Echigosanzan-Tadami
越後三山只見

Hyōnosen-Ushiroyama-Nagisen
氷ノ山後山那岐山

Echizen-
Kagakaigan
越前加賀海岸

Myōgi-Arafune-Sakukōgen
妙義荒船佐久高原

Hiba-Dōgo-Taishaku
比婆道後帝釈

Yatsugatake-
Chūshinkōgen
八ヶ岳中信高原

Suigō-Tsukuba
水郷筑波

Nishi-chūgoku-sanchi
西中国山地

Wakasa-wan
若狭湾

Meijinomori-Takao
明治の森高尾

Kitanagato-kaigan
北長門海岸

Biwa-ko
琵琶湖

Minami-Bōsō
南房総

Kitakyūshū
北九州

Tanzawa-Oyama
丹沢大山

岐対馬
-Tsushima

Genkai
玄海

Akiyoshidai
秋吉台

Mikawa-wan
三河湾

Tenryū-Okumikawa
天竜奥三河

Yaba-Hita-
Hikōsan
馬日田英彦山

Ishizuchi
石鎚

Muroto-
Anankaigan
室戸阿南海岸

Kongō-Ikoma
金剛生駒

Aichi-Kōgen
愛知高原

Kyūshū-
ɪɪŪō-sanchi
州中央山地

Tsurugisan
剣山

Kōya-Ryūjin
高野竜神

Nippō-kaigan
日豊海岸

Nichinan-kaigan
日南海岸

Sobo-katamuki
祖母傾

① Meijinomori-Minō 明治の森箕面
② Yamato-aogaki 大和青垣
③ Murō-Akame-Aoyama 室生赤目青山
④ Suzuka 鈴鹿
⑤ Ibi -Sekigahara-Yōrō 揖斐関ヶ原養老
⑥ Hida-Kisogawa 飛騨木曽川

Amami-guntō
奄美群島

Okinawa-Kaigan
沖縄海岸

Okinawa Senseki
沖縄戦跡

99

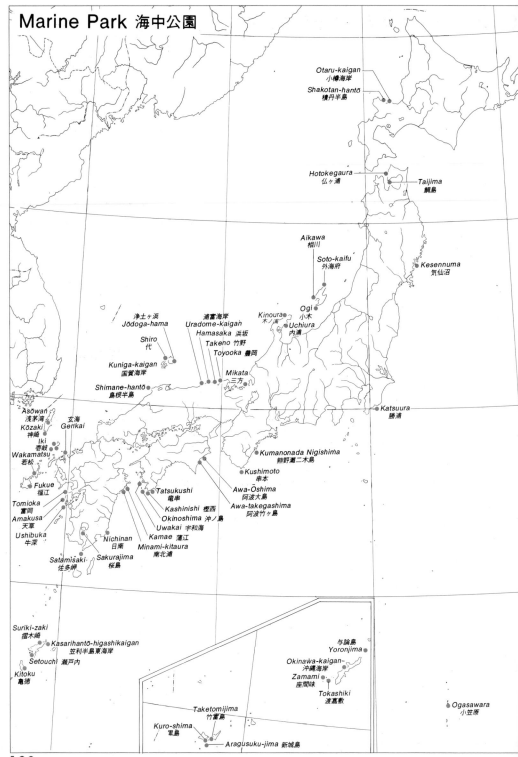

Marine Park 海中公園

Otaru-kaigan
小樽海岸
Shakotan-hantō
積丹半島

Hotokegaura
仏ヶ浦

Taijima
鯛島

Aikawa
相川

Soto-kaifu
外海府

Kesennuma
気仙沼

浄土ヶ浜
Jōdoga-hama

浦富海岸
Uradome-kaigan
Hamasaka 浜坂
Takeno 竹野
Toyooka 豊岡

Kinoura
木ノ浦
Ogi
小木
Uchiura
内浦

Shiro
代

Kuniga-kaigan
国賀海岸

Mikata
三方

Shimane-hantō
島根半島

Katsuura
勝浦

Asōwan
浅茅湾
Kōzaki
神崎
Iki
壱岐
Wakamatsu
若松

玄海
Genkai

Kumanonada Nigishima
熊野灘二木島

Kushimoto
串本

Awa-Ōshima
阿波大島

Awa-takegashima
阿波竹ヶ島

Fukue
福江

Tatsukushi
竜串

Kashinishi 樫西

Tomioka
富岡
Amakusa
天草
Ushibuka
牛深

Okinoshima 沖ノ島

Uwakai 宇和海

Satamisaki
佐多岬

Nichinan
日南

Sakurajima
桜島

Kamae 蒲江
Minami-kitaura
南北浦

Suriki-zaki
摺木崎

Kasarihantō-higashikaigan
笠利半島東海岸

Setouchi 瀬戸内

与論島
Yoronjima

Okinawa-kaigan
沖縄海岸

Kitoku
亀徳

Zamami
座間味

Tokashiki
渡嘉敷

Ogasawara
小笠原

Taketomijima
竹富島

Kuro-shima
黒島

Aragusuku-jima 新城島

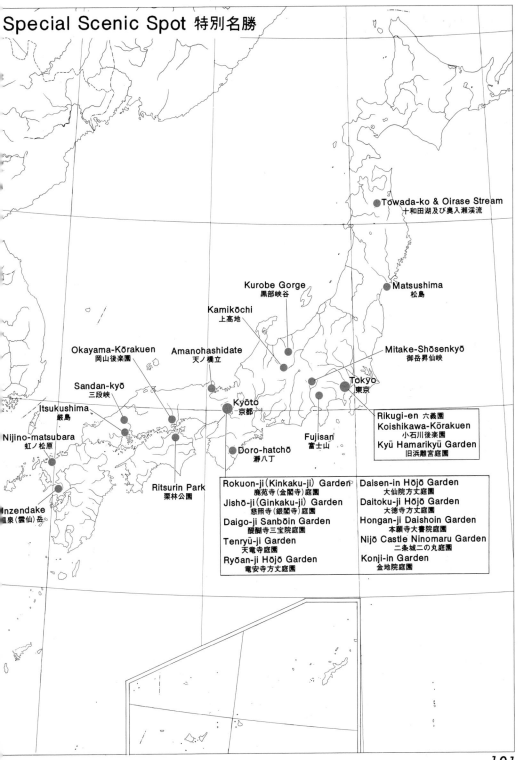

Special Scenic Spot 特別名勝

Towada-ko & Oirase Stream
十和田湖及び奥入瀬渓流

Kurobe Gorge
黒部峡谷

Matsushima
松島

Kamikōchi
上高地

Amanohashidate
天ノ橋立

Mitake-Shōsenkyō
御岳昇仙峡

Okayama-Kōrakuen
岡山後楽園

Tokyo
東京

Sandan-kyō
三段峡

Itsukushima
厳島

Kyōto
京都

Nijino-matsubara
虹ノ松原

Fujisan
富士山

Doro-hatchō
瀞八丁

Rikugi-en 六義園
Koishikawa-Kōrakuen
小石川後楽園
Kyū Hamarikyū Garden
旧浜離宮庭園

Ritsurin Park
栗林公園

Unzendake
温泉(雲仙)岳

Rokuon-ji(Kinkaku-ji) Garden 鹿苑寺(金閣寺)庭園	Daisen-in Hōjō Garden 大仙院方丈庭園
Jishō-ji(Ginkaku-ji) Garden 慈照寺(銀閣寺)庭園	Daitoku-ji Hōjō Garden 大徳寺方丈庭園
Daigo-ji Sanbōin Garden 醍醐寺三宝院庭園	Hongan-ji Daishoin Garden 本願寺大書院庭園
Tenryū-ji Garden 天竜寺庭園	Nijō Castle Ninomaru Garden 二条城二の丸庭園
Ryōan-ji Hōjō Garden 竜安寺方丈庭園	Konji-in Garden 金地院庭園

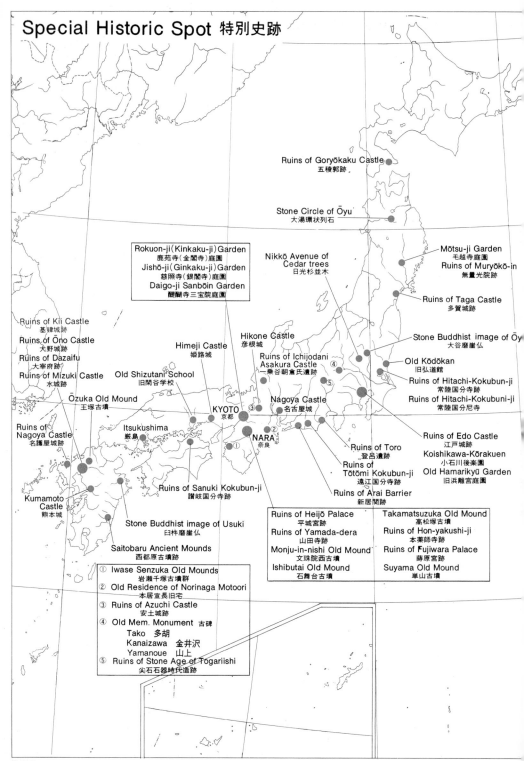

Special Historic Spot 特別史跡

Ruins of Goryōkaku Castle
五稜郭跡

Stone Circle of Ōyu
大湯環状列石

Mōtsu-ji Garden
毛越寺庭園
Ruins of Muryōkō-in
無量光院跡

Rokuon-ji(Kinkaku-ji)Garden
鹿苑寺(金閣寺)庭園
Jishō-ji(Ginkaku-ji)Garden
慈照寺(銀閣寺)庭園
Daigo-ji Sanbōin Garden
醍醐寺三宝院庭園

Nikkō Avenue of
Cedar trees
日光杉並木

Ruins of Taga Castle
多賀城跡

Hikone Castle
彦根城

Stone Buddhist image of Ōya
大谷磨崖仏

Ruins of Kii Castle
基肄城跡

Himeji Castle
姫路城

Ruins of Ichijodani
Asakura Castle
一乗谷朝倉氏遺跡

Old Kōdōkan
旧弘道館

Ruins of Ōno Castle
大野城跡

Old Shizutani School
旧閑谷学校

Ruins of Hitachi-Kokubun-ji
常陸国分寺跡

Ruins of Dazaifu
大宰府跡

Ruins of Mizuki Castle
水城跡

Nagoya Castle
名古屋城

Ruins of Hitachi-Kokubuni-ji
常陸国分尼寺

Ōzuka Old Mound
王塚古墳

KYOTO
京都

Ruins of Edo Castle
江戸城跡

Ruins of
Nagoya Castle
名護屋城跡

Itsukushima
厳島

NARA
奈良

Ruins of Toro
登呂遺跡

Koishikawa-Kōrakuen
小石川後楽園

Old Hamarikyū Garden
旧浜離宮庭園

Ruins of
Tōtōmi Kokubun-ji
遠江国分寺跡

Ruins of Sanuki Kokubun-ji
讃岐国分寺跡

Ruins of Arai Barrier
新居関跡

Kumamoto
Castle
熊本城

Stone Buddhist image of Usuki
臼杵磨崖仏

Ruins of Heijō Palace
平城宮跡

Takamatsuzuka Old Mound
高松塚古墳

Ruins of Yamada-dera
山田寺跡

Ruins of Hon-yakushi-ji
本薬師寺跡

Saitobaru Ancient Mounds
西都原古墳跡

Monju-in-nishi Old Mound
文珠院西古墳

Ruins of Fujiwara Palace
藤原宮跡

Ishibutai Old Mound
石舞台古墳

Suyama Old Mound
単山古墳

① Iwase Senzuka Old Mounds
岩瀬千塚古墳群
② Old Residence of Norinaga Motoori
本居宣長旧宅
③ Ruins of Azuchi Castle
安土城跡
④ Old Mem. Monument 古碑
　Tako 多胡
　Kanaizawa 金井沢
　Yamanoue 山上
⑤ Ruins of Stone Age of Togariishi
尖石石器時代遺跡

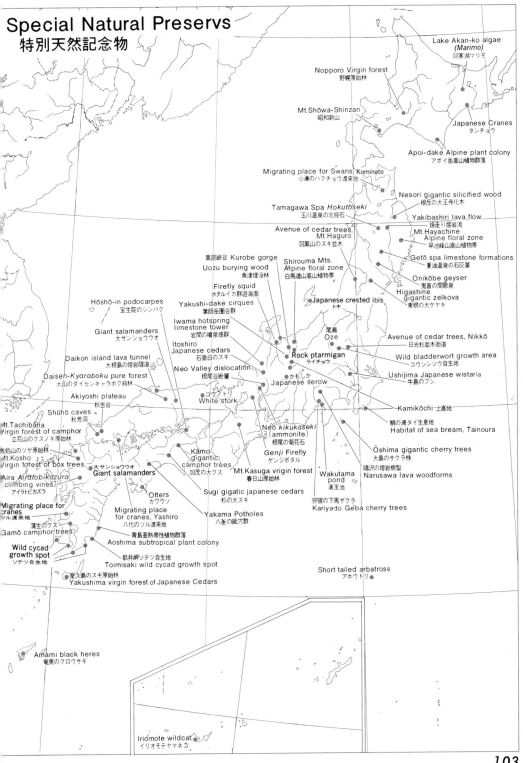

Special Natural Preservs
特別天然記念物

Lake Akan-ko algae
(Marimo)
阿寒湖マリモ

Nopporo Virgin forest
野幌原始林

Mt.Shōwa-Shinzan
昭和新山

Japanese Cranes
タンチョウ

Apoi-dake Alpine plant colony
アポイ岳高山植物群落

Migrating place for Swans, Kominato
小湊のハクチョウ渡来地

Nesori gigantic silicified wood
根反の大王寺化木

Tamagawa Spa *Hokutōseki*
玉川温泉の北投石

Yakibashiri lava flow
焼走り熔岩流

Mt.Hayachine
Alpine floral zone
早池峰山高山植物群落

Avenue of cedar trees,
Mt.Haguro
羽黒山のスギ並木

黒部峡谷 Kurobe gorge
Uozu burying wood
魚津埋・没林

Shirouma Mts.
Alpine floral zone
白馬連山高山植物帯

Getō spa limestone formations
夏油温泉の石灰華

Onikōbe geyser
鬼首の間歇泉

Higashine
gigantic zelkova
東根の大ケヤキ

Firefly squid
ホタルイカ群遊海面

Yakushi-dake cirques
薬師岳圏谷群

Japanese crested ibis
トキ

Hōshō-in podocarpes
宝生院のシンパク

Iwama hotspring
limestone tower
岩間の噴泉塔群

尾瀬
Oze

Avenue of cedar trees, Nikkō
日光杉並木街道

Giant salamanders
大サンショウウオ

Itoshiro
Japanese cedars
石徹白のスギ

Wild bladderwort growth area
コウシンソウ自生地

Daikon island lava tunnel
大根島の熔岩隧道

Neo Valley dislocation
根尾谷断層

Rock ptarmigan
ライチョウ

Ushijima Japanese wistaria
牛島のフジ

Daisen-*Kyaraboku* pure forest
大山のダイセンキャラボク純林

かもしか

Japanese serow

Akiyoshi plateau
秋吉台

コウノトリ
White stork

Kamikōchi 上高地

Shūhō caves
秋芳洞

Mt.Tachibana
Virgin forest of camphor
立花山のクスノキ原始林

鯛の浦タイ生息地
Habitat of sea bream, Tainoura

Mt.Kosho
Virgin forest of box trees
石鎚山のツゲ原始林

Neo *kikukaseki*
(ammonite)
根尾の菊花石

Ōshima gigantic cherry trees
大島のサクラ株

Aira *Airdfobikazura*
climbing vines
アイラトビカズラ

Kamo
gigantic
camphor trees
加茂のクス

Genji Firefly
ゲンジボタル

Wakutama
pond
湧玉池

鳴沢の熔岩樹型
Narusawa lava woodforms

大サンショウウオ
Giant salamanders

Mt.Kasuga virgin forest
春日山原始林

Migrating place for
cranes
ツル渡来地

Otters
カワウソ

Migrating place
for cranes, Yashiro
八代のツル渡来地

Sugi gigatic japanese cedars
杉の大スギ

狩宿の下馬ザクラ
Kariyado Geba cherry trees

Gamō camphor trees
蒲生のクス

Yakama Potholes
八釜の甌穴群

Wild cycad
growth spot
ソテツ自生地

青島亜熱帯性植物群落
Aoshima subtropical plant colony

Short tailed arbatross
アホウドリ

都井岬ソテツ自生地
Toimisaki wild cycad growth spot

屋久島のスギ原始林
Yakushima virgin forest of Japanese Cedars

Amami black heres
奄美のクロウサギ

Iridomote wildcat
イリオモテヤマネコ

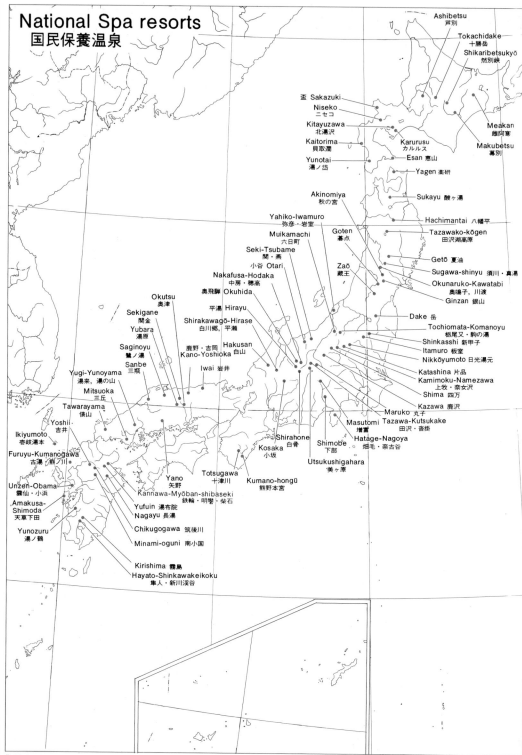

National Spa resorts
国民保養温泉

Ashibetsu 芦別
Tokachidake 十勝岳
Shikaribetsukyō 然別峡

盃 Sakazuki
Niseko ニセコ
Kitayuzawa 北湯沢
Kaitorima 貝取澗
Yunotai 湯ノ岱

Meakan 雌阿寒
Makubetsu 幕別
Karurusu カルルス
Esan 恵山
Yagen 薬研

Akinomiya 秋の宮
Sukayu 酸ヶ湯
Hachimantai 八幡平
Tazawako-kōgen 田沢湖高原

Yahiko-Iwamuro 弥彦・岩室
Muikamachi 六日町
Seki-Tsubame 関・燕
Otari 小谷
Nakafusa-Hodaka 中房・穂高
Okuhida 奥飛騨
Hirayu 平湯
Shirakawagō-Hirase 白川郷・平瀬
Hakusan 白山
Kano-Yoshioka 鹿野・吉岡
Iwai 岩井

Goten 碁点
Zaō 蔵王
Getō 夏油
Sugawa-shinyu 須川・真湯
Okunaruko-Kawatabi 奥鳴子、川渡
Ginzan 銀山
Dake 岳
Tochiomata-Komanoyu 栃尾又・駒の湯
Shinkasshi 新甲子
Itamuro 板室
Nikkōyumoto 日光湯元
Katashina 片品
Kamimoku-Namezawa 上牧・奈女沢
Shima 四万
Kazawa 鹿沢

Okutsu 奥津
Sekigane 関金
Yubara 湯原
Saginoyu 鷺ノ湯
Sanbe 三瓶
Yugi-Yunoyama 湯来、湯の山
Mitsuoka 三丘
Tawarayama 俵山
Yoshii 吉井
Ikiyumoto 壱岐湯本
Furuyu-Kumanogawa 古湯・熊ノ川
Unzen-Obama 雲仙・小浜
Amakusa-Shimoda 天草下田
Yunozuru 湯ノ鶴
Yano 矢野
Kannawa-Myōban-shibaseki 鉄輪・明礬・柴石
Yufuin 湯布院
Nagayu 長湯
Chikugogawa 筑後川
Minami-oguni 南小国
Kirishima 霧島
Hayato-Shinkawakeikoku 隼人・新川渓谷

Maruko 丸子
Masutomi 増富
Tazawa-Kutsukake 田沢・沓掛
Hatage-Nagoya 畑毛・奈古谷
Shirahone 白骨
Kosaka 小坂
Shimobe 下部
Utsukushigahara 美ヶ原
Totsugawa 十津川
Kumano-hongū 熊野本宮

104

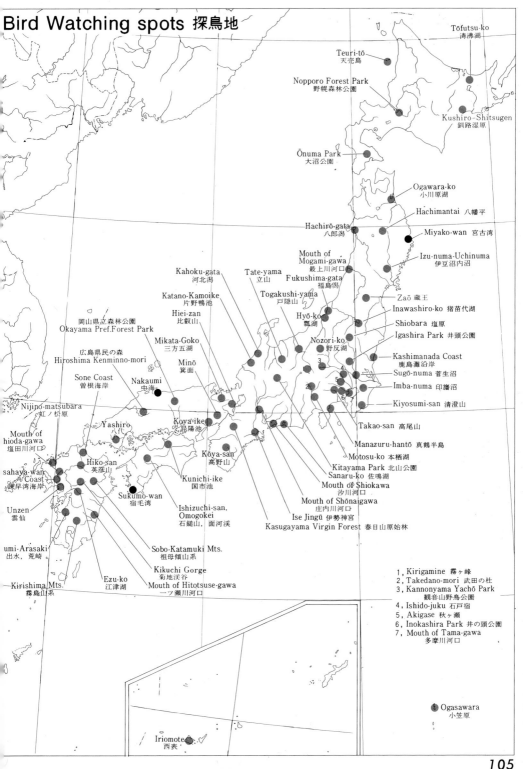

Bird Watching spots 探鳥地

Teuri-tō 天売島

Nopporo Forest Park 野幌森林公園

Tōfutsu-ko 涛沸湖

Kushiro-Shitsugen 釧路湿原

Ōnuma Park 大沼公園

Ogawara-ko 小川原湖

Hachimantai 八幡平

Hachirō-gata 八郎潟

Miyako-wan 宮古湾

Mouth of Mogami-gawa 最上川河口

Izu-numa-Uchinuma 伊豆沼内沼

Kahoku-gata 河北潟

Tate-yama 立山

Fukushima-gata 福島潟

Zaō 蔵王

Katano-Kamoike 片野鴨池

Togakushi-yama 戸隠山

Inawashiro-ko 猪苗代湖

Hiei-zan 比叡山

Hyō-ko 瓢湖

Shiobara 塩原

岡山県立森林公園
Okayama Pref.Forest Park

Mikata-Goko 三方五湖

Nozori-ko 野反湖

Igashira Park 井頭公園

広島県民の森
Hiroshima Kenminno-mori

Minō 箕面

Kashimanada Coast 鹿島灘沿岸

Sugō-numa 菅生沼

Sone Coast 曽根海岸

Nakaumi 中海

Imba-numa 印旛沼

Nijino-matsubara 虹ノ松原

Yashiro 八代

Kōya-ike 昆陽池

Kiyosumi-san 清澄山

Mouth of hioda-gawa 塩田川河口

Hiko-san 英彦山

Kōya-san 高野山

Takao-san 高尾山

sahaya-wan Coast 諫早湾海岸

Manazuru-hantō 真鶴半島

Kunichi-ike 国市池

Motosu-ko 本栖湖

Unzen 雲仙

Sukumo-wan 宿毛湾

Kitayama Park 北山公園

Sanaru-ko 佐鳴湖

Ishizuchi-san, Omogokei 石鎚山, 面河渓

Mouth of Shiokawa 汐川河口

Mouth of Shōnaigawa 庄内川河口

umi-Arasaki 出水, 荒崎

Sobo-Katamuki Mts. 祖母傾山系

Ise Jingū 伊勢神宮

Kasugayama Virgin Forest 春日山原始林

Kikuchi Gorge 菊地渓谷

Mouth of Hitotsuse-gawa 一ツ瀬川河口

Kirishima Mts. 霧島山系

Ezu-ko 江津湖

1, Kirigamine 霧ヶ峰
2, Takedano-mori 武田の杜
3, Kannonyama Yachō Park 観音山野鳥公園
4, Ishido-juku 石戸宿
5, Akigase 秋ヶ瀬
6, Inokashira Park 井の頭公園
7, Mouth of Tama-gawa 多摩川河口

Ogasawara 小笠原

Iriomote 西表

105

HOKKAIDŌ
北海道

Fujina-yaki
布志名焼

清水焼
Kiyomizu-yaki

Mijiro-yaki
御代焼

Izushi-yaki
出石焼

Echizen-
越前焼

Iwami-yaki
石見焼

SHIMANE
島根

TOTTORI
鳥取

Wakasa-
若狭焼

Hosshōji-yaki
法勝寺焼

Imari-Arita-yaki
伊万里, 有田焼

Koishihara-yaki
小石原焼

萩焼
Hagi-yaki

HIROSHIMA

OKAYAMA
岡山

KYŌTO
京都

Karatsu-yaki
唐津焼

YAMAGUCHI
山口

備前焼
Bizen-yaki

Tanba-Tachikui-yaki
丹波立杭焼

2

Takatori-yaki
高取焼

Miyajima-yaki 広島
宮島焼

Sakatsu-yaki
酒津焼

HYŌGO
兵庫

4

Mikawachi-yaki
三川内焼

Horikoshi-yaki
堀越焼

Mimaya-yaki
御廏焼

Akahada
赤膚焼

FUKUOKA
福岡

Agano-yaki
上野焼

KAGAWA
香川

OSAKA

SAGA
佐賀

Kikuma Kawara
菊間瓦

Minato-yaki
湊焼

Hasami-yaki
波佐見焼

Shiroishi-yaki
白石焼

Onta-yaki
小鹿田焼

Tobe-yaki
砥部焼

NARA
奈良

NAGASAKI
長崎

OITA

TOKUSHIMA
徳島

Otani-yaki
大谷焼

Uchida Sarayama-yaki
内田皿山焼

Kōzan-yaki
広山焼

EHIME
愛媛

阿波粘土瓦
Awa Nendogawara

WAKAYAMA
和歌山

Shōdai-yaki
小代焼

KŌCHI
高知

Uchiharano-yaki
内原野焼

Shig

Takahama-yaki
高浜焼

KUMAMOTO
熊本

Mizunohira-yaki
水の平焼

Takata-yaki 高田焼

Isshōchi-yaki
膳地焼

Odo-yaki 尾戸焼
Nosayama-Yaki
能茶山焼

Maruo-yaki
丸尾焼

MIYAZAKI
宮崎

Satsuma-yaki
さつま焼

Hioki Kawara
日置瓦

KAGOSHIMA
鹿児島

1, Mushiake-yaki　虫明焼
2, Kyō-gawara　京瓦
3, Zeze-yaki　膳所焼
4, Shimoda-yaki　下田焼
5, Hachiman-gawara　八幡瓦
6, Hatta-yaki　八田焼
7, Kuwana Banko-yaki　桑名万古焼
8, Akogi-yaki　阿漕焼
9, Matsusaka Banko-yaki　松阪万古焼

106

Ceramic kiln areas
陶磁器産地

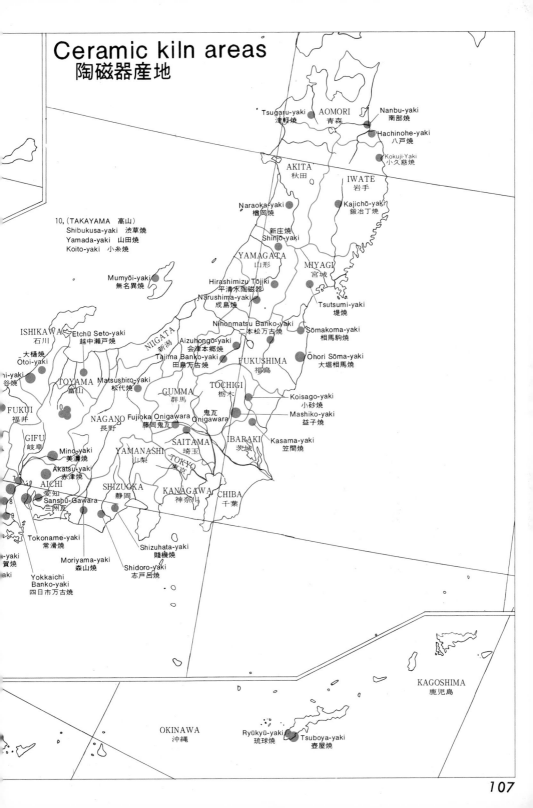

Tsugaru-yaki 津軽焼
AOMORI 青森
Nanbu-yaki 南部焼
Hachinohe-yaki 八戸焼
Kokuji-Yaki 小久慈焼

AKITA 秋田

IWATE 岩手

Naraoka-yaki 楢岡焼
Kajichō-yaki 鍛冶丁焼

新庄焼
Shinjo-yaki

10, (TAKAYAMA 高山)
Shibukusa-yaki 渋草焼
Yamada-yaki 山田焼
Koito-yaki 小糸焼

YAMAGATA 山形

MIYAGI 宮城

Mumyōi-yaki 無名異焼

Hirashimizu Tojiki 平清水陶磁器
Narushima-yaki 成島焼

Tsutsumi-yaki 堤焼

ISHIKAWA 石川
Etchū Seto-yaki 越中瀬戸焼

NIIGATA 新潟

Nihonmatsu Banko-yaki 二本松万古焼
Sōmakoma-yaki 相馬駒焼

大樋焼
Ōtoi-yaki

Aizuhongo-yaki 会津本郷焼
Tajima Banko-yaki 田島万古焼

FUKUSHIMA 福島

Ōhori Sōma-yaki 大堀相馬焼

-yaki
谷焼

TOYAMA 富山
Matsushiro-yaki 松代焼

GUMMA 群馬

TOCHIGI 栃木

Koisago-yaki 小砂焼
Mashiko-yaki 益子焼

FUKUI 福井

NAGANO 長野
Fujioka Onigawara 藤岡鬼瓦
Onigawara 鬼瓦

10

SAITAMA 埼玉

IBARAKI 茨城

Kasama-yaki 笠間焼

GIFU 岐阜

YAMANASHI 山梨

Mino-yaki 美濃焼
Akatsu-yaki 赤津焼

AICHI 愛知
Sanshū-Gawara 三州瓦

SHIZUOKA 静岡

TOKYO

KANAGAWA 神奈川

CHIBA 千葉

Tokoname-yaki 常滑焼

Shizuhata-yaki 賤機焼

-yaki
焼

Moriyama-yaki 森山焼
Shidoro-yaki 志戸呂焼

焼
yaki

Yokkaichi
Banko-yaki
四日市万古焼

KAGOSHIMA 鹿児島

OKINAWA 沖縄

Ryūkyū-yaki 琉球焼
Tsuboya-yaki 壺屋焼

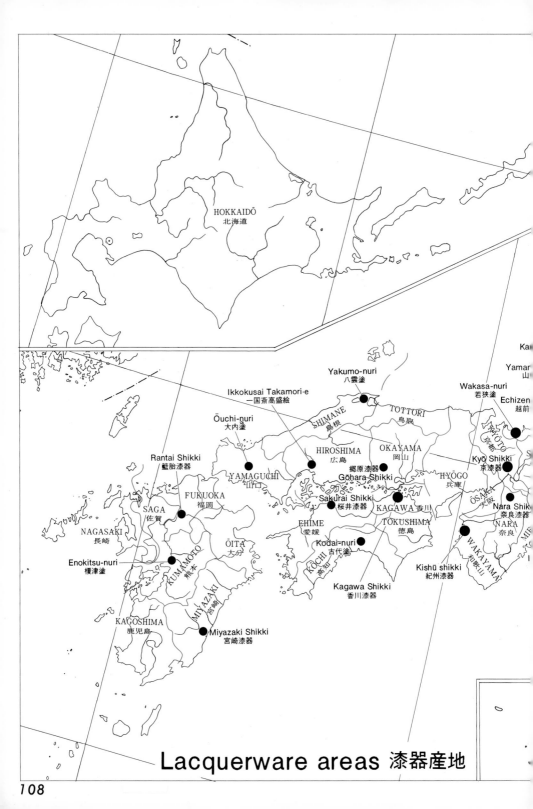

HOKKAIDŌ
北海道

Yakumo-nuri
八雲塗

Ikkokusai Takamori-e
一国斎高盛絵

Ōuchi-nuri
大内塗

SHIMANE
島根

TOTTORI
鳥取

Wakasa-nuri
若狭塗

Echizen
越前

Yamar
山

Ka

HIROSHIMA
広島

OKAYAMA
岡山

KYŌTO
京都

Kyō Shikki
京漆器

Rantai Shikki
藍胎漆器

YAMAGUCHI
山口

Gōhara Shikki
郷原漆器

HYŌGO
兵庫

OSAKA
大阪

Nara Shik
奈良漆器

FUKUOKA
福岡

Sakurai Shikki
桜井漆器

KAGAWA 香川

NARA
奈良

SAGA
佐賀

EHIME
愛媛

TOKUSHIMA
徳島

MI

NAGASAKI
長崎

ŌITA
大分

KŌCHI
高知

Kodai-nuri
古代塗

WAKAYAMA
和歌山

Kishū shikki
紀州漆器

Enokitsu-nuri
榎津塗

KUMAMOTO
熊本

MIYAZAKI
宮崎

KAGOSHIMA
鹿児島

Kagawa Shikki
香川漆器

Miyazaki Shikki
宮崎漆器

Lacquerware areas 漆器産地

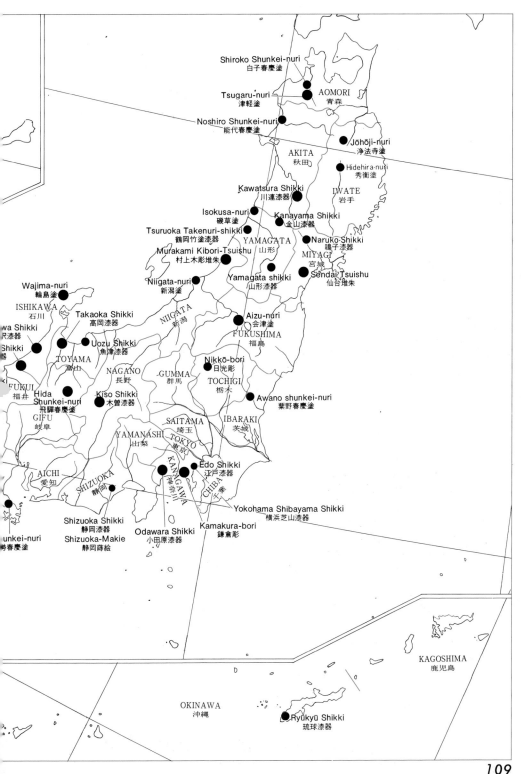

Shiroko Shunkei-nuri
白子春慶塗

Tsugaru-nuri
津軽塗

AOMORI
青森

Noshiro Shunkei-nuri
能代春慶塗

Jōhōji-nuri
浄法寺塗

AKITA
秋田

Hidehira-nuri
秀衡塗

Kawatsura Shikki
川連漆器

IWATE
岩手

Isokusa-nuri
磯草塗

Kanayama Shikki
金山漆器

Tsuruoka Takenuri-shikki
鶴岡竹塗漆器

YAMAGATA
山形

Naruko-Shikki
鳴子漆器

Murakami Kibori-Tsuishu
村上木彫堆朱

MIYAGI
宮城

Niigata-nuri
新潟塗

Yamagata shikki
山形漆器

Sendai Tsuishu
仙台堆朱

Wajima-nuri
輪島塗

ISHIKAWA
石川

Takaoka Shikki
高岡漆器

NIIGATA
新潟

Aizu-nuri
会津塗

wa Shikki
尺漆器

FUKUSHIMA
福島

Shikki
器

Uozu Shikki
魚津漆器

TOYAMA
富山

NAGANO
長野

GUMMA
群馬

Nikkō-bori
日光彫

ki
FUKUI
福井

Hida
Shunkei-nuri
飛騨春慶塗

GIFU
岐阜

Kiso Shikki
木曽漆器

TOCHIGI
栃木

Awano shunkei-nuri
粟野春慶塗

SAITAMA
埼玉

IBARAKI
茨城

AICHI
愛知

YAMANASHI
山梨

TOKYO
東京

Edo Shikki
江戸漆器

KANAGAWA
神奈川

CHIBA
千葉

SHIZUOKA
静岡

Shizuoka Shikki
静岡漆器

Shizuoka-Makie
静岡蒔絵

Odawara Shikki
小田原漆器

Kamakura-bori
鎌倉彫

Yokohama Shibayama Shikki
横浜芝山漆器

unkei-nuri
崎春慶塗

KAGOSHIMA
鹿児島

OKINAWA
沖縄

Ryūkyū Shikki
琉球漆器

109

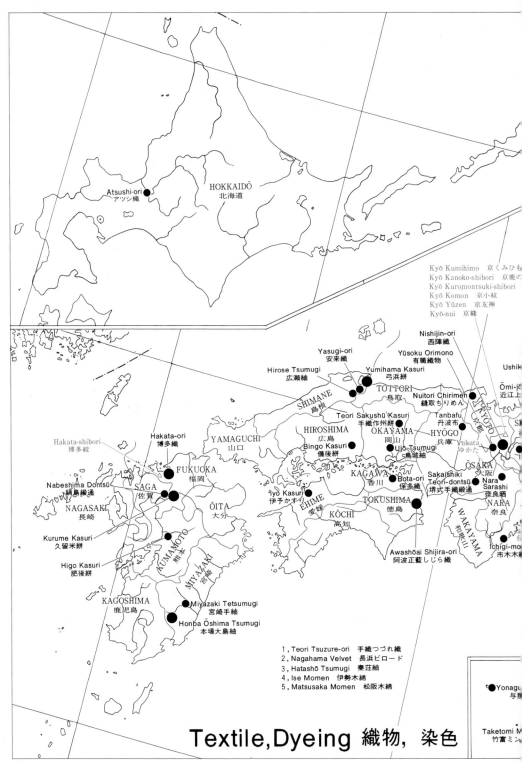

Atsushi-ori
アツシ織

HOKKAIDŌ
北海道

Kyō Kumihimo 京くみひも
Kyō Kanoko-shibori 京鹿の
Kyō Kuromontsuki-shibori
Kyō Komon 京小紋
Kyō Yūzen 京友禅
Kyō-nui 京縫

Nishijin-ori
西陣織

Yasugi-ori
安来織

Yūsoku Orimono
有職織物

Hirose Tsumugi
広瀬紬

Yumihama Kasuri
弓浜絣

Ushik

SHIMANE
島根

TOTTORI
鳥取

Nuitori Chirimen
縫取ちりめん

Ōmi-jo
近江上

Hakata-shibori
博多絞

Hakata-ori
博多織

YAMAGUCHI
山口

Teori Sakushū Kasuri
手織作州絣

Tanbafu
丹波布

KYOTO
京都

HIROSHIMA
広島

OKAYAMA
岡山

HYŌGO
兵庫

Yukata
ゆかた

Bingo Kasuri
備後絣

Ujō Tsumugi
鳥城紬

FUKUOKA
福岡

Nabeshima Dontsū
鍋島緞通

SAGA
佐賀

KAGAWA
香川

Bota-ori
保多織

Sakaishiki
Teori-dontsū
堺式手織緞通

ŌSAKA
大阪

Nara
Sarashi
奈良晒

NARA
奈良

NAGASAKI
長崎

ŌITA
大分

Iyo Kasuri
伊予かすり

EHIME
愛媛

TOKUSHIMA
徳島

WAKAYAMA
和歌山

Kurume Kasuri
久留米絣

KŌCHI
高知

Ichigi-mo
市木木綿

Higo Kasuri
肥後絣

KUMAMOTO
熊本

Awashōai Shijira-ori
阿波正藍しじら織

MIYAZAKI
宮崎

KAGOSHIMA
鹿児島

Miyazaki Tetsumugi
宮崎手紬

Honba Ōshima Tsumugi
本場大島紬

1, Teori Tsuzure-ori 手織つづれ織
2, Nagahama Velvet 長浜ビロード
3, Hatashō Tsumugi 秦荘紬
4, Ise Momen 伊勢木綿
5, Matsusaka Momen 松阪木綿

Yonagu

Taketomi M
竹富ミン

Textile, Dyeing 織物, 染色

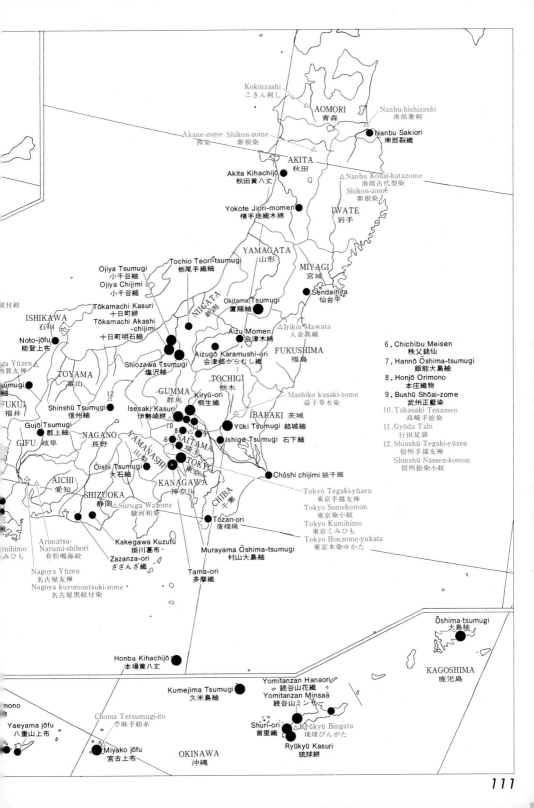

Kokinzashi
こきん刺し

Nanbu-hishizashi
南部菱刺

AOMORI
青森

Nanbu Sakiori
南部裂織

Akane-zome Shikon-zome
茜染 紫根染

AKITA
秋田

Akita Kihachijō
秋田黄八丈

IWATE
岩手

Nanbu Kodai-katazome
南部古代型染
Shikon-zome
紫根染

Yokote Jiori-momen
横手地織木綿

Tochio Teori-tsumugi
栃尾手織紬

YAMAGATA
山形

MIYAGI
宮城

Ojiya Tsumugi
小千谷紬
Ojiya Chijimi
小千谷縮

Okitama Tsumugi
置賜紬

Sendaihira
仙台平

Tōkamachi Kasuri
十日町絣
Tōkamachi Akashi
-chijimi
十日町明石綿

ISHIKAWA
石川

NIIGATA
新潟

Aizu Momen
会津木綿

Irikin Mawata
入金真綿

Noto-jōfu
能登上布

Aizugō Karamushi-ori
会津郷からむし織

FUKUSHIMA
福島

TOYAMA
富山

Shiozawa Tsumugi
塩沢紬

TOCHIGI
栃木

FUKUI
福井

Shinshū Tsumugi
信州紬

GUMMA
群馬

Kiryū-ori
桐生織

Mashiko kusaki-zome
益子草木染

Gujō Tsumugi
郡上紬

Isesaki Kasuri
伊勢崎絣

IBARAKI
茨城

GIFU
岐阜

NAGANO
長野

SAITAMA
埼玉

Yūki Tsumugi
結城紬

Ishige Tsumugi
石下紬

YAMANASHI
山梨

Ōishi Tsumugi
大石紬

TOKYO
東京

AICHI
愛知

SHIZUOKA
静岡

KANAGAWA
神奈川

Chōshi chijimi 銚子縮

Suruga Wazome
駿河和染

CHIBA
千葉

Tōzan-ori
唐棧織

Arimatsu-
Narumi-shibori
有松鳴海絞

Kakegawa Kuzufu
掛川葛布
Zazanza-ori
ざざんざ織

Murayama Ōshima-tsumugi
村山大島紬

Tokyo Tegaki-yūzen
東京手描友禅
Tokyo Somekomon
東京染小紋
Tokyo Kumihimo
東京くみひも
Tokyo Honzome-yukata
東京本染ゆかた

Nagoya Yūzen
名古屋友禅
Nagoya kuromontsuki-zome
名古屋黒紋付染

Tama-ori
多摩織

Honba Kihachijō
本場黄八丈

Ōshima-tsumugi
大島紬

KAGOSHIMA
鹿児島

Kumejima Tsumugi
久米島紬

Yomitanzan Hanaori
読谷山花織
Yomitanzan Minsaa
読谷山ミンサー

Choma Tetsumugi-ito
苧麻手紡糸

Yaeyama jōfu
八重山上布

Shuri-ori
首里織

Ryūkyū Bingata
琉球びんがた

Miyako jōfu
宮古上布

OKINAWA
沖縄

Ryūkyū Kasuri
琉球絣

6, Chichibu Meisen
秩父銘仙
7, Hannō Ōshima-tsumugi
飯能大島紬
8, Honjō Orimono
本庄織物
9, Bushū Shōai-zome
武州正藍染
10, Takasaki Tenassen
高崎手捺染
11, Gyōda Tabi
行田足袋
12, Shinshū Tegaki-yūzen
信州手描友禅
Shinshū Nassen-kōmon
信州捺染小紋

111

INDEX 索引

A

Aba-son	阿波村	15	I 3
Abashiri-ko	網走湖	33	G3
Abashiri-shi	網走市	33	G3
Abiko-shi	我孫子市	41	G2
Abu-cho	阿武町	14	B5
Abu-gawa	阿武川	14	B5
Abukuma-gawa	阿武隈川	27	H4
Abuta-cho	虻田町	30	D4
Achi-mura	阿智村	21	E4
Adachi-machi	安達町	27	F5
Adogawa-cho	安曇川町	19	G4
Agano-gawa	阿賀野川	26	C4
Agatsuma-machi	吾妻町	25	H2
Agawa-mura	吾川村	17	F4
Agematsu-machi	上松町	20	E3
Ageo-shi	上尾市	40	E2
Ago-cho	阿児町	18	D7
Ago Wan	英虞湾	18	D6
Agui-cho	阿久比町	38	C5
Aguni-son	粟国村	4	D4
Aibetsu-cho	愛別町	32	C4
Aida-cho	英田町	15	I 4
Aikawa-machi	愛川町	40	C5
Aikawa-machi	合川町	28	E3
Aikawa-machi	相川町	26	A4
Aimi-cho	会見町	15	G3
Aino-cho	愛野町	12	E6
Aioi-cho	相生町	17	I 3
Aioi-shi	相生市	19	F1
Aira-cho	姶良町	11	F3
Aira-cho	吾平町	11	G4
Aito-cho	愛東町	19	G5
Aizubange-machi	会津坂下町	26	E5
Aizumi-cho	藍住町	17	I 3
Aizutakada-machi	会津高田町	26	E6
Aizuwakamatsu-shi	会津若松市	27	F5
Aji-cho	庵治町	17	H2
Ajigasawa-machi	鰺ヶ沢町	29	G2
Ajikata-mura	味方村	26	C5③
Ajimu-machi	安心院町	13	H4
Ajisu-cho	阿知須町	14	B7
Aka-mura	赤村	44	E3
Akabane-cho	赤羽根町	29	D7⑩
Akabira-shi	赤平市	32	B5
Akabori-machi	赤堀町	25	H3
Akadomari-mura	赤泊村	26	B5
Akagi-cho	赤来町	15	F4
Akagi-mura	赤城村	78	A6
Akagi-san	赤城山	25	H3
Akaigawa-mura	赤井川村	30	D2
Akaike-machi	赤池町	44	D3
Akaishi-dake	赤石岳	21	F4
Akan-cho	阿寒町	33	F6
Akan-ko	阿寒湖	33	F5
Akaoka-cho	赤岡町	17	G4
Akasaka-cho	赤坂町	15	I 4
Akasaki-cho	赤碕町	15	H2
Akashi-shi	明石市	34	C4
Akashi Kaikyo	明石海峡	18	E2
Akashina-machi	明科町	23	F6
Akechi-cho	明智町	20	E5
Akehama-cho	明浜町	16	C5
Akeno-machi	明野町	25	G5
Akeno-mura	明野村	21	G3⑧
Aki-machi	安岐町	13	I 4
Aki-shi	安芸市	17	G4
Akigawa-shi	秋川市	40	C3
Akishima-shi	昭島市	40	C4

Akita-machi	飽田町	70	D6
Akita-shi	秋田市	28	D2
Akitsu-cho	安芸津町	15	F6
Akiyama-mura	秋山村	77	E2
Akiyoshidai	秋吉台	14	B6
Akkeshi-cho	厚岸町	33	H6
Akō-shi	赤穂市	15	J4
Akune-shi	阿久根市	11	E2
Ama-cho	海士町	14	A2
Amagasaki-shi	尼崎市	34	E3
Amagase-machi	天瀬町	13	G5
Amagi-cho	天城町	10	A3
Amagi-san	天城山	24	C2
Amagi-shi	甘木市	44	C5
Amagiyugashima-cho	天城湯ヶ島町	21	H6
Amakusa-machi	天草町	10	E1
Amakusa Nada	天草灘	10	C1
Amakusa Shoto	天草諸島	10	E1
Amami-Ōshima	奄美大島	10	A2
Amami Shoto	奄美諸島	4	E5
Amanohashidate	天ノ橋立	19	H3
Amarume-machi	余目町	28	A2
Amatsukominato-machi	天津小湊町	24	D5
Ami-machi	阿見町	41	I 1
Amino-cho	網野町	19	H2
Ampachi-cho	安八町	38	B2
Anabuki-cho	穴吹町	17	H3
Anamizu-machi	穴水町	22	C3
Anan-cho	阿南町	21	F4
Anan-shi	阿南市	17	I 3
Ando-cho	安堵町	35	G4
Ani-machi	阿仁町	28	E3
Anjō-shi	安城市	20	D6
Annaka-shi	安中市	25	H2
Anō-cho	安濃町	38	A6
Ao-shima	青島	16	D4
Aogaki-cho	青垣町	19	G2
Aogashima-mura	青ヶ島村	7	H6
Aoki-mura	青木村	21	F1①
Aomori-shi	青森市	29	G4
Aoshima	青島	11	H2
Aoya-cho	青谷町	15	I 2
Aoyama-cho	青山町	18	E5
Ara-kawa	荒川	40	B2
Arafune-yama	荒船山	25	G1
Arai-cho	新居町	20	E6
Arai-shi	新井市	23	F4
Arakawa-machi	荒川町	26	D4
Arakawa-mura	荒川村	40	A2
Arao-shi	荒尾市	13	F6
Ariake-cho	有明町	12	E5
Ariake-cho	有明町	11	G3
Ariake-machi	有明町	13	E6
Ariake-machi	有明町	12	E7
Ariake Kai	有明海	12	E6
Arida-shi	有田市	18	D2
Arie-cho	有家町	13	E6
Arikawa-cho	有川町	12	B6
Arita-machi	有田町	12	D5
Asaba-cho	浅羽町	39	J7
Asago-cho	朝来町	19	G1
Asahi-cho	旭町	14	D4
Asahi-cho	旭町	15	H4
Asahi-cho	旭町	20	E5
Asahi-cho	朝日町	22	A7
Asahi-cho	朝日町	32	C3
Asahi-cho	朝日町	38	B4
Asahi-dake	朝日岳	26	E3
Asahi-gawa	旭川	15	H4
Asahi-machi	朝日町	22	E4
Asahi-machi	朝日町	27	E3
Asahi-mura	旭村	25	G6
Asahi-mura	朝日村	20	D2
Asahi-mura	朝日村	21	F2④

Asahi-mura	朝日村	26	D3
Asahi-mura	朝日村	26	E2
Asahi-shi	旭市	25	F6
Asahi-son	旭村	14	B6
Asahikawa-shi	旭川市	32	C4
Asaji-machi	朝地町	13	H5
Asaka-shi	朝霞市	43	J2
Asakawa-machi	浅川町	27	G7
Asakura-machi	朝倉町	17	F4
Asakura-mura	朝倉村	16	E3
Asama-yama	浅間山	23	G6
Asama spa	浅間温泉	23	F7
Asashina-mura	浅科村	21	G2③
Ashibe-cho	芦辺町	12	D3
Ashibetsu-shi	芦別市	32	B5
Ashigawa-mura	芦川村	76	B2
Ashikaga-shi	足利市	25	H3
Ashikari-cho	芦刈町	12	E5⑩
Ashikita-machi	芦北町	11	F1
Ashino-ko	芦ノ湖	40	A7
Ashio-machi	足尾町	25	H3
Ashiro-cho	安代町	28	E5
Ashitaka-yama	愛鷹山	24	D2
Ashiwada-mura	足和田村	76	B3
Ashiya-machi	芦屋町	44	C1
Ashiya-shi	芦屋市	36	D4
Ashiyasu-mura	芦安村	76	A1
Ashyoro-cho	足寄町	33	E6
Aso-machi	阿蘇町	13	G6
Asō-machi	麻生町	25	G6
Aso-san	阿蘇山	13	G6
Asō Wan	浅茅湾	12	B2
Assabu-cho	厚沢部町	30	C6
Asuka-mura	明日香村	35	H5
Asuke-cho	足助町	20	D5
Atami-shi	熱海市	21	I 5
Atō-cho	阿東町	14	C5
Atsugi-shi	厚木市	40	C5
Atsuma-cho	厚真町	31	F3
Atsumi-cho	渥美町	20	D7
Atsumi-machi	温海町	26	D2
Atsumi Hantō	渥美半島	20	D7
Atsushiokanō-mura	熱塩加納村	26	E5
Atsuta-mura	厚田村	30	E1
Awa-cho	阿波町	17	H3
Awaji-cho	淡路町	34	C4
Awaji-shima	淡路島	18	E2
Awano-machi	粟野町	25	H4
Awara-cho	芦原町	22	A6
Awashimaura-mura	粟島浦村	26	C3
Aya-cho	綾町	11	H2
Ayabe-shi	綾部市	19	G3
Ayakami-cho	綾上町	17	G2③
Ayama-cho	阿山町	19	F5
Ayase-shi	綾瀬市	40	C5
Ayauta-cho	綾歌町	17	G2②
Azai-cho	浅井町	19	H5
Azuchi-cho	安土町	19	G5
Azuchi-Ōshima	的山大島	12	C4
Azuma-cho	吾妻町	70	A5
Azuma-cho	東町	10	E1
Azuma-mura	東村	25	F6⑧
Azuma-mura	東村	25	H2①
Azuma-mura	東村	25	H3
Azumaya-san	四阿山	21	F2
Azumi-mura	安曇村	21	E2
Azusagawa-mura	梓川村	21	F2

B

Bandai-machi	磐梯町	27	E5
Bandai-san	磐梯山	27	F5
Batō-machi	馬頭町	25	I 5
Beppu-shi	別府市	13	H5

Besshiyama-mura 別子山村 17 F3
Bessho-spa 別所温泉 23 F6
Betsukai-cho 別海町 33 I5
Bibai-shi 美唄市 31 F1
Bicchu-mura 備中町 15 G4
Biei-cho 美瑛町 32 C5
Bifuka-cho 美深町 32 C2
Bihoro-cho 美幌町 33 F4
Biratori-cho 平取町 31 G3
Bisai-shi 尾西市 38 C2
Bisei-cho 美星町 15 H5
Biwa-cho びわ町 19 G5⑧
Biwa-ko 琵琶湖 19 G5
Bizen-shi 備前市 15 I5
Bōnotsu-cho 坊津町 10 E4
Bōsō Hantō 房総半島 24 D5
Bungo Suidō 豊後水道 16 C6
Bungotakada-shi 豊後高田市 13 H4
Bunsui-machi 分水町 26 C5
Buzen-shi 豊前市 13 G4

C

Chatan-cho 北谷町 69 A5
Chiba-shi 千葉市 41 H4
Chibu-mura 知夫村 14 A2
Chiburi-jima 知夫里島 14 A2
Chichi-jima 父島 9 I5
Chichibu-shi 秩父市 40 B1
Chigasaki-shi 茅ヶ崎市 40 D6
Chihayaakasaka-mura 千早赤阪村 35 F5
Chijiwa-machi 千々石町 12 E6
Chikubu-shima 竹生島 19 H5
Chikugo-gawa 筑後川 12 G5
Chikugo-shi 筑後市 44 B6
Chikuho-machi 筑穂町 44 C3
Chikuma-gawa 千曲川 23 F6
Chikura-cho 千倉町 24 D5
Chikusa-cho 千種町 19 G1
Chikushino-shi 筑紫野市 44 B4
China-cho 知名町 4 E5②
Chinen-son 知念村 69 B6
Chino-shi 茅野市 21 F3
Chinzei-cho 鎮西町 12 D4
Chippubetsu-cho 秩父別町 32 B4
Chiran-cho 知覧町 11 F4
Chiryu-shi 知立市 38 D4
Chita Hantō 知多半島 20 C6
Chita-shi 知多市 38 C4
Chitose-mura 千歳村 13 H5
Chitose-shi 千歳市 31 E3
Chiyoda-cho 千代田町 14 E5
Chiyoda-cho 千代田町 44 A6
Chiyoda-machi 千代田町 25 G3⑬
Chiyoda-mura 千代田村 25 G5
Chiyokawa-mura 千代川村 25 G5⑥
Chizu-cho 智頭町 15 I3
Chōfu-shi 調布市 43 G1
Chōkai-machi 鳥海町 28 B3
Chōkai-san 鳥海山 28 B2
Chōmon-kyō 長門峡 14 C6
Chōnan-machi 長南町 41 I6
Chōsei-mura 長生村 41 J6
Chōshi-shi 銚子市 25 F7
Chōyō-mura 長陽村 71 F5
Chūka-son 中村町 15 H3
Chūnan-machi 仲南町 17 G2
Chūō-cho 中央町 15 I4
Chūō-machi 中央町 70 E6
Chūrui-mura 忠類村 31 I3
Chūzenji-ko 中禅寺湖 25 I3
Chūzu-cho 中主町 19 G5

D

Daian-cho 大安町 38 A3
Daiei-cho 大栄町 15 H2
Daigo-machi 大子町 25 I5
Daimon-machi 大門町 22 C5
Dainichiga-take 大日ヶ岳 20 C3
Daiō-cho 大王町 18 D7
Daiō-zaki 大王崎 18 D7
Daisen-cho 大山町 15 G2
Daisen 大山 15 H3
Daitō-cho 大東町 15 F3
Daitō-cho 大東町 21 F6
Daitō-cho 大東町 28 B5
Daitō-shi 大東市 37 I4
Daitō Shotō 大東諸島 4 C6
Daiwa-cho 大和町 15 F5
Daiwa-mura 大和村 15 E4
Danjō Guntō 男女群島 5 H5
Daruma-yama 達磨山 21 H6
Date-machi 伊達町 27 G4
Date-shi 伊達市 30 D4
Dazaifu-shi 太宰府市 44 B4
Dejima-mura 出島村 25 G5
Dōgashima 堂ヶ島 24 C1
Dōgo-yama 道後山 15 G3
Dōgo 島後 14 B1
Doi-cho 土居町 17 F3
Donari-cho 土成町 17 H2
Dorohatchō 瀞八丁 18 C4
Dōshi-mura 道志村 77 E3
Dōzen 島前 14 A2

E

Ebetsu-shi 江別市 30 E2
Ebina-shi 海老名市 40 D6
Ebino-shi えびの市 11 G2
Echigawa-cho 愛知川町 19 G5③
Echizen-cho 越前町 19 I4
Echizen-misaki 越前岬 20 A3
Edosaki-machi 江戸崎町 41 I2
Ei-cho 　町 11 F4
Eigenji-cho 永源寺町 19 G5
Eiheiji-cho 永平寺町 22 B7
Emukae-cho 江迎町 12 C5
Ena-san 恵那山 20 E4
Ena-shi 恵那市 20 E4
Enbetsu-cho 遠別町 32 B1
Engaru-cho 遠軽町 32 E3
Eniwa-shi 恵庭市 31 E3
Enoshima 江ノ島 40 D6
Enzan-shi 塩山市 21 H3
Erimo-cho えりも町 31 I5
Erimo-misaki 襟裳岬 31 I5
Esan-cho 恵山町 30 D6
Esashi-cho 恵山町 30 B6
Esashi-cho 枝幸町 33 H2
Esashi-shi 江刺市 28 D5
Etajima-cho 江田島町 14 E6
Etorofu-to 択捉島 9 I1
Ezuriko-mura 江釣子村 28 C5

F

Fuchū-cho 府中町 14 E5⑤
Fuchū-machi 婦中町 22 D5
Fuchū-shi 府中市 15 G5
Fuchū-shi 府中市 40 D4
Fudai-mura 普代村 28 E6
Fuji-cho 富士町 12 E4
Fuji-kawa 富士川 24 D1
Fuji-san 富士山 24 E2
Fuji-shi 富士市 21 H5
Fujieda-shi 藤枝市 21 G6
Fujihashi-mura 藤橋村 20 B4

Fujiidera-shi 藤井寺市 37 I6
Fujikawa-cho 富士川町 21 H5
Fujimi-machi 富士見町 21 G3
Fujimi-mura 富士見村 78 A1
Fujimi-shi 富士見市 40 E2
Fujino-machi 藤野町 40 B4
Fujinomiya-shi 富士宮市 21 H5
Fujioka-cho 藤岡町 39 E3
Fujioka-machi 藤岡町 25 G4
Fujioka-shi 藤岡市 25 G2
Fujisaki-machi 藤崎町 29 G3
Fujisato-machi 藤里町 29 E3
Fujisawa-cho 藤沢町 28 A5
Fujisawa-shi 藤沢市 40 D6
Fujishima-machi 藤島町 28 A2
Fujishiro-machi 藤代町 41 H2
Fujiwara-cho 藤原町 38 A3
Fujiwara-machi 藤原町 25 I4
Fujiyoshida-shi 富士吉田市 21 H4
Fukada-mura 深田村 11 A1
Fukae-cho 深江町 13 E6
Fukagawa-shi 深川市 32 B4
Fukaura-machi 深浦町 29 F2
Fukaya-shi 深谷市 25 G3
Fukiage-cho 吹上町 11 F3
Fukiage-hama 吹上浜 11 E3
Fukiage-machi 吹上町 40 D1
Fukube-son 福部村 15 J2
Fukuchi-mura 福地村 29 F5
Fukuchiyama-shi 福知山市 19 G2
Fukude-cho 福田町 39 I7
Fukudomi-machi 福富町 12 E5⑨
Fukue-jima 福江島 12 A7
Fukue-shi 福江市 12 B7
Fukue-son 福栄村 16 A1
Fukui-shi 福井市 22 A7
Fukuma-machi 福間町 44 B2
Fukumitsu-machi 福光町 22 C5
Fukuno-machi 福野町 22 C5
Fukuoka-cho 福岡町 20 E4
Fukuoka-machi 福岡町 22 C5
Fukuoka-shi 福岡市 44 A4
Fukuroi-shi 袋井市 21 F6
Fukusaki-cho 福崎町 34 A1
Fukushima-cho 福島町 12 D4
Fukushima-cho 福島町 30 C7
Fukushima-shi 福島市 27 G5
Fukutomi-cho 福富町 15 F5
Fukuyama-cho 福山町 11 G3
Fukuyama-shi 福山市 15 G5
Funabashi-shi 船橋市 41 G3
Funagata-machi 舟形町 28 A3
Funahashi-mura 船橋村 22 D5
Funao-cho 船穂町 15 H5
Funaoka-cho 船岡町 15 I3
Funehiki-machi 船引町 27 G5
Funo-son 布野村 15 F4
Furano-shi 富良野市 31 G1
Fūren-cho 風連町 32 C2
Fūren-ko 風連湖 33 I5
Furubira-cho 古平町 30 D1
Furudono-machi 古殿町 27 G5
Furukawa-cho 古川町 20 D2
Furukawa-shi 古川市 27 G2
Fuse-mura 布施村 14 B1
Fusō-cho 扶桑町 38 C2
Fussa-shi 福生市 40 C3
Futaba-cho 双葉町 76 A1
Futaba-machi 双葉町 27 H5
Futago-yama 両子山 13 H4
Futai-jima 蓋井島 14 A6
Futami-cho 双海町 17 F4
Futami-cho 二見町 18 E7
Futatsui-machi 二ツ井町 28 E3

Futsu-cho	布津町	70	B6
Futtsu-shi	富津市	41	G7

G

Gamagōri-shi	蒲郡市	20	D6
Gamo-cho	蒲生町	19	F5
Geihoku-cho	芸北町	14	E4
Geinō-cho	芸濃町	19	E5
Geisei-mura	芸西村	17	G4
Genkai-cho	玄海町	12	D4
Genkai-machi	玄海町	44	B1
Genkai Nada	玄界灘	12	E2
Gero-cho	下呂町	20	D3
Gifu-shi	岐阜市	20	C4
Ginan-cho	岐南町	38	C1
Ginowan-shi	宜野湾市	10	A6
Ginoza-son	宜野座村	10	B6
Gō-gawa	江川	14	D3
Gobō-shi	御坊市	18	C2
Gōdo-cho	神戸町	38	B1
Gogo-shima	興居島	16	D3
Gohoku-son	吾北村	17	F4
Gojō-shi	五條市	35	G6
Gojōme-machi	五城目町	28	D2
Goka-mura	五箇村	14	B1
Goka-mura	五霞村	25	G4⑨
Gokase-cho	五ヶ瀬町	13	H6
Gokase-gawa	五ヶ瀬川	13	I7
Gokashō-cho	五個荘町	19	G5⑤
Gonohe-machi	五戸町	29	F5
Gōnoura-cho	郷ノ浦町	12	D3
Gose-shi	御所市	35	G5
Gosen-shi	五泉市	26	C5
Goshiki-cho	五色町	34	A5
Goshikidai	五色台	15	I6
Goshogawara-shi	五所川原市	29	G3
Goshonoura-cho	御所浦町	11	F1
Gotemba-shi	御殿場市	21	H4
Gotō Rettō	五島列島	12	A6
Gōtsu-shi	江津市	14	D4
Gozaisho-yama	御在所山	20	B5
Gozenyama-mura	御前山村	25	H5
Gumma-machi	群馬町	25	H2⑤
Gushikami-son	具志頭村	69	A7
Gushikawa-shi	具志川市	10	A6
Gushikawa-son	具志川村	4	D4④
Gusukube-cho	城辺町	4	C3⑦
Gyōda-shi	行田市	25	G3
Gyokutō-machi	玉東町	70	D4

H

Habikino-shi	羽曳野市	37	H7
Habomai Shotō	歯舞諸島	9	H2
Haboro-cho	羽幌町	32	A2
Hachijō-machi	八丈町	7	H6
Hachikai-mura	八開村	38	B3
Hachiman-cho	八幡町	20	C3
Hachimori-machi	八森町	29	F2
Hachinohe-shi	八戸市	29	F5
Hachiōji-shi	八王子市	40	C4
Hachirōgata-machi	八郎潟町	28	D2
Hachiryū-machi	八竜町	28	E2
Hadano-shi	秦野市	40	E6
Haebaru-cho	南風原町	69	E5
Haga-cho	芳賀町	19	G1
Haga-machi	芳賀町	25	H5④
Hagi-shi	萩市	14	E4
Hagiwara-cho	萩原町	20	D3
Haguro-machi	羽黒町	28	A2
Haha-jima	母島	9	I5
Haibara-cho	榛原町	21	G6
Haibara-cho	榛原町	35	I5
Haki-machi	杷木町	13	F4
Hekinan-shi	碧南市	38	D5

Hakkoda-san	八甲田山	29	G4
Hakodate-shi	函館市	30	D6
Hakone-machi	箱根町	40	B7
Hakone-yama	箱根山	40	A7
Haku-san	白山	22	B6
Hakuba-mura	白馬村	23	F5
Hakui-shi	羽咋市	22	C4
Hakusan-cho	白山町	18	E5
Hakushū-machi	白州町	21	G3
Hakusui-mura	白水村	71	G5
Hakuta-cho	伯太町	15	G3
Hakuta-cho	伯方町	17	E2
Hamada-shi	浜田市	14	D4
Hamajima-cho	浜島町	18	D6
Hamakita-shi	浜北市	21	F6
Hamamasu-mura	浜益村	32	A4
Hamamatsu-shi	浜松市	21	E6
Hamana-ko	浜名湖	20	E6
Hamanaka-cho	浜中町	33	I6
Hamaoka-cho	浜岡町	21	F6
Hamasaka-cho	浜坂町	19	H1
Hamatama-cho	浜玉町	12	E4
Hamatonbetsu-cho	浜頓別町	33	H2
Hamochi-machi	羽茂町	26	A5
Hamura-machi	羽村町	40	C3
Hanaizumi-machi	花泉町	28	A5
Hanamaki-shi	花巻市	28	C5
Hanawa-machi	塙町	25	J6
Hanayama-mura	花山村	27	G1
Hanazono-machi	花園町	25	G3④
Hanazono-mura	花園村	18	D3
Hanazura-misaki	鼻面岬	16	D6
Handa-cho	半田町	17	H3
Handa-shi	半田市	20	C5
Hannan-cho	阪南町	34	D6
Hannō-shi	飯能市	40	C2
Hanoura-cho	羽ノ浦町	17	I3
Hanyū-shi	羽生市	25	G4
Hanzan-cho	飯山町	17	A2
Hara-mura	原村	21	G3
Haramachi-shi	原町市	27	H5
Harima-cho	播磨町	34	B3
Harima Nada	播磨灘	18	E1
Harue-cho	春江町	22	A6
Haruhi-mura	春日村	39	H1
Haruna-machi	榛名町	25	H2
Haruna-san	榛名山	25	H2
Haruno-cho	春野町	17	F4
Haruno-cho	春野町	21	F6
Hasaki-machi	波崎町	25	F7
Hasama-cho	挟間町	13	H5
Hasama-machi	迫町	27	H2
Hasami-cho	波佐見町	12	D5
Hase-mura	長谷村	21	F3
Hashikami-machi	階上町	29	F6
Hashima-shi	羽島市	38	B2
Hashimoto-shi	橋本市	35	G6
Hashira-jima	柱島	14	E7
Hasuda-shi	蓮田市	41	E1
Hasumi-mura	羽須美村	15	E4
Hasunuma-mura	蓮沼村	25	E6④
Hata-machi	羽田町	22	E7
Hatano-machi	畑野町	26	B4
Hatashō-cho	秦荘町	19	G5④
Hateruma-jima	波照間島	4	C2
Hatogaya-shi	鳩ヶ谷市	41	F2
Hatoma-jima	鳩間島	4	C2
Hatoyama-mura	鳩山村	40	C1
Hatsukaichi-shi	廿日市市	14	E6
Hatta-mura	八田村	76	A1
Hattō-cho	八東町	15	J3
Hayachine-san	早池峰山	28	C5
Hayakawa-cho	早川町	21	G4

Hayakita-cho	早来町	31	F3
Hayama-machi	葉山町	40	E7
Hayama-mura	葉山村	17	E4
Hayashima-cho	早島町	15	H5
Hayato-cho	隼人町	11	F2
Hazu-cho	幡豆町	38	E6
Heda-mura	戸田村	21	H5
Hedo-misaki	辺土岬	10	B5
Heguri-cho	平群町	35	G4
Heigun-to	平郡島	16	C3
Heiwa-cho	平和町	38	C3
Heki-son	日置村	14	A5
Hekinan-shi	碧南市	38	D5
Hiba-yama	比婆山	15	F3
Hibiki Nada	響灘	13	F2
Hiburi-shima	日振島	16	C5
Hichisō-cho	七宗町	20	D4
Hidaka-cho	日高町	18	C2
Hidaka-cho	日高町	19	H1
Hidaka-cho	日高町	31	G3
Hidaka-gawa	日高川	18	C2
Hidaka-machi	日高町	40	C2
Hidaka-mura	日高村	17	F4
Hiezu-son	日吉津村	15	G2
Higashi-mura	東村	27	F6
Higashi-son	東村	10	B5
Higashiawakura-son	東粟倉村	15	I3
Higashichichibu-mura	東秩父村	40	B1
Higashidori-mura	東通村	29	I5
Higashihiroshima-shi	東広島市	15	F5
Higashiichiki-cho	東市来町	11	E3
Higashiiiyama-son	東祖谷山村	17	G3
Higashiizu-cho	東伊豆町	21	I6
Higashiizumo-cho	東出雲町	15	G2
Higashikagura-cho	東神楽町	32	C4
Higashikawa-cho	東川町	32	C4
Higashikurume-shi	東久留米市	43	I1
Higashikushira-cho	東串良町	11	G4
Higashimatsuyama-shi	東松山市	40	D3
Higashimokoto-mura	東藻琴村	33	G4
Higashimurayama-shi	東村山市	40	D3
Higashinaruse-mura	東成瀬村	28	B4
Higashine-shi	東根市	27	F3
Higashino-cho	東野町	15	F6
Higashiōsaka-shi	東大阪市	37	I4
Higashirishiri-cho	東利尻町	33	E1
Higasefuri-son	東脊振村	44	A5
Higashishirakawa-mura	東白川村	20	D4
Higashisonogi-cho	東彼杵町	12	D5
Higashiura-cho	東浦町	34	C5
Higashiura-cho	東浦町	38	D4
Higashiyama-cho	東山町	28	B5
Higashiyama spa	東山温泉	27	E6
Higashiyamato-shi	東大和市	40	D3
Higashiyoka-cho	東与賀町	44	A6
Higashiyoshino-mura	東吉野村	35	I6
Higashiyuri-machi	東由利町	28	B3
Hii-gawa	斐伊川	15	F3
Hiji-kawa	肱川	16	D4
Hiji-machi	日出町	13	H4
Hijikawa-cho	肱川町	16	D4
Hikami-cho	氷上町	19	G2
Hikari-machi	光町	25	F6②
Hikari-shi	光市	14	C7
Hikata-machi	干潟町	25	F6
Hikawa-cho	斐川町	15	F3
Hiketa-cho	引田町	17	I2
Hikigawa-cho	日置川町	18	B3
Hikimi-cho	匹見町	14	D5
Hiko-san	英彦山	13	G4
Hikone-shi	彦根市	19	G5
Hime-kawa	姫川	23	E5

114

Himedo-machi	姫戸町	11	F1③
Himeji-shi	姫路市	34	A2
Himeshima-mura	姫島村	13	I3
Himi-shi	氷見市	22	C5
Hinai-machi	比内町	28	E3
Hinase-cho	日生町	15	I5
Hino-cho	日野町	15	G3
Hino-cho	日野町	19	G5
Hino-misaki	日ノ御崎	18	C2
Hino-misaki	日御碕	14	E2
Hino-shi	日野市	77	H1
Hinode-machi	日の出町	40	C3
Hinoemata-mura	檜枝岐村	26	D7
Hinohara-mura	檜原村	40	B3
Hinokage-cho	日之影町	13	H6
Hira-san	比良山	19	G4
Hira-shima	平島	12	C6
Hirado-shima	平戸島	12	C5
Hirado-shi	平戸市	12	C4
Hiraizumi-cho	平泉町	28	B5
Hiraka-machi	平鹿町	28	B3
Hiraka-machi	平賀町	29	F3
Hirakata-shi	枚方市	37	J2
Hiranai-machi	平内町	29	G4
Hirao-cho	平生町	14	D7
Hirara-shhi	平良市	4	C3
Hirata-cho	平田町	38	B2
Hirata-machi	平田町	28	A2
Hirata-mura	平田村	27	G6
Hirata-shi	平田市	15	F2
Hiraya-mura	平谷村	20	E5
Hirogawa-cho	広川町	18	C2
Hirokami-mura	広神村	26	C6
Hirokawa-machi	広川町	13	F5⑤
Hiromi-cho	広見町	16	D5
Hirono-machi	広野町	27	H6
Hiroo-cho	広尾町	31	I4
Hirosaki-shi	弘前市	29	F3
Hirose-machi	広瀬町	15	G3
Hiroshima-cho	広島町	31	E2
Hiroshima-shi	広島市	14	E5
Hirota-mura	広田村	16	E4
Hiru-zen	蒜山	15	H3
Hirukawa-mura	蛭川村	20	D4
Hisai-shi	久居市	38	A7
Hisaka-jima	久賀島	12	B6
Hisayama-machi	久山町	44	B3
Hishikari-cho	菱刈町	11	F2
Hita-shi	日田市	13	G4
Hitachi-shi	日立市	25	H6
Hitachiōta-shi	常陸太田市	25	H6
Hitoyoshi-shi	人吉市	11	G1
Hiuchi Nada	燧灘	17	F3
Hiwa-cho	比和町	15	F4
Hiwaki-cho	樋脇町	11	F2
Hiwasa-cho	日和佐町	17	I4
Hiyoshi-cho	日吉町	11	F3
Hiyoshi-cho	日吉町	19	G3
Hiyoshi-mura	日吉村	16	E5
Hiyoshi-mura	日義村	21	E3
Hizen-cho	肥前町	12	D4
Hobara-machi	保原町	27	G4
Hobetsu-cho	穂別町	31	G3
Hōfu-shi	防府市	14	C6
Hōhoku-cho	豊北町	14	A6
Hōjō-cho	北条町	15	H2
Hōjō-machi	方城町	44	D3
Hōjō-shi	北条市	16	E3
Hokota-machi	鉾田町	25	G6
Hokubō-cho	北房町	15	H2
Hokubu-machi	北部町	70	D5
Hokudan-cho	北淡町	34	B5
Hokuryū-cho	北竜町	32	B4
Hokusei-cho	北勢町	38	A3
Honai-cho	保内町	16	D4
Honami-machi	穂波町	44	C3
Honbetsu-cho	本別町	33	E6
Hondo-shi	本渡市	12	E7
Hongawa-mura	本川村	17	F4
Hongō-cho	本郷町	15	F5
Hongō-machi	本郷町	26	E6
Hongō-son	本郷村	14	D6
Hongū-cho	本宮町	18	C4
Honjō-mura	本匠村	13	I6
Honjō-mura	本城村	23	F6
Honjō-shi	本荘市	28	C2
Honjō-shi	本庄市	25	G3
Honkawane-cho	本川根町	21	F5
Honyabaki-machi	本耶馬溪町	13	G4
Horado-mura	洞戸村	20	C4
Horai-cho	鳳来町	20	E6
Horaiji-san	鳳来寺山	20	E5
Horigane-mura	堀金村	22	E7⑤
Horinouchi-machi	堀之内町	26	C6
Horokanai-cho	幌加内町	32	B3
Horonobe-cho	幌延町	33	G2
Hoshino-mura	星野村	13	F5
Hoshuyama-mura	宝珠山村	13	G4
Hosoe-cho	細江町	39	H6
Hosoiri-mura	細入村	22	D6
Hotaka-dake	穂高岳	22	E6
Hotaka-machi	穂高町	21	E2
Hotaka-yama	武尊山	25	I3
Hōya-shi	保谷市	43	I2
Hōyo Kaikyō	豊予海峡	13	I4
Hozumi-cho	穂積町	38	B1
Hyōno-sen	氷ノ山	15	J3
Hyūga-shi	日向市	11	I1

I

Ibara-shi	井原市	15	G5
Ibaraki-machi	茨城町	25	G6
Ibaraki-shi	茨木市	37	H2
Ibi-gawa	揖斐川	38	B4
Ibigawa-mura	揖斐川町	20	B4
Ibogawa-cho	揖保川町	19	F1
Ibuki-cho	伊吹町	19	G5
Ibuki-yama	伊吹山	20	B4
Ibusuki-shi	指宿市	11	F4
Icchiu-son	一宇村	17	H3
Ichiba-cho	市場町	17	H3
Ichifusa-yama	市房山	11	G1
Ichihara-shi	市原市	41	H5
Ichihasama-cho	一迫町	27	G2
Ichijima-cho	市島町	19	G2
Ichikai-machi	市貝町	25	H5
Ichikawa-cho	市川町	34	A1
Ichikawa-shi	市川市	41	G3
Ichikawadaimon-cho	市川大門町	76	A3
Ichiki-cho	市来町	11	F3
Ichinohe-machi	一戸町	28	E5
Ichinomiya-cho	一宮町	19	G1
Ichinomiya-cho	一宮町	34	B5
Ichinomiya-cho	一宮町	39	G5
Ichinomiya-cho	一宮町	76	C2
Ichinomiya-machi	一の宮町	13	G6
Ichinomiya-machi	一宮町	41	J6
Ichinomiya-shi	一宮市	20	C5
Ichinoseki-shi	一関市	28	A5
Ichishi-cho	一志町	18	E6⑪
Ide-cho	井手町	35	H3
Ie-jima	伊江島	10	A5
Ie-son	伊江村	10	A5
Ieshima-cho	家島町	19	E1
Iga-cho	伊賀町	19	F5
Iheya-son	伊平屋村	10	B4
Iida-shi	飯田市	21	F4
Iidate-mura	飯舘村	27	G5
Iide-machi	飯豊町	26	E4
Iide-san	飯豊山	26	E4
Iijima-machi	飯島町	21	F3
Iimori-cho	飯盛町	12	E6
Iinan-cho	飯南町	18	E5
Iino-machi	飯野町	27	G5
Iioka-machi	飯岡町	25	F7
Iitagawa-machi	飯高川町	28	D2
Iitaka-cho	飯高町	18	E5
Iiyama-shi	飯山市	23	G5
Iizuka-shi	飯塚市	44	C3
Ijira-mura	伊自良村	20	C4
Ijuin-cho	伊集院町	11	F3
Ikaho-machi	伊香保町	25	H2
Ikarigaseki-mura	碇ヶ関村	29	F4
Ikaruga-cho	斑鳩町	35	G4
Ikata-cho	伊方町	16	C4
Ikawa-cho	井川町	17	G3
Ikawa-machi	井川町	28	D2
Ikazaki-cho	五十崎町	16	D4
Ikeda-cho	池田町	17	G3
Ikeda-cho	池田町	17	H1
Ikeda-cho	池田町	19	I5
Ikeda-cho	池田町	31	J3
Ikeda-ko	池田湖	11	F4
Ikeda-machi	池田町	21	F1
Ikeda-machi	池田町	38	A1
Ikeda-machi	池田町	37	F2
Ikegawa-cho	池川町	17	E4
Iki	壱岐	12	D3
Ikina-mura	生名村	17	F2⑤
Ikitsuki-cho	生月町	12	C4
Ikitsuki-shima	生月島	12	C4
Ikoma-shi	生駒市	35	G4
Ikuno-cho	生野町	19	G2
Ikusaka-mura	生坂村	23	E6
Ikutahara-cho	生田原町	32	E4
Imabari-shi	今治市	16	E3
Imabetsu-machi	今別町	29	H3
Imadate-cho	今立町	19	I5
Imagane-cho	今金町	30	B4
Imaichi-shi	今市市	25	I4
Imajō-cho	今庄町	19	I5
Imari-shi	伊万里市	12	D5
Imazu-cho	今津町	19	H4
Imba-mura	印旛村	41	H3
Imba-numa	印旛沼	41	H3
Ina-machi	伊奈町	40	E1
Ina-machi	伊奈町	41	H2
Ina-mura	伊南村	26	D6
Ina-shi	伊那市	21	F3
Inabe-cho	員弁町	38	A4
Inabu-cho	稲武町	20	E5
Inagaki-mura	稲垣村	29	G3
Inagawa-cho	猪名川町	34	E2
Inagi-shi	稲城市	43	H1
Inakadate-mura	田舎館村	29	F3
Inakawa-machi	稲川町	28	B4
Inami-cho	稲美町	34	B3
Inami-cho	印南町	18	C3
Inami-machi	井波町	22	C5
Inasa-cho	引佐町	39	H6
Inatsuki-machi	稲築町	44	C3
Inawashiro-ko	猪苗代湖	27	F5
Inawashiro-machi	猪苗代町	27	F5
Inazawa-shi	稲沢市	38	C3
Ine-cho	伊根町	19	H3
Innai-machi	院内町	13	H4
Innoshima-shi	因島市	15	G6
Ino-cho	伊野町	17	F4
Inokuchi-mura	井口村	22	C6
Inubo-zaki	犬吠埼	25	F7
Inukai-machi	犬飼町	13	H5

Inuyama-shi 犬山市 ………… 20 D4
Inzai-machi 印西町 ………… 41 H3
Iōjima-cho 伊王島町 ………… 12 D6
Ipponmatsu-cho 一本松町 …… 16 D6
Irabu-cho 伊良部町 ………… 4 C3⑩
Irago-misaki 伊良湖岬 ……… 20 D7
Irihirose-mura 入広瀬村 …… 26 C6
Iriki-cho 入来町 …………… 11 F2
Iriomote-jima 西表島 ……… 4 C2
Irō-zaki 石廊崎 …………… 24 B2
Iruma-shi 入間市 ………… 40 D3
Isahaya-shi 諫早市 ………… 12 E6
Isawa-cho 石和町 ………… 25 F1
Isawa-cho 胆沢町 ………… 28 B5
Ise-shi 伊勢市 …………… 18 E6
Isehara-shi 伊勢原市 ……… 40 C6
Isen-cho 伊仙町 …………… 10 A4
Isesaki-shi 伊勢崎市 ……… 25 H4
Ise Wan 伊勢湾 …………… 20 C6
Ishibashi-machi 石橋町 …… 25 H4
Ishibe-cho 石部町 ………… 19 G5
Ishida-cho 石田町 ………… 12 D3
Ishidoriya-cho 石鳥谷町 …… 28 C5
Ishigaki-jima 石垣島 ……… 4 C2
Ishigaki-shi 石垣市 ………… 4 C2
Ishige-machi 石下町 ……… 44 G1
Ishii-cho 石井町 …………… 17 I3
Ishikari-cho 石狩町 ………… 30 E1
Ishikari-gawa 石狩川 ……… 30 E1
Ishikawa-machi 石川町 …… 27 G6
Ishikawa-shi 石川市 ……… 10 A6
Ishiki-cho 一色町 ………… 20 D6
Ishikoshi-machi 石越町 …… 27 H1
Ishinomaki-shi 石巻市 …… 27 H2
Ishioka-shi 石岡市 ………… 25 G5
Ishizuchi-san 石鎚山 ……… 16 E3
Isobe-cho 磯部町 ………… 18 D7
Isumi-machi 夷隅町 ………… 41 I6
Itadori-mura 板取村 ……… 20 C3
Itako-machi 潮来町 ………… 25 F6
Itakura-machi 板倉町 ……… 23 G4
Itakura-machi 板倉町 ……… 25 G4
Itami-shi 伊丹市 …………… 37 F2
Itano-cho 板野町 ………… 17 I2
Itayanagi-machi 板柳町 …… 29 G3
Ito-shi 伊東市 …………… 21 I5
Itoda-machi 糸田町 ………… 44 D3
Itoigawa-shi 糸魚川市 …… 23 E4
Itoman-shi 糸満市 ………… 10 A7
Itonuki-cho 糸貫町 ………… 38 B1
Itsukaichi-machi 五日市町 … 40 B3
Itsuki-mura 五木村 ………… 11 G1
Itsuku-shima 厳島 ………… 14 D6
Itsuwa-machi 五和町 ……… 12 E7
Iwade-cho 岩出町 ………… 34 E7
Iwadeyama-machi 岩出山町 … 27 G2
Iwagi-mura 岩城村 ………… 17 E2
Iwai-jima 祝島 …………… 16 B3
Iwai-shi 岩井市 …………… 41 F1
Iwaizumi-cho 岩泉町 ……… 28 D6
Iwaki-machi 岩木町 ………… 28 C2
Iwaki-machi 岩木町 ………… 29 F3
Iwaki-san 岩木山 ………… 29 F3
Iwaki-shi いわき市 ………… 27 H7
Iwakuni-shi 岩国市 ………… 14 D6
Iwakura-shi 岩倉市 ………… 38 C2
Iwama-machi 岩間町 ……… 25 H5
Iwami-machi 岩美町 ……… 15 J2
Iwami-cho 石見町 ………… 14 E4
Iwamizawa-shi 岩見沢市 …… 31 F2
Iwamura-cho 岩村町 ……… 20 E4
Iwamuro-mura 岩室村 …… 26 C5
Iwanai-cho 岩内町 ………… 30 C2

Iwanuma-shi 岩沼市 ……… 27 G3
Iwasaki-mura 岩崎村 ……… 29 F2
Iwase-machi 岩瀬町 ……… 25 H5
Iwase-mura 岩瀬村 ………… 27 F6
Iwashiro-machi 岩代町 …… 27 G5
Iwata-shi 磐田市 ………… 21 F6
Iwataki-cho 岩滝町 ………… 19 H2
Iwate-machi 岩手町 ………… 28 E5
Iwate-san 岩手山 ………… 28 D4
Iwatsuki-shi 岩槻市 ……… 41 E2
Iwō-jima 硫黄島 …………… 10 E5
Iwō-jima 硫黄島 …………… 9 I6
Iyo-shi 伊予市 …………… 16 D4
Iyomishima-shi 伊予三島市 … 17 F3
Izena-son 伊是名村 ………… 10 A4
Izu-numa 伊豆沼 ………… 27 H2
Izu Hantō 伊豆半島 ……… 24 C2
Izuhara-machi 巌原町 ……… 12 C2
Izumi-mura 泉村 …………… 13 G7
Izumi-mura 和泉村 ………… 19 I6
Izumi-shi 出水市 ………… 11 F2
Izumi-shi 和泉市 ………… 35 E5
Izumiōtsu-shi 泉大津市 …… 34 E5
Izumisano-shi 泉佐野市 …… 34 E6
Izumizaki-mura 泉崎村 …… 27 F6
Izumo-shi 出雲市 ………… 15 F3
Izumozaki-machi 出雲崎町 … 26 B5
Izunagaoka-cho 伊豆長岡町 … 21 H5
Izushi-cho 出石町 ………… 19 H2
Izu Shotō 伊豆諸島 ……… 24 B4

J
Jimokuji-cho 甚目寺町 …… 39 G2
Jinseki-cho 神石町 ………… 15 G4
Jinzū-gawa 神通川 ………… 22 D5
Jōetsu-shi 上越市 ………… 23 F4
Jōge-cho 上下町 …………… 15 G5
Jōhana-machi 城端町 ……… 22 C5
Jōhen-cho 城辺町 ………… 16 D6
Jōhōji-machi 浄法寺町 …… 28 E5
Jōhoku-machi 常北町 ……… 25 H6
Jōjima-machi 城島町 ……… 44 B6
Jōnan-machi 城南町 ………… 70 D6
Jōyō-machi 上陽町 ………… 13 F5
Jōyō-shi 城陽市 …………… 35 H2
Jōzankei-spa 定山渓温泉 …… 30 E2
Jūmonji-machi 十文字町 …… 28 B3
Jūo-machi 十王町 ………… 25 I6
Jūsan-ko 十三湖 …………… 29 H3
Jūshiyama-mura 十四山村 …… 38 C4

K
Kaba-shima 椛島 …………… 12 B6
Kadena-cho 嘉手納町 ……… 69 A5
Kadogawa-cho 門川町 …… 13 H7
Kadoma-shi 門真市 ………… 37 H3
Kaga-shi 加賀市 …………… 22 B6
Kagami-cho 香我美町 ……… 17 G4
Kagami-machi 鏡町 ………… 13 F7
Kagami-mura 鏡村 ………… 17 F4
Kagamiishi-machi 鏡石町 …… 27 F6
Kagamino-cho 鏡野町 ……… 15 I3
Kagawa-cho 香川町 ………… 17 H2
Kagoshima-shi 鹿児島市 …… 11 F3
Kagoshima Wan 鹿児島湾 …… 11 F3
Kaho-machi 嘉穂町 ………… 44 D4
Kahoku-cho 河北町 ………… 27 H2
Kahoku-cho 香北町 ………… 17 F3
Kahoku-machi 河北町 ……… 27 F3
Kahoku-machi 鹿北町 ……… 13 F5
Kaibara-cho 柏原町 ………… 19 G2
Kaida-mura 開田村 ………… 20 E3
Kaifu-cho 海部町 …………… 17 H4
Kaimon-cho 開聞町 ………… 11 F4

Kaimon-dake 開聞岳 ……… 11 F4
Kainan-cho 海南町 ………… 17 H4
Kainan-shi 海南市 ………… 18 D2
Kaisei-machi 開成町 ………… 40 E6
Kaita-cho 海田町 ………… 14 E6
Kaita-machi 穎田町 ………… 44 D3
Kaizu-cho 海津町 ………… 38 B3
Kaizuka-shi 貝塚市 ………… 34 E5
Kajikazawa-cho 鰍沢町 …… 21 G4
Kajiki-cho 加治木町 ……… 11 F3
Kajikawa-mura 加治川村 …… 26 D4
Kakaji-cho 香々地町 ……… 13 H3
Kakamigahara-shi 各務原市 … 38 C1
Kakara-shima 加唐島 ……… 12 D4
Kake-cho 加計町 ………… 14 E5
Kakegawa-shi 掛川市 ……… 21 F6
Kakeroma-jima 加計呂麻島 … 10 A2
Kakeya-machi 掛合町 ……… 15 F3
Kakinoki-mura 柿木村 …… 14 C5
Kakizaki-machi 柿崎町 …… 23 G4
Kakogawa-shi 加古川市 …… 34 B3
Kakuda-shi 角田市 ………… 27 G4
Kakunodate-machi 角館町 … 28 C3
Kamae-cho 蒲江町 ………… 13 I6
Kamagari-cho 蒲刈町 ……… 15 F6
Kamagaya-shi 鎌ヶ谷市 …… 41 G3
Kamaishi-shi 釜石市 ……… 28 B6
Kamakura-shi 鎌倉市 ……… 40 E6
Kambara-cho 蒲原町 ……… 21 G5
Kameda-machi 亀田町 …… 26 C4
Kameoka-shi 亀岡市 ……… 19 F3
Kameyama-shi 亀山市 ……… 38 A5
Kami-cho 香美町 ………… 19 G2
Kami-mura 可美村 ………… 39 H7
Kami-mura 上村 …………… 21 F4
Kamiagata-cho 上県町 …… 12 C1
Kamifukuoka-shi 上福岡市 … 40 D2
Kamifurano-cho 上富良野町 … 31 G1
Kamigōri-cho 上郡町 ……… 15 J4
Kamigotō-cho 上五島町 …… 12 B6
Kamihayashi-mura 神林村 … 26 D3
Kamiichi-machi 上市町 …… 22 D5
Kamiishizu-cho 上石津町 …… 38 A2
Kamiiso-cho 上磯町 ………… 30 C6
Kamiita-cho 上板町 ………… 17 I2
Kamiizumi-mura 神泉村 …… 25 G2①
Kamikatsu-cho 上勝町 …… 17 I3
Kamikawa-cho 上川町 …… 32 D4
Kamikawa-machi 神川町 …… 25 G2
Kamikawa-mura 上川村 …… 26 D5
Kamikawachi-mura 上河内村 … 25 I4①
Kamikita-machi 上北町 …… 29 G5
Kamikitayama-mura 上北山村 … 18 D3
Kamikoani-mura 上小阿仁村 … 28 E3
Kamikochi 上高地 ………… 22 E7
Kamikoshiki-mura 上甑町 …… 10 D2
Kamikuishiki-mura 上九一色村 … 76 B3
Kamimine-cho 上峰町 …… 44 B5
Kaminaka-cho 上中町 ……… 19 H4
Kaminaka-cho 上那賀町 …… 17 H3
Kaminoho-mura 上之保村 …… 20 D4
Kaminokawa-machi 上三川町 … 25 H6
Kaminokuni-cho 上ノ国町 …… 30 B6
Kaminoseki-cho 上関町 …… 16 C3
Kaminoyama-shi 上山市 …… 27 F3
Kamioka-cho 神岡町 ……… 20 D2
Kamioka-machi 神岡町 …… 28 C3
Kamisaibara-son 上斎原村 …… 15 I3
Kamisato-machi 上斎原村 …… 21 F4
Kamisato-machi 上里町 …… 25 G3
Kamishihi-mura 上志比村 …… 22 B7②
Kamishihoro-cho 上士幌町 … 31 I1
Kamisu-machi 神栖町 ……… 25 F6
Kamisunagawa-cho 上砂川町 … 31 F1

Kamitaira-mura	上平村	22	C6
Kamitakara-mura	上宝村	20	D2
Kamitonda-cho	上富田町	18	B3
Kamitsue-mura	上津江村	13	G5
Kamitsushima-cho	上対馬町	12	C1
Kamiura-cho	上浦町	16	E2
Kamiura-machi	上浦町	13	I5
Kamiyahagi-cho	上矢作町	20	E5
Kamiyaku-cho	上屋久町	11	F6
Kamiyama-cho	上山町	17	H3
Kamiyamada-machi	上山田町	21	F1
Kamiyūbetsu-cho	上湧別町	32	E3
Kammaki-cho	上牧町	35	G4
Kamo-cho	加茂町	15	I3
Kamo-cho	加茂町	35	H3
Kamō-cho	蒲生町	11	F2
Kamo-machi	加茂町	15	F3
Kamo-mura	賀茂村	21	H6
Kamo-shi	加茂市	26	C5
Kamoenai-mura	神恵内村	30	C2
Kamogata-cho	鴨方町	15	H5
Kamogawa-cho	加茂川町	15	H4
Kamogawa-shi	鴨川市	24	D5
Kamojima-cho	鴨島町	17	H3
Kamoto-machi	鹿本町	13	F5
Kamui-misaki	神威岬	30	C1
Kanada-machi	金田町	44	D3
Kanagi-cho	金城町	14	D4
Kanagi-cho	金木町	29	G3
Kanai-machi	金井町	26	A4
Kanan-cho	河南町	35	G5
Kanasagō-mura	金砂郷村	25	H4
Kanaya-cho	金屋町	18	D2
Kanaya-cho	金谷町	21	F6
Kanayama-cho	金山町	20	D4
Kanazawa-shi	金沢市	22	C5
Kanazu-cho	金津町	22	A6
Kanda-machi	苅田町	44	E2
Kanegasaki-cho	金ヶ崎町	28	B5
Kaneyama-cho	兼山町	38	E1
Kaneyama-machi	金山町	28	A3
Kani-shi	可児市	38	E1
Kanie-cho	蟹江町	38	C3
Kanita-machi	蟹田町	29	H4
Kanmon Kaikyō	関門海峡	13	G3
Kanmuri-yama	冠山	14	D5
Kannabe-cho	神辺町	15	G5
Kannami-cho	函南町	76	E7
Kannari-cho	金成町	27	G1
Kannon-zaki	観音崎	41	F7
Kano-cho	鹿野町	14	C4
Kanonji-shi	観音寺市	17	G2
Kanose-machi	鹿瀬町	26	D5
Kanoya-shi	鹿屋市	11	G4
Kanra-machi	甘楽町	25	G2
Kanuma-shi	鹿沼市	25	H4
Kanzaki-cho	神崎町	34	A1
Kanzaki-machi	神埼町	44	A5
Kaō-machi	鹿央町	70	D4
Karakuwa-cho	唐桑町	27	I1
Karasu-cho	香良洲町	19	E6
Karasuyama-machi	烏山町	25	I5
Karatsu-shi	唐津市	12	D4
Karikachi-tōge	狩勝峠	31	H2
Kariwa-mura	刈羽村	23	G3
Kariya-shi	刈谷市	38	D4
Karuizawa-machi	軽井沢町	21	G1
Karumai-machi	軽米町	29	F5
Kasado-shima	笠戸島	14	C7
Kasagi-cho	笠置町	35	H3
Kasahara-cho	笠原町	38	E2
Kasai-shi	加西市	34	B2
Kasakake-mura	笠懸村	25	H3⑨
Kasama-shi	笠間市	25	H5
Kasamatsu-cho	笠松町	38	C2
Kasaoka-shi	笠岡市	15	G5
Kasari-cho	笠利町	10	C1
Kasasa-cho	笠沙町	10	E4
Kaseda-shi	加世田市	11	E4
Kashiba-cho	香芝町	35	G5
Kashihara-shi	橿原市	35	H5
Kashima-cho	鹿島町	15	F2
Kashima-machi	嘉島町	70	E6
Kashima-machi	鹿島町	22	C4
Kashima-machi	鹿島町	25	G6
Kashima-machi	鹿島町	27	H5
Kashima-mura	鹿島村	10	D2
Kashima-shi	鹿島市	12	E5
Kashimadai-machi	鹿島台町	27	H2
Kashima Nada	鹿島灘	25	H7
Kashimo-mura	加子母村	20	E3
Kashiwa-mura	柏村	29	G3
Kashiwa-shi	柏市	41	G2
Kashiwara-shi	柏原市	37	I6
Kashiwazaki-shi	柏崎市	26	B6
Kasuga-cho	春日町	19	G2
Kasuga-mura	春日村	38	A1
Kasuga-shi	春日市	44	B4
Kasugai-cho	春日町	76	B1
Kasugai-shi	春日井市	38	D2
Kasukabe-shi	春日部市	41	F2
Kasukawa-mura	粕川村	25	H3⑥
Kasumi-cho	香住町	19	H1
Kasumiga-ura	霞ヶ浦	25	G6
Kasuya-machi	粕屋町	44	B3
Katahigashi-mura	潟東村	26	C5②
Katamuki-yama	傾山	13	H6
Katano-shi	交野市	37	J2
Katashina-mura	片品村	25	I3
Katsumoto-cho	勝本町	12	D3
Katsunuma-cho	勝沼町	25	F2
Katsura-mura	桂村	25	H5
Katsuragi-cho	かつらぎ町	35	F6
Katsuragi-san	葛城山	18	D3
Katsurahama	桂浜	17	F4
Katsurao-mura	葛尾村	27	G5
Katsuren-cho	勝連町	69	B5
Katsuta-cho	勝田町	15	I3
Katsuta-shi	勝田市	25	H6
Katsuura-cho	勝浦町	17	I3
Katsuura-shi	勝浦市	24	D6
Katsuyama-cho	勝山町	15	H3
Katsuyama-machi	勝山町	44	E3
Katsuyama-mura	勝山村	76	C3
Katsuyama-shi	勝山市	22	B7
Kawaba-mura	川場村	25	I3
Kawabe-cho	川辺町	18	C3
Kawabe-cho	川辺町	38	E1
Kawabe-machi	河辺町	28	D3
Kawabe-mura	河辺村	16	D4
Kawachi-cho	河内町	25	I4
Kawachi-machi	河内町	70	D5
Kawachi-mura	河内村	22	B6
Kawachi-mura	河内村	41	I2
Kawachinagano-shi	河内長野市	35	F5
Kawage-cho	河芸町	38	A6
Kawagoe-cho	川越町	38	B4
Kawagoe-shi	川越市	40	D2
Kawaguchi-machi	川口町	26	C6
Kawaguchi-shi	川口市	43	J4
Kawaguchiko-machi	河口湖町	76	C2
Kawahara-cho	河原町	15	I3
Kawahigashi-mura	河東村	26	E5①
Kawai-cho	河合町	35	G5
Kawai-mura	河合村	20	D2
Kawai-mura	川井村	28	D6
Kawajima-machi	川島町	40	D2
Kawajiri-cho	川尻町	15	F6
Kawakami-cho	川上町	15	H4
Kawakami-mura	川上村	21	G2
Kawakami-mura	川上村	35	I6
Kawakami-son	川上村	14	B5
Kawakami-son	川上村	15	H3
Kawakita-machi	川北町	22	B6
Kawamata-machi	川俣町	27	G5
Kawaminami-cho	川南町	11	I1
Kawamoto-machi	川本町	14	E4
Kawamoto-machi	川本町	25	G3
Kawanabe-cho	川辺町	11	F4
Kawane-cho	川根町	21	F6
Kawanishi-cho	川西町	35	G4
Kawanishi-machi	川西町	23	H4
Kawanishi-machi	川西町	27	F4
Kawanishi-shi	川西市	37	F1
Kawanoe-shi	川之江市	17	F3
Kawara-machi	香春町	44	D3
Kawasaki-cho	川崎町	27	G3
Kawasaki-machi	川崎町	44	D3
Kawasaki-mura	川崎村	28	A5
Kawasaki-shi	川崎市	42	D5
Kawasato-mura	川里村	40	D1
Kawashima-cho	川島町	17	H3
Kawashima-cho	川島町	38	C2
Kawasoe-machi	川副町	44	A6
Kawatana-cho	川棚町	12	D5
Kawauchi-cho	川内町	16	E3
Kawauchi-machi	川内町	29	H4
Kawauchi-mura	川内村	27	G6
Kawaue-mura	川上村	20	E4
Kawaura-machi	河浦町	10	E1
Kawazu-cho	河津町	21	I6
Kaya-cho	加悦町	19	H2
Kayo-cho	賀陽町	15	H4
Kazamaura-mura	風間浦村	29	I4
Kazan(Iwo) Rettō	火山(硫黄)列島	9	I6
Kazo-shi	加須市	40	E1
Kazuno-shi	鹿角市	28	E4
Kazusa-machi	加津佐町	12	E7
Kedōin-cho	祁答院町	11	F2
Keihoku-cho	京北町	19	G4
Keisen-machi	桂川町	44	C3
Kenbuchi-cho	剣淵町	32	C3
Kerama Retto	慶良間列島	4	D4
Kesennuma-shi	気仙沼市	27	I1
Ketaka-cho	気高町	15	I2
Kibi-cho	吉備町	18	D2
Kihō-cho	紀宝町	18	C4
Kihoku-cho	輝北町	11	G3
Kiinagashima-cho	紀伊長島町	18	D5
Kiire-cho	喜入町	11	F4
Kii Suido	紀伊水道	18	C2
Kijimadaira-mura	木島平村	23	G3
Kijō-cho	木城町	11	H1
Kikai-shima	喜界島	5	E6
Kikai-shima	喜界島	4	E6
Kikonai-cho	木古内町	30	C6
Kikuchi-shi	菊池市	13	G6
Kikugawa-cho	菊川町	14	A6
Kikugawa-cho	菊川町	21	F6⑨
Kikuka-machi	菊鹿町	13	F5
Kikuma-cho	菊間町	16	E3
Kikusui-machi	菊水町	13	F6
Kikuyo-machi	菊陽町	70	E5
Kimita-son	君田村	15	F4
Kimitsu-shi	君津市	41	G6
Kimobetsu-cho	喜茂別町	30	D3
Kimpō-cho	金峰町	11	F3
Kin-cho	金武町	10	A4
Kinasa-mura	鬼無里村	23	F5
Kinkai-cho	琴海町	12	D6
Kino-kawa	紀ノ川	18	D3
Kinoe-cho	木江町	15	F6

Kinomoto-cho	木之本町	19	H5
Kinosaki-cho	城崎町	19	H2
Kinpoku-san	金北山	23	G1
Kinu-gawa	鬼怒川	25	G4
Kira-cho	吉良町	38	B6
Kirigamine	霧ヶ峰	21	F2
Kirishima-cho	霧島町	11	G2
Kirishima-yama	霧島山	11	G2
Kiryu-shi	桐生市	25	H3
Kisa-cho	吉舎町	15	F5
Kisai-machi	騎西町	40	E1
Kisakata-machi	象潟町	28	B2
Kisarazu-shi	木更津市	41	G6
Kisawa-son	木沢村	17	H3
Kisei-cho	紀勢町	18	D6
Kishigawa-cho	貴志川町	34	E7
Kishimoto-cho	岸本町	15	G3
Kishiwada-shi	岸和田市	34	E5
Kishuku-cho	岐宿町	12	A6
Kiso-gawa	木曽川	20	C6
Kiso-mura	木祖村	21	E3
Kisofukushima-machi	木曽福島町	21	E3
Kisogawa-cho	木曽川町	38	C2
Kisozaki-cho	木曽岬町	38	B4
Kisuki-cho	木次町	15	F5
Kita-mura	木村	31	F1
Kita-ura	北浦	25	G6
Kitaaiki-mura	北相木村	21	G2
Kitaaizu-mura	北会津村	26	E5
Kitaarima-cho	北有馬町	70	A6
Kitadaito-son	北大東村	4	D6
Kitagata-cho	北方町	38	B1
Kitagata-machi	北方町	12	E5
Kitagawa-cho	北川町	13	I6
Kitagawa-mura	北川村	17	H4
Kitagi-shima	北木島	17	F2
Kitago-cho	北郷町	11	H3
Kitago-son	北郷村	13	H7
Kitahata-mura	北波多村	12	D4⑦
Kitahiyama-cho	北檜山町	30	D4
Kitaibaraki-shi	北茨城市	25	I6
Kitaiwō-jima	北硫黄島	9	I6
Kitajima-cho	北島町	17	I2
Kitakami-gawa	北上川	27	H1
Kitakami-machi	北上町	27	I2
Kitakami-shi	北上市	28	B5
Kitakata-cho	北方町	13	H7
Kitakata-shi	喜多方市	26	E5
Kitakawabe-machi	北川辺町	25	G4③
Kitakyushu-shi	北九州市	44	D2
Kitami-shi	北見市	33	F4
Kitamimaki-mura	北御牧村	23	G7
Kitamoto-shi	北本市	40	D1
Kitanakagusuku-son	北中城村	69	B5
Kitano-machi	北野町	44	C5
Kitashigeyasu-cho	北茂安町	44	B5
Kitashiobara-mura	北塩原村	26	E5
Kitatachibana-mura	北橘村	78	A4
Kitaura-cho	北浦町	13	I6
Kitaura-mura	北浦村	25	G6
Kitayama-mura	北山村	18	C4
Kitō-son	木頭村	17	H4
Kitsuki-shi	杵築市	13	H4
Kitsuregawa-machi	喜連川町	25	I5
Kiwa-cho	紀和町	18	C4
Kiyama-cho	基山町	44	B5
Kiyokawa-mura	清川村	13	H6
Kiyokawa-mura	清川村	40	C5
Kiyomi-mura	清見村	20	D2
Kiyone-son	清音村	15	H5③
Kiyosato-cho	清里町	33	H4
Kiyosato-mura	清里村	23	G4
Kiyose-shi	清瀬市	43	I1
Kiyosu-cho	清洲町	38	C3
Kiyosumi-san	清澄山	24	D5
Kiyotake-cho	清武町	11	H2
Kizu-cho	木津町	35	H3
Kizukuri-machi	木造町	29	G3
Kobayashi-shi	小林市	11	G2
Kōbe-shi	神戸市	34	D3
Kobuchizawa-cho	小淵沢町	21	G3
Kobushiga-dake	甲武信岳	25	F1
Kōchi-cho	河内町	15	F5
Kōchi-shi	高知市	17	F4
Kochinda-cho	東風平町	69	D5
Kōda-cho	甲田町	15	F5
Kodaira-shi	小平市	43	H1
Kodama-machi	児玉町	25	G3
Kōdera-cho	香寺町	34	A2
Kodomari-mura	小泊村	29	H3
Kōfu-cho	江府町	15	H3
Kōfu-shi	甲府市	21	G3
Koga-machi	古賀町	44	B2
Koga-shi	古河市	25	G4
Koganei-shi	小金井市	43	H1
Kōge-cho	郡家町	15	I3
Kogota-cho	小牛田町	27	G2
Kohoku-cho	湖北町	19	H5
Kōhoku-machi	江北町	12	E5
Koide-machi	小出町	26	C6
Koishiwara-mura	小石原村	13	F4
Kōka-cho	甲賀町	19	F5
Kokawa-cho	粉河町	34	E7
Kokonoe-machi	九重町	13	G5
Kokubu-shi	国分市	11	G3
Kokubunji-cho	国分寺町	17	G2
Kokubunji-machi	国分寺町	25	H4
Kokubunji-shi	国分寺市	40	D4
Kokufu-cho	国府町	15	J2
Kokufu-cho	国府町	20	D2
Komae-shi	狛江市	43	H2
Komaga-take(Kiso)	駒ヶ岳(木曽)	21	F3
Komaga-take(Yamanashi)	駒ヶ岳(山梨)	21	G3
Komagane-shi	駒ヶ根市	21	F3
Komaga-take(Hokkaidō)	駒ヶ岳(北海道)	30	D5
Komaki-shi	小牧市	38	D2
Komatsu-cho	小松町	17	E3
Komatsu-shi	小松市	22	B6
Komatsushima-shi	小松島市	17	I3
Komochi-mura	子持村	25	H2
Komono-cho	菰野町	38	A4
Komoro-shi	小諸市	21	G1
Konagai-cho	小長井町	12	E6
Kōnan-cho	甲南町	19	F5
Kōnan-cho	香南町	17	G2
Kōnan-machi	甲南町	25	G3⑤
Kōnan-shi	江南市	38	C2
Konda-cho	今田町	34	C1
Konkō-cho	金光町	15	H5
Kōno-mura	河野村	19	I5
Kōnosu-shi	鴻巣市	40	D1
Konoura-machi	金浦町	28	B2
Kōnu-cho	甲奴町	15	F5
Kōra-cho	甲良町	19	G5②
Kōri-machi	桑折町	27	F4
Kōriyama-cho	郡山町	11	F3
Kōriyama-shi	郡山市	27	F4
Koromogawa-mura	衣川村	28	B5
Kōryō-cho	湖陵町	15	F5
Kōryō-cho	広陵町	35	G5
Kōsa-machi	甲佐町	13	G6
Kōsai-machi	河西町	76	A2
Kosai-shi	湖西市	20	E6
Kosaka-machi	小坂町	29	F4
Kosaza-cho	小佐々町	12	C5
Kōsei-cho	甲西町	19	G5⑨
Koshigaya-shi	越谷市	41	F2
Kōshi-machi	合志町	70	E5
Koshiji-machi	越路町	23	H4
Koshikijima Rettō	甑島列島	10	D2
Koshimizu-cho	小清水町	33	G4
Koshino-mura	越廼村	22	A7
Kōshoku-shi	更埴市	21	F1
Kosudo-machi	小須戸町	26	C5
Kosuge-mura	小菅村	25	F2
Kosugi-machi	小杉町	22	D5
Kōta-cho	幸田町	20	D6
Kotake-machi	小竹町	44	C3
Kotō-cho	湖東町	19	G5⑥
Kotohira-cho	琴平町	17	G2
Kotonami-cho	琴南町	17	G2
Kotooka-machi	琴丘町	28	E2
Koumi-machi	小海町	21	G2
Kōya-cho	高野町	35	F7
Koyadaira-son	木屋平村	17	H3
Kōyagi-cho	香焼町	12	D6
Kōyaguchi-cho	高野口町	35	F6
Kōyama-cho	高山町	11	G4
Koza-cho	古座町	18	B4
Kozagawa-cho	古座川町	18	B4
Kōzakai-cho	小坂井町	39	F6
Kōzaki-machi	神崎町	41	I2
Kōzan-cho	甲山町	15	F5
Kōzan-cho	上月町	15	J4
Kōzushima-mura	神津島村	24	A3
Kubiki-mura	頸城村	23	G4
Kubokawa-cho	窪川町	17	E5
Kubota-cho	久保田町	44	A6
Kuchierabu-jima	口永良部島	10	E6
Kuchinotsu-cho	口之津町	12	E7
Kuchiwa-cho	口和町	15	F4
Kudaka-jima	久高島	10	A7
Kudamatsu-shi	下松市	14	C7
Kudoyama-cho	九度山町	35	F6
Kuga-cho	玖珂町	14	D6
Kugino-mura	久木野村	71	F5
Kuguno-cho	久々野町	20	D2
Kui-cho	久井町	15	F5
Kuji-shi	久慈市	28	E6
Kujō-machi	九条町	13	H5
Kujū-san	九重山	13	H5
Kujūku-shima	九十九島	12	C5
Kujūkuri-machi	九十九里町	25	I6
Kujūkurihama	九十九里浜	24	E6
Kuka-cho	久賀町	14	D7
Kuki-shi	久喜市	41	E1
Kukizaki-mura	茎崎村	41	H1
Kuma-cho	久万町	16	E4
Kuma-gawa	球磨川	11	F1
Kuma-mura	球磨村	11	F1
Kumagaya-shi	熊谷市	25	G3
Kumage-cho	熊毛町	14	D6⑥
Kumaishi-cho	熊石町	30	B5
Kumamoto-shi	熊本市	13	F6
Kumano-cho	熊野町	15	E6
Kumano-gawa	熊野川	18	C4
Kumano-shi	熊野市	18	C4
Kumanogawa-cho	熊野川町	18	C4
Kumano Nada	熊野灘	18	C6
Kumatori-cho	熊取町	34	E6
Kumayama-cho	熊山町	15	I4
Kume-jima	久米島	4	D3
Kume-cho	久米町	15	H4
Kumenan-cho	久米南町	15	I4
Kumihama-cho	久美浜町	19	H2
Kumiyama-cho	久御山町	35	G2
Kumotori-yama	雲取山	25	F2
Kunashiri-to	国後島	9	H1
Kuni-mura	六合村	25	H1
Kunigami-son	国頭村	10	B5
Kunimi-cho	国見町	13	E6
Kunimi-cho	国見町	13	I3

118

Kunimi-dake	国見岳	13	G7
Kunimi-machi	国見町	27	G4
Kunisaki-machi	国東町	13	I 4
Kunitachi-shi	国立市	40	D4
Kunitomi-cho	国富町	11	H2
Kunneppu-cho	訓子府町	33	F4
Kunohe-mura	九戸村	28	E5
Kurabuchi-mura	倉渕村	25	H2④
Kurahashi-cho	倉橋町	14	E6
Kuraishi-mura	倉石村	29	F5
Kurashiki-shi	倉敷市	15	H5
Kuratake-machi	倉岳町	11	F1②
Kurate-machi	鞍手町	44	C2
Kurayoshi-shi	倉吉市	15	H2
Kure-shi	呉市	14	E6
Kurihashi-machi	栗橋町	25	G4
Kurikoma-machi	栗駒町	27	G1
Kurikoma-yama	栗駒山	28	B4
Kurimoto-machi	栗源町	25	F6
Kurino-cho	栗野町	11	G2
Kurisawa-cho	栗沢町	31	F2
Kuriyama-cho	栗山町	31	F2
Kuriyama-mura	栗山村	25	I 4
Kuro-shima	黒島	10	D5
Kurobane-machi	黒羽町	25	I 5
Kurobe-gawa	黒部川	22	D4
Kurobe-ko	黒部湖	22	E6
Kurobe-shi	黒部市	22	D5
Kurobe-gorge	黒部峡谷	22	E5
Kurodashō-cho	黒田庄町	34	B1
Kurogi-machi	黒木町	13	F5
Kurohone-mura	黒保根村	25	H3
Kuroishi-shi	黒石市	29	F4
Kuroiso-shi	黒磯市	25	I 5
Kurokawa-mura	黒川村	26	D4
Kuromatsunai-cho	黒松内町	30	C3
Kurono-seto	黒之瀬戸	10	E7
Kurosaki-cho	黒埼町	26	C5
Kurose-cho	黒瀬町	15	E6
Kurotaki-mura	黒滝村	35	H6
Kurume-shi	久留米市	44	C5
Kusagaki Guntō	草垣群島	10	C5
Kusatsu-machi	草津町	25	H1
Kusatsu-shi	草津市	19	F4
Kuse-cho	久世町	15	H3
Kushibiki-machi	櫛引町	28	A2
Kushigata-machi	櫛形町	21	G4
Kushihara-mura	串原村	20	D5
Kushikino-shi	串木野市	10	E3
Kushima-shi	串間市	11	H3
Kushimoto-cho	串本町	18	B4
Kushira-cho	串良町	11	G4
Kushiro-cho	釧路町	33	G6
Kushiro-shi	釧路市	33	G6
Kussharo-ko	屈斜路湖	33	G4
Kusu-cho	楠町	38	B5
Kusu-machi	玖珠町	13	H6
Kusunoki-cho	楠町	14	B6
Kutchan-cho	倶知安町	30	D3
Kutsuki-mura	朽木村	19	G4
Kuwana-shi	桑名市	38	B4
Kuze-mura	久瀬村	20	B4
Kuzumaki-machi	葛巻町	28	E5
Kuzuryu-gawa	九頭竜川	22	A4
Kuzuu-machi	葛生町	25	H4
Kyōga-saki	経ヶ岬	19	I 3
Kyōgase-mura	京ヶ瀬村	26	C4
Kyōgoku-cho	京極町	30	D3
Kyokushi-mura	旭志村	70	E4
Kyonan-machi	鋸南町	24	D4
Kyōto-shi	京都市	35	G1
Kyōwa-cho	共和町	30	C2
Kyōwa-machi	協和町	25	H5④
Kyōwa-machi	協和町	28	C3

Kyūragi-machi	厳木町	12	E5

M

Mabi-cho	真備町	15	H5
Machida-shi	町田市	40	D5
Madara-shima	馬渡島	12	D4
Maebaru-machi	前原町	12	E4
Maebashi-shi	前橋市	25	H2
Maesawa-cho	前沢町	28	B5
Maetsue-mura	前津江村	13	G5
Maihara-cho	米原町	19	G5
Maisaka-cho	舞坂町	20	E6
Maizuru-shi	舞鶴市	19	H3
Makabe-machi	真壁町	25	G5
Maki-machi	巻町	26	C5
Maki-mura	牧村	23	G4
Makino-cho	マキノ町	19	H5
Makioka-cho	牧丘町	25	F2
Makizono-cho	牧園町	11	G2
Makkari-mura	真狩村	30	D3
Makubetsu-cho	幕別町	31	I 2
Makurazaki-shi	枕崎市	11	E4
Mamba-machi	万場町	25	G2
Mamurogawa-machi	真室川町	28	A3
Manatsuru-machi	真鶴町	24	D3
Mannō-cho	満濃町	17	G2①
Mano-machi	真野町	26	A4
Marugame-shi	丸亀市	17	G2
Maruko-cho	丸子町	21	G2
Marumori-machi	丸森町	27	G4
Maruoka-cho	丸岡町	22	A6
Maruseppu-cho	丸瀬布町	32	E3
Maruyama-machi	丸山町	24	D5
Masaki-cho	松前町	16	D3
Mashike-cho	増毛町	32	A4
Mashiki-machi	益城町	70	E6
Mashiko-machi	益子町	25	H5
Mashu-ko	摩周湖	33	G4
Masuda-cho	増田町	28	B3
Masuda-shi	益田市	14	C5
Masuho-cho	増穂町	76	A4
Matama-cho	真玉町	13	H4
Matsu-shima	松島	12	C6
Matsubara-shi	松原市	37	H6
Matsubase-machi	松橋町	70	D6
Matsubushi-machi	松伏町	41	F2
Matsuda-machi	松田町	40	B6
Matsudai-machi	松代町	23	G4
Matsudo-shi	松戸市	43	I 7
Matsue-shi	松江市	15	F2
Matsuida-machi	松井田町	25	H2
Matsukawa-machi	松川町	21	F4
Matsukawa-mura	松川村	21	E1⑥
Matsukawaura	松川浦	27	H4
Matsumae-cho	松前町	30	B7
Matsumoto-cho	松元町	11	F3
Matsumoto-shi	松本市	21	F2
Matsuno-cho	松野町	16	D5
Matsunoyama-machi	松之山町	23	G4
Matsuo-machi	松尾町	25	F6
Matsuo-mura	松尾村	28	E4
Matsuoka-cho	松岡町	22	A6
Matsusaka-shi	松阪市	18	E6
Matsushige-cho	松茂町	17	I 2
Matsushima-cho	松島町	27	H2
Matsushima-machi	松島町	13	F7
Matsutō-shi	松任市	22	B5
Matsuura-shi	松浦市	12	D4
Matsuyama-cho	松山町	11	G3
Matsuyama-machi	松山町	27	H2
Matsuyama-machi	松山町	28	A2
Matsuyama-shi	松山市	16	E3
Matsuzaki-cho	松崎町	21	H6
Maze-mura	馬瀬村	20	D3

Meiwa-cho	明和町	18	E6
Meiwa-mura	明和村	25	G3⑭
Memanbetsu-cho	女満別町	33	G4
Memuro-cho	芽室町	31	I 2
Menda-machi	免田町	11	G1
Menuma-machi	妻沼町	25	G3
Mi-shima	見島	14	B4
Miasa-mura	美麻村	23	F6
Mibu-machi	壬生町	25	H4
Midori-cho	美土里町	14	E5
Midori-cho	緑町	34	B6
Mie-machi	三重町	13	H5
Mifune-machi	御船町	13	G6
Mihama-cho	御浜町	18	C5
Mihama-cho	美浜町	18	C2
Mihama-cho	美浜町	19	H4
Mihama-cho	美浜町	38	C6
Mihara-cho	三原町	34	A6
Mihara-cho	美原町	37	F5
Mihara-mura	三原村	16	E6
Mihara-shi	三原市	15	F5
Mihara-yama	三原山	24	C3
Miharu-machi	三春町	27	G6
Miho-mura	美浦村	41	I 1
Miho	三保	21	G5
Mihonoseki-cho	美保関町	15	G2
Miiraku-cho	三井楽町	12	A6
Mikame-cho	三瓶町	16	C5
Mikamo-cho	三加茂町	17	G3
Mikamo-son	美甘村	15	H3
Mikasa-shi	三笠市	31	F1
Mikata-cho	三方町	19	H4
Mikata-cho	美方町	19	H1
Mikatsuki-cho	三日月町	12	E5⑧
Mikawa-cho	三川町	14	D6
Mikawa-machi	三加和町	13	F5
Mikawa-machi	三川町	28	A2
Mikawa-machi	美川町	22	B5
Mikawa-mura	三川村	26	D5
Mikawa-mura	美川村	16	E4
Mikawa Wan	三河湾	20	D6
Mikazuki-cho	三日月町	19	F1
Miki-cho	三木町	17	H2
Miki-shi	三木市	34	C4
Mikkabi-cho	三ヶ日町	20	E6
Mikumo-cho	三雲町	18	E6⑫
Mikuni-cho	三国町	22	A6
Mikurajima-mura	御蔵島村	7	H5
Mima-cho	三間町	16	D5
Mima-cho	美馬町	17	H3
Mimasaka-cho	美作町	15	I 4
Mimata-cho	三股町	11	H3
Mimi-kawa	耳川	11	I 1
Minabe-cho	南部町	18	C3
Minabegawa-mura	南部川村	18	C3
Minakami-machi	水上町	25	I 2
Minakuchi-cho	水口町	19	F5
Minamata-shi	水俣市	11	F1
Minami-mura	美並村	20	C4
Minamitane-cho	南種子町	11	G7
Minamiaiki-mura	南相木村	21	G2
Minamiarima-cho	南有馬町	12	E7
Minamiashigara-shi	南足柄市	40	B6
Minamichita-cho	南知多町	38	D6
Minamidaitō-son	南大東村	4	D6
Minamifurano-cho	南富良野町	31	H2
Minamiiwō-jima	南硫黄島	9	I 7
Minamiizu-cho	南伊豆町	21	H6
Minamikata-machi	南方町	27	H2
Minamikawachi-cho	南河内町	25	H4
Minamikawara-mura	南河原村	25	G3⑦
Minamikayabe-cho	南茅部町	30	D6
Minamikushiyama-cho	南串山町	70	A6
Minamimaki-mura	南牧村	21	G2

Minamiminowa-mura　南箕輪村‥ 21 F3⑤
Minaminasu-machi　南那須町‥ 25 I5
Minamioguni-machi　南小国町‥ 13 G5⑬
Minamishinano-mura　南信濃村‥ 21 F4
Minamitori-shima　南鳥島‥‥ 3
Minamiyamashiro-mura　南山城村‥ 35 I3
Minano-machi　皆野町‥‥ 40 B1
Minase-mura　皆瀬村‥‥ 28 B4
Mine-cho　三根町‥‥ 44 B5
Mine-shi　美祢市‥‥ 14 B6
Mine-son　峰村‥‥ 12 C1
Minehama-mura　峰浜村‥‥ 29 E2
Mineyama-cho　峰山町‥‥ 19 H2
Minmaya-mura　三厩村‥‥ 29 H3
Mino-cho　三野町‥‥ 17 G2
Mino-cho　三野町‥‥ 17 G3
Mino-shi　美濃市‥‥ 20 C4
Minobu-cho　身延町‥‥ 21 G4
Minokamo-shi　美濃加茂市‥ 20 D4
Minoo-shi　箕面市‥‥ 37 G1
Minori-machi　美野里町‥‥ 25 G6
Minowa-machi　箕輪町‥‥ 21 F3
Mirasaka-cho　三良坂町‥‥ 15 F4
Misaka-cho　御坂町‥‥ 76 C2
Misaki-cho　三崎町‥‥ 16 C5
Misaki-cho　岬町‥‥ 34 D6
Misaki-machi　岬町‥‥ 41 J6
Misakubo-cho　水窪町‥‥ 21 F5
Misasa-cho　三朝町‥‥ 15 H3
Misato-cho　美里町‥‥ 18 D2
Misato-machi　美里町‥‥ 25 G3
Misato-machi　箕郷町‥‥ 25 H2
Misato-mura　三郷村‥‥ 22 E7
Misato-mura　美里村‥‥ 19 E5
Misato-shi　三郷市‥‥ 41 F3
Misato-son　美郷村‥‥ 17 H3
Misawa-shi　三沢市‥‥ 29 G5
Mishima-machi　三島町‥‥ 26 B6
Mishima-machi　三島町‥‥ 26 E6
Mishima-mura　三島村‥‥ 10 D5
Mishima-shi　三島市‥‥ 21 H5
Mishō-cho　御荘町‥‥ 16 B6
Misono-mura　御薗村‥‥ 18 D6
Misugi-mura　美杉村‥‥ 18 E6
Misumi-cho　三隅町‥‥ 14 B5
Misumi-cho　三隅町‥‥ 14 D4
Misumi-machi　三角町‥‥ 13 F7
Mitagawa-cho　三田川町‥‥ 44 A5
Mitaka-shi　三鷹市‥‥ 43 H2
Mitake-cho　御嵩町‥‥ 38 E1
Mitake-mura　三岳村‥‥ 20 E3
Mitake-Shōsenkyō　御岳昇仙峡‥ 21 G3
Mitama-cho　三珠町‥‥ 76 B2
Mito-cho　御津町‥‥ 39 F6
Mito-cho　御津町‥‥ 14 D5
Mitō-cho　美東町‥‥ 14 B6
Mito-shi　水戸市‥‥ 25 H6
Mitomi-mura　三富村‥‥ 21 F2
Mitoya-cho　三刀屋町‥‥ 15 F3
Mitsu-cho　御津町‥‥ 15 H4
Mitsu-cho　御津町‥‥ 21 G7
Mitsue-mura　御杖村‥‥ 35 J5
Mitsugi-cho　御調町‥‥ 15 G5
Mitsuishi-machi　三石町‥‥ 44 B7
Mitsuishi-cho　三石町‥‥ 31 H4
Mitsukaidō-shi　水海道市‥‥ 41 G1
Mitsuke-shi　見附市‥‥ 26 C5
Mitsumine-san　三峰山‥‥ 40 A2
Mitsuse-mura　三瀬村‥‥ 12 E4
Mitsushima-cho　美津島町‥‥ 12 C2
Miura-shi　三浦市‥‥ 24 D4
Miura Hantō　三浦半島‥‥ 24 D4
Miwa-cho　三和町‥‥ 15 G5
Miwa-cho　三和町‥‥ 19 G3

Miwa-cho　美和町‥‥ 38 C3
Miwa-cho　美和町‥‥ 14 D6
Miwa-machi　三輪町‥‥ 44 C4
Miwa-mura　美和村‥‥ 25 I5①
Miya-mura　宮村‥‥ 20 D1
Miyagawa-mura　宮川村‥‥ 18 D5
Miyagawa-mura　宮川村‥‥ 20 D2
Miyagi-mura　宮城村‥‥ 78 B7
Miyahara-machi　宮原町‥‥ 13 F7
Miyajima-cho　宮島町‥‥ 14 E6
Miyake-cho　三宅町‥‥ 35 H4
Miyake-mura　三宅村‥‥ 24 A4
Miyako-jima　宮古島‥‥ 4 C3
Miyako-shi　宮古市‥‥ 28 D7
Miyakoji-mura　都路村‥‥ 27 G5
Miyakonojō-shi　都城市‥‥ 11 G3
Miyako Shotō　宮古諸島‥‥ 4 D3
Miyama-cho　海山町‥‥ 18 D5
Miyama-cho　美山町‥‥ 19 G3
Miyama-cho　美山町‥‥ 19 I5
Miyama-cho　美山町‥‥ 20 C4
Miyama-mura　美山村‥‥ 18 C3
Miyamori-mura　宮守村‥‥ 28 C5
Miyanojō-cho　宮之城町‥‥ 11 F2
Miyanoura-dake　宮之浦岳‥‥ 11 F7
Miyashiro-machi　宮代町‥‥ 41 F1
Miyata-machi　宮田町‥‥ 44 C2
Miyata-mura　宮田村‥‥ 21 F3
Miyazaki-cho　宮崎町‥‥ 27 G2
Miyazaki-mura　宮崎村‥‥ 19 I5
Miyazaki-shi　宮崎市‥‥ 11 H2
Miyazu-shi　宮津市‥‥ 19 H2
Miyoshi-cho　三好町‥‥ 17 G3
Miyoshi-cho　三芳町‥‥ 38 E4
Miyoshi-machi　三芳町‥‥ 40 D3
Miyoshi-mura　三芳村‥‥ 24 A4
Miyoshi-shi　三次市‥‥ 15 F4
Miyota-machi　御代田町‥‥ 21 G2
Mizobe-cho　溝辺町‥‥ 11 F2
Mizoguchi-cho　溝口町‥‥ 15 G3
Mizuho-cho　瑞穂町‥‥ 14 E4
Mizuho-cho　瑞穂町‥‥ 19 G3
Mizuho-cho　瑞穂町‥‥ 70 A5
Mizuho-machi　瑞穂町‥‥ 40 C3
Mizukami-mura　水上村‥‥ 11 G3
Mizuma-machi　三潴町‥‥ 44 B6
Mizumaki-machi　水巻町‥‥ 44 C1
Mizunami-shi　瑞浪市‥‥ 20 D4
Mizusawa-shi　水沢市‥‥ 28 B5
Mobara-shi　茂原市‥‥ 41 I6
Mochigase-cho　用瀬町‥‥ 15 I3
Mochizuki-machi　望月町‥‥ 21 G2
Mogami-gawa　最上川‥‥ 28 A1
Mogami-machi　最上町‥‥ 28 A3
Mombetsu-shi　紋別市‥‥ 32 E2
Momoishi-mura　百石町‥‥ 29 F5
Momoyama-cho　桃山町‥‥ 34 E7
Monbetsu-cho　門別町‥‥ 31 G4
Monobe-gawa　物部川‥‥ 17 G4
Monobe-mura　物部村‥‥ 17 G4
Monou-cho　桃生町‥‥ 27 H2
Monzen-machi　門前町‥‥ 22 C3
Mooka-shi　真岡市‥‥ 25 I5
Mori-machi　森町‥‥ 21 F6
Mori-machi　森町‥‥ 30 C5
Moriguchi-shi　守口市‥‥ 37 H3
Moriokā-shi　盛岡市‥‥ 28 D5
Morita-mura　森田村‥‥ 29 G3
Moriya-machi　守谷町‥‥ 41 G2
Moriyama-cho　森山町‥‥ 12 E6⑪
Moriyama-shi　守山市‥‥ 19 G4
Moriyoshi-machi　森吉町‥‥ 28 E3
Morodomi-cho　諸富町‥‥ 44 A6

Morotsuka-son　諸塚村‥‥ 13 H7
Moroyama-machi　毛呂山町‥‥ 40 C2
Moseushi-cho　妹背牛町‥‥ 32 B4
Motegi-machi　茂木町‥‥ 25 H5
Motobu-cho　本部町‥‥ 10 A5
Motomiya-machi　本宮町‥‥ 27 F5
Motono-mura　本埜村‥‥ 41 H3
Motosu-cho　本巣町‥‥ 38 B1
Motoyama-cho　本山町‥‥ 17 F4
Motoyoshi-cho　本吉町‥‥ 27 I1
Mugegawa-cho　武芸川町‥‥ 20 C4
Mugi-cho　武儀町‥‥ 20 D4
Mugi-cho　牟岐町‥‥ 17 I4
Muika-machi　六日町‥‥ 23 H5
Muikaichi-machi　六日市町‥‥ 14 C6
Mukabaki-yama　背門山‥‥ 13 H6
Mukaihara-cho　向原町‥‥ 15 F5
Mukaishima-cho　向島町‥‥ 15 G6
Mukawa-cho　鵡川町‥‥ 31 F3
Mukawa-mura　武川村‥‥ 21 G3
Mukō-shi　向日市‥‥ 35 G2
Munakata-shi　宗像市‥‥ 44 B2
Murakami-shi　村上市‥‥ 26 D3
Muramatsu-machi　村松町‥‥ 26 C5
Muraoka-cho　村岡町‥‥ 19 H1
Murata-machi　村田町‥‥ 27 G3
Murayama-shi　村山市‥‥ 27 F2
Mure-cho　牟礼町‥‥ 17 H2
Mure-mura　牟礼村‥‥ 23 F5
Muro-mura　室生村‥‥ 35 I4
Murone-mura　室根村‥‥ 28 B5
Muroran-shi　室蘭市‥‥ 30 E4
Muroto-shi　室戸市‥‥ 17 H5
Muroto-zaki　室戸岬‥‥ 17 H5
Musashi-machi　武蔵町‥‥ 13 I4
Musashi-murayama-shi　武蔵村山市‥ 40 C3
Musashino-shi　武蔵野市‥‥ 43 H2
Mutsu-shi　むつ市‥‥ 29 I5
Mutsumi-mura　むつみ村‥‥ 14 C5
Mutsu Wan　陸奥湾‥‥ 29 H4
Mutsuzawa-machi　睦沢町‥‥ 41 J6
Myōgata-mura　明方村‥‥ 20 D3
Myōgi-machi　妙義町‥‥ 25 G2
Myōgi-san　妙義山‥‥ 25 G2
Myōken-yama　妙見山‥‥ 19 F3
Myōkō-mura　妙高村‥‥ 23 F5
Myōkō-san　妙高山‥‥ 23 F5
Myōkōkōgen-machi　妙高高原町‥ 23 F5

N
Nabari-shi　名張市‥‥ 18 E5
Nachi-san　那智山‥‥ 18 C4
Nachikatsuura-cho　那智勝浦町‥ 18 B4
Nadachi-machi　名立町‥‥ 23 F4
Nadasaki-cho　灘崎町‥‥ 15 H5
Naeba-san　苗場山‥‥ 25 I1
Naga-cho　那賀町‥‥ 35 E7
Nagahama-cho　長浜町‥‥ 16 D4
Nagahama-shi　長浜市‥‥ 19 G5
Nagai-shi　長井市‥‥ 26 E4
Nagaizumi-cho　長泉町‥‥ 76 D6
Nagakute-cho　長久手町‥‥ 38 D3
Nagano-shi　長野市‥‥ 23 F6
Naganohara-machi　長野原町‥‥ 25 H1
Naganuma-cho　長沼町‥‥ 31 F2
Naganuma-machi　長沼町‥‥ 27 F6
Nagao-cho　長尾町‥‥ 17 H2
Nagaoka-shi　長岡市‥‥ 26 C6
Nagaokakyō-shi　長岡京市‥‥ 35 G2
Nagara-gawa　長良川‥‥ 38 C1
Nagara-machi　長柄町‥‥ 41 I5
Nagareyama-shi　流山市‥‥ 41 G2
Nagasaka-cho　長坂町‥‥ 21 G3⑦
Nagasaki-bana　長崎鼻‥‥ 11 F4

120

Name	漢字	Page	Grid
Nagasaki-shi	長崎市	12	D6
Nagashima-cho	長島町	10	E1
Nagashima-cho	長島町	38	B4
Nagasu-machi	長洲町	13	F6
Nagato-machi	長門町	21	G2
Nagato-shi	長門市	14	B5
Nagatoro-machi	長瀞町	40	B1
Nagatoro	長瀞	25	G3
Nagawa-machi	名川町	29	F5
Nagawa-mura	奈川村	21	E2
Nagayo-cho	長与町	12	D6
Nagi-cho	奈義町	15	I3
Nagi-sen	那岐山	15	I3
Nagiso-machi	南木曽町	20	E4
Nago-shi	名護市	10	B5
Nagoya-shi	名古屋市	20	C5
Naguri-mura	名栗村	40	B2
Naha-shi	那覇市	10	A6
Nahari-cho	奈半利町	17	H5
Naie-cho	奈井江町	31	F1
Naka-cho	中町	34	B1
Naka-gawa	那珂川	25	H6
Naka-machi	那珂町	25	H6
Naka Umi	中海	15	G2
Nakayama-machi	中山町	27	F3
Nakabaru-cho	中原町	44	B5
Nakada-cho	中田町	27	H2
Nakadōri-jima	中通島	12	B5
Nakafurano-cho	中富良野町	31	G1
Nakagawa-cho	中川町	32	B1
Nakagawa-cho	那賀川町	17	I3
Nakagawa-machi	那珂川町	44	B4
Nakagawa-mura	中川村	21	F4
Nakagō-mura	中郷村	23	F5
Nakagusuku-son	中城村	69	B6
Nakaheji-cho	中辺路町	18	C3
Nakai-machi	中井町	40	B6
Nakaizu-cho	中伊豆町	21	I5
Nakajima-cho	中島町	16	D3
Nakajima-machi	中島町	22	C4
Nakajima-mura	中島村	27	F6
Nakajō-machi	中条町	26	D4
Nakajō-mura	中条村	23	F6
Nakakawane-cho	中川根町	21	E5
Nakama-shi	中間市	44	C2
Nakamichi-cho	中道町	76	B2
Nakaminato-shi	那珂湊市	25	H6
Nakamura-shi	中村市	16	E6
Nakaniida-machi	中新田町	27	G2
Nakano-shima	中ノ島	14	A2
Nakano-shi	中野市	23	G5
Nakanojō-machi	中之条町	25	H2
Nakanokuchi-mura	中之口村	26	C5
Nakanoshima-machi	中之島町	26	C5
Nakasato-machi	中里町	29	G3
Nakasato-mura	中里村	23	H5
Nakasato-mura	中里村	25	G2
Nakasatsunai-mura	中礼内村	31	I3
Nakasen-machi	中仙町	28	C3
Nakashibetsu-cho	中標津町	33	H5
Nakatane-cho	中種子町	11	G6
Nakatomi-cho	中富町	21	G4
Nakatonbetsu-cho	中頓別町	33	H2
Nakatosa-cho	中土佐町	17	F5
Nakatsu-mura	中津村	18	C3
Nakatsu-shi	中津市	13	G4
Nakatsue-mura	中津江村	13	G5
Nakatsugawa-shi	中津川市	20	E4
Nakayama-cho	中山町	15	H2
Nakayama-mura	中山村	16	D4
Nakazato-son	仲里村	4	D4③
Nakijin-son	今帰仁村	10	B5
Namegawa-machi	滑川町	40	C1
Namerikawa-shi	滑川市	22	D5
Nambu-cho	南部町	21	G5
Nambu-machi	南部町	29	F5
Namiai-mura	浪合村	20	E4
Namie-machi	浪江町	27	H5
Namikata-cho	波方町	16	E2
Namino-son	波野村	71	G4
Namioka-machi	浪岡町	29	G4
Nammoku-mura	南牧村	25	G2
Nanae-cho	七飯町	30	D6
Nanakai-mura	七会村	25	H5③
Nanao-shi	七尾市	22	C4
Nanatsuka-machi	七塚町	22	C5
Nanayama-mura	七山村	12	E4⑥
Nandan-cho	南淡町	34	A7
Nangai-mura	南外村	28	C3
Nangō-cho	南郷町	11	H3
Nangō-cho	南郷町	27	H2③
Nangō-mura	南郷村	26	D6
Nangō-mura	南郷村	29	F5
Nangō-son	南郷村	11	H1
Nanjō-cho	南条町	19	I5
Nankan-machi	南関町	13	F5
Nankō-cho	南光町	15	J4
Nankoku-shi	南国市	17	G4
Nannō-cho	南濃町	38	B3
Nanporo-cho	南幌町	31	F2
Nansei-cho	南勢町	18	D6
Nansei Shotō	南西諸島	4	E3
Nantai-zan	男体山	25	I4
Nantō-cho	南島町	18	D6
Nanyō-shi	南陽市	27	F4
Naoiri-machi	直入町	13	H5
Naokawa-son	直川村	13	I6
Naoshima-cho	直島町	17	H1
Nara-ken	奈良県	35	H3
Naraha-machi	楢葉町	27	H6
Narakawa-mura	楢川村	21	F3
Narao-cho	奈良尾町	12	B6
Narashino-shi	習志野市	41	H4
Narita-shi	成田市	41	I3
Nariwa-cho	成羽町	15	H4
Naru-cho	奈留町	12	B6
Naru-shima	奈留島	12	B6
Naruko-cho	鳴子町	27	G2
Narusawa-mura	鳴沢村	76	C4
Naruse-machi	鳴瀬町	27	H2
Naruto-kaikyō	鳴門海峡	18	D1
Narutō-machi	成東町	41	J4
Naruto-shi	鳴門市	17	I2
Nasu-dake	那須岳	25	J5
Nasu-machi	那須町	25	J5
Natashō-mura	名田庄村	19	G3
Natori-shi	名取市	27	G3
Nawa-cho	名和町	15	G2
Nayoro-shi	名寄市	32	C2
Naze-shi	名瀬市	10	B2
Neagari-machi	根上町	22	B6
Neba-mura	根羽村	20	E5
Nejime-cho	根占町	11	G4
Nemuro-shi	根室市	33	J5
Neo-mura	根尾村	20	C4
Neyagawa-shi	寝屋川市	37	I3
Nezamenotoko	寝覚ノ床	20	E3
Nichihara-cho	日原町	14	C5
Nichinan-cho	日南町	15	G3
Nichinan-shi	日南市	11	H3
Nihonmatsu-shi	二本松市	27	F5
Niibo-mura	新穂村	26	B4
Niigata-shi	新潟市	26	C4
Niihama-shi	新居浜市	17	F3
Niihari-mura	新治村	25	G5③
Niiharu-mura	新治村	25	I2
Niijimahon-mura	新島本村	24	B3
Niikappu-cho	新冠町	31	G4
Niimi-shi	新見市	15	G4
Niisato-mura	新里村	25	H3⑦
Niisato-mura	新里村	28	C6
Niitsu-shi	新津市	26	C5
Niitsuru-mura	新鶴村	26	E5③
Niiza-shi	新座市	43	J2
Nijino-Matsubara	虹の松原	12	E4
Nijō-machi	二丈町	12	E4
Nikaho-machi	仁賀保町	28	B2
Niki-cho	仁木町	30	D2
Nikkō-shi	日光市	25	I4
Nima-cho	仁摩町	14	E3
Ninohe-shi	二戸市	29	E5
Ninomiya-machi	二宮町	25	H5
Ninomiya-machi	二宮町	40	C7
Nio-cho	仁尾町	17	G2
Nirasaki-shi	韮崎市	21	G3
Nirayama-cho	韮山町	76	E7
Niseko-cho	ニセコ町	30	D3
Nishiaizu-machi	西会津町	26	E5
Nishiarie-cho	西有家町	70	B6
Nishiarita-cho	西有田町	12	D5
Nishiawakura-son	西粟倉村	15	I3
Nishiazai-cho	西浅井町	19	H5
Nishibiwajima-cho	西枇杷島町	38	C3
Nishigō-mura	西郷村	27	F6
Nishigōshi-machi	西合志町	70	D4
Nishihara-cho	西原町	69	A6
Nishihara-mura	西原村	71	E5
Nishiharu-cho	西春町	39	H1
Nishiiyayama-son	西祖谷山村	17	G3
Nishiizu-cho	西伊豆町	21	H6
Nishikata-mura	西方村	25	H4
Nishikatsura-cho	西桂町	76	D2
Nishikawa-machi	西川町	26	C5
Nishikawa-machi	西川町	27	F3
Nishiki-cho	錦町	14	D6
Nishiki-cho	西紀町	19	F3
Nishiki-gawa	錦川	14	D6
Nishiki-machi	錦町	11	G1
Nishiki-mura	西木村	28	C3
Nishime-machi	西目町	28	C2
Nishimera-son	西米良村	11	H1
Nishimeya-mura	西目屋村	29	F3
Nishinasuno-machi	西那須野町	25	I5
Nishine-cho	西根町	28	D5
Nishinomiya-shi	西宮市	36	E3
Nishinoomote-shi	西之表市	11	G6
Nishinoshima-Shintō	西之島新島	9	I5
Nishinoshima-cho	西ノ島町	14	A2
Nishio-shi	西尾市	20	D6
Nishiokoppe-mura	西興部村	32	D2
Nishisemboku-machi	西仙北町	28	C3
Nishisonogi Hantō	西彼杵半島	12	D6
Nishitosa-mura	西土佐村	16	D5
Nishiumi-cho	西海町	16	D6
Nishiwaki-shi	西脇市	34	B1
Nishiyama-machi	西山町	23	H3
Nishiyoshino-mura	西吉野村	35	G7
Nisshin-cho	日進町	38	D3
Nita-machi	仁多町	15	F3
Nitta-machi	新田町	25	G3⑪
Niyodo-gawa	仁淀川	17	F4
Niyodo-mura	仁淀村	16	E4
Nobeoka-shi	延岡市	13	I7
Noboribetsu-shi	登別市	30	E4
Noda-cho	野田町	11	E2
Noda-mura	野田村	28	E6
Noda-shi	野田市	41	F2
Nodagawa-cho	野田川町	19	H2
Nōgata-shi	直方市	44	D2
Nogi-machi	野木町	25	G4③
Nōgō-hakusan	能郷白山	20	B3
Noheji-machi	野辺地町	29	G5

Noichi-cho 野市町	17 G4		
Nojima-zaki 野島崎	24 C4		
Nojiri-cho 野尻町	11 H2		
Nojiri-ko 野尻湖	23 F5		
Nokami-cho 野上町	18 D2		
Nokogiri-yama 鋸山	24 D4		
Noma-misaki 野間岬	10 E4		
Nōmi-cho 能美町	14 E6		
Nomozaki-cho 野母崎町	12 D7		
Nomura-cho 野村町	16 D5		
Nonoichi-machi 野々市町	22 B5		
Norikura-dake 乗鞍岳	22 D7		
Nosaka-machi 野栄町	25 F6③		
Nose-cho 能勢町	35 E1		
Nosegawa-mura 野迫川村	18 D4		
Noshiro-shi 能代市	28 E2		
Nossapu-misaki 納沙布岬	33 J5		
Noto-Kongō 能登金剛	22 C4		
Noto-machi 能都町	22 D3		
Notogawa-cho 能登川町	19 G5		
Notojima-machi 能登島町	22 D4		
Notoro-ko 能取湖	33 G3		
Notsu-machi 野津町	13 I5		
Notsuharu-machi 野津原町	13 H5		
Nou-machi 能生町	23 F4		
Nozaki-jima 野崎島	12 B5		
Nozawaonsen-mura 野沢温泉村	23 G5		
Nukata-cho 額田町	39 F5		
Numakuma-cho 沼隈町	15 G5		
Numata-cho 沼田町	32 B4		
Numata-shi 沼田市	25 H2		
Numazu-shi 沼津市	21 H5		
Nuwa-jima 怒和島	14 E7		
Nyūkawa-mura 丹生川村	20 D2		
Nyūzen-machi 入善町	22 E4		

O

Ōamishirasato-machi 大網白里町	41 I5		
Ōarai-machi 大洗町	25 H6		
Ōasa-cho 大朝町	14 E4		
Obama-cho 小浜町	12 E6		
Obama-shi 小浜市	19 H4		
Obanazawa-shi 尾花沢市	27 F2		
Obara-mura 小原村	20 D5		
Ōbata-cho 小俣町	18 E6⑬		
Ōbatake-cho 大畠町	14 D7		
Obihiro-shi 帯広市	31 I2		
Ōbira-cho 小平町	32 A3		
Oboke 大歩危	17 G3		
Ōbu-shi 大府市	38 D4		
Obuse-machi 小布施町	23 G5		
Ochi-cho 越知町	17 F4		
Ōchi-cho 相知町	12 E4		
Ōchi-cho 邑智町	14 E3		
Ochiai-cho 落合町	15 H4		
Oda-cho 小田町	14 E3		
Ōda-shi 大田市	14 E3		
Ōdai-cho 大台町	18 E5		
Ōdaigahara-zan 大台ヶ原山	18 D5		
Ōdaka-machi 大高町	27 H5		
Ōdate-shi 大館市	29 E3		
Odawara-shi 小田原市	40 B7		
Ōe-cho 大江町	19 G2		
Ōe-machi 大江町	27 F3		
Ōfunato-shi 大船渡市	28 B6		
Ofuyu-misaki 雄冬岬	32 A4		
Oga-shi 男鹿市	28 D2		
Ōgachi-machi 雄勝町	28 B3		
Oga Hantō 男鹿半島	28 D1		
Ōgaki-cho 大柿町	14 E6		
Ōgaki-shi 大垣市	18 E5		
Ogano-machi 小鹿野町	40 A1		
Ogasa-cho 小笠町	21 F6		
Ogasawara-mura 小笠原村	9 I5		

Ogasawara Shotō 小笠原諸島	9 I6		
Ogata-cho 大方町	16 E6		
Ogata-machi 緒方町	13 H5		
Ogata-machi 大潟町	23 G4		
Ogata-mura 大潟村	28 E2		
Ogatsu-cho 雄勝町	27 I2		
Ogawa-machi 小川町	13 F7		
Ogawa-machi 小川町	25 G6		
Ogawa-machi 小川町	25 I5		
Ogawa-machi 小川町	40 C1		
Ogawa-mura 緒川村	25 H5②		
Ogawa-mura 小川村	23 F6		
Ogawara-machi 大河原町	27 G4		
Ogi-machi 荻町	13 H6		
Ogi-machi 小城町	12 E5		
Ogi-machi 小木町	26 A5		
Ōgimi-son 大宜味村	10 B5		
Ogino-sen 扇ノ山	15 J2		
Ōgo-machi 大胡町	25 H3		
Ōgoe-machi 大越町	27 G6		
Ogori-cho 小郡町	14 B6		
Ogori-shi 小郡市	44 C5		
Ogose-machi 越生町	40 C2		
Ōguchi-cho 大口町	38 D2		
Oguni-machi 小国町	23 H4		
Oguni-machi 小国町	26 E4		
Oguni-machi 小国町	13 G5		
Ōhara-cho 大原町	15 J3		
Ōhara-cho 大原町	24 D6		
Ōharu-cho 大治町	39 G2		
Ōhasama-machi 大迫町	28 C5		
Ōhata-machi 大畑町	29 I5		
Ōhira-machi 大平町	25 H4②		
Ōhira-mura 大衡村	27 G4		
Ōhito-cho 大仁町	21 H5		
Ōi-cho 大飯町	19 H4		
Ōi-gawa 大井川	21 G6		
Ōi-machi 大井町	40 B6		
Ōi-machi 大井町	40 D2		
Ōigawa-cho 大井川町	21 G6		
Ōirase-gawa 奥入瀬川	29 F4		
Ōishida-machi 大石田町	27 F2		
Ōiso-machi 大磯町	40 C7		
Ōita-shi 大分市	13 I5		
Ōiwake-cho 追分町	31 F3		
Ōizumi-mura 大泉村	21 G3		
Ōizumi-machi 大泉町	25 G3		
Ōji-cho 王寺町	35 G4		
Ojika-cho 小値賀町	12 B5		
Ojika-jima 小値賀島	12 B5		
Ojika Hantō 牡鹿半島	27 I3		
Ojima-machi 尾島町	25 G3		
Ojiya-shi 小千谷市	26 B6		
Okabe-machi 岡部町	25 G3③		
Okabe-cho 岡部町	21 G6		
Okagaki-machi 岡垣町	44 C1		
Okaharu-mura 岡原村	11 G1		
Ōkawa-cho 大川町	17 H2		
Ōkawa-mura 大川村	17 F3		
Ōkawa-shi 大川市	44 A6		
Ōkawachi-mura 大河内町	19 G1		
Okaya-shi 岡谷市	21 F2		
Okayama-shi 岡山市	15 H5		
Okazaki-shi 岡崎市	20 D6		
Okegawa-shi 桶川市	40 E1		
Ōketo-cho 置戸町	32 E4		
Ōki-machi 大木町	44 B6		
Okidaitō-jima 沖大東島	4 C6		
Okierabu-jima 沖永良部島	4 E5		
Okimi-cho 沖美町	14 E6		
Okinawa-shi 沖縄市	10 A6		
Okinawa Hontō 沖縄本島	10 B6		
Okino-shima 沖ノ島	12 D7		
Okino-shima 沖ノ島	16 D7		

Okinotori-shima 沖ノ鳥島	3		
Oki Shotō 隠岐諸島	14 A1		
Okoppe-cho 興部町	32 D2		
Oku-cho 邑久町	15 I5		
Ōkuchi-mura 尾口村	22 B6		
Ōkuchi-shi 大口市	11 F2		
Ōkuma-machi 大熊町	27 H6		
Ōkura-mura 大蔵村	28 A3		
Okushiri-cho 奥尻町	30 A5		
Okushiri-to 奥尻島	30 A5		
Okutadami-ko 奥只見湖	26 D7		
Okutama-ko 奥多摩湖	25 F2		
Okutama-machi 奥多摩町	40 B3		
Okutango Hantō 奥丹後半島	19 H2		
Okutone-ko 奥利根湖	25 I2		
Okutsu-cho 奥津町	15 I3		
Ōkuwa-mura 大桑村	21 E3		
Ōma-machi 大間町	29 I4		
Ōmachi-cho 大町町	12 E5		
Ōmachi-shi 大町市	21 F1		
Ōmae-zaki 御前崎	21 G7		
Ōmaezaki-cho 御前崎町	21 G7		
Ōmagari-shi 大曲市	28 C3		
Ōmama-machi 大間々町	25 H3		
Ōme-shi 青梅市	40 C1		
Ōmi-cho 青海町	19 G5⑦		
Ōmi-machi 青海町	23 F4		
Ōmi-mura 麻績村	23 F6		
Ōmi-shima 大三島	14 B5		
Omigawa-machi 小見川町	25 F6		
Ōmihachiman-shi 近江八幡市	19 G5		
Ōmishima-cho 大三島町	16 E2		
Ōmiya-cho 大宮町	18 D6		
Ōmiya-cho 大宮町	19 H2		
Ōmiya-machi 大宮町	25 H6		
Ōmiya-shi 大宮市	40 E2		
Omogo-mura 面河村	16 E4		
Omogokei 面河渓	16 E4		
Omono-gawa 雄物川	28 D2		
Omonogawa-machi 雄物川町	28 B3		
Ōmori-machi 大森町	28 C3		
Ōmotego-mura 表郷村	27 F7		
Ōmu-cho 雄武町	32 D2		
Ōmura-shi 大村市	12 D6		
Ōmura Wan 大村湾	12 D6		
Ōmuta-shi 大牟田市	13 E5		
Onagawa-cho 女川町	27 I2		
Onbetsu-cho 音別町	33 F7		
Ondo-cho 音戸町	14 E6		
Onejime-cho 大根占町	11 G4		
Onga-cho 遠賀町	44 C1		
Ōnishi-cho 大西町	16 E3		
Ōnishi-machi 鬼石町	25 G2		
Onjuku-machi 御宿町	24 D6		
Onna-son 恩納村	10 A6		
Ōno-cho 大野町	14 D6		
Ōno-cho 大野町	20 C4		
Ōno-cho 大野町	30 C6		
Ōno-gawa 大野川	13 I5		
Ono-machi 小野町	27 G6		
Ōno-machi 大野町	13 H5		
Ōno-mura 大野村	25 G5		
Ōno-mura 大野村	29 F5		
Ono-shi 小野市	34 B2		
Ōno-shi 大野市	22 B7		
Onoda-machi 小野田町	27 G2		
Onoda-shi 小野田市	14 B7		
Onoe-machi 尾上町	29 H2		
Ōnogami-mura 小野上村	25 H2		
Ōnohara-cho 大野原町	17 G3		
Ōnojo-shi 大野城市	44 B4		
Ōnomi-son 大野見村	17 E5		
Onomichi-shi 尾道市	15 G5		
Onsen-cho 温泉町	19 H1		

Ontake-san 御岳山 …… 20 E3
Ōnuma 大沼 …… 30 D5
Ōoka-mura 大岡村 …… 23 F6
Ōra-machi 邑楽町 …… 25 G3⑫
Ōsa-cho 大佐町 …… 15 H3
Osafune-cho 長船町 …… 15 I5
Ōsaka-sayama-shi 大阪狭山市 …… 35 F5
Ōsaka-shi 大阪市 …… 35 E4
Ōsaka-cho 小坂町 …… 20 D3
Ōsaka Wan 大阪湾 …… 18 E3
Ōsaki-cho 大崎町 …… 11 G3
Ōsaki-cho 大崎町 …… 15 F6
Ōsato-cho 大郷町 …… 27 G2
Ōsato-mura 大里村 …… 25 G3⑥
Ōsawano-machi 大沢野町 …… 22 D5
Ōseto-cho 大瀬戸町 …… 12 D5
Oshamambe-cho 長万部町 …… 30 C4
Oshika-cho 牡鹿町 …… 27 I3
Ōshika-mura 大鹿村 …… 21 F4
Ōshima(Izu) 大島(伊豆) …… 24 C3
Ōshima(Yashiro-jima) 大島(屋代島) …… 14 E7
Ōshima-cho 大島町 …… 12 D5
Ōshima-cho 大島町 …… 14 D7
Ōshima-machi 大島町 …… 22 C5
Ōshima-machi 大島町 …… 24 C3
Ōshima-mura 大島村 …… 12 C4
Ōshima-mura 大島村 …… 23 G4
Ōshima-mura 大島村 …… 44 B1
Ōshimizu-machi 押水町 …… 22 C5
Oshino-mura 忍野村 …… 76 D3
Osore-zan 恐山 …… 29 H4
Ōsuka-cho 大須賀町 …… 21 F6
Ōsumi Hantō 大隅半島 …… 11 G4
Ōsumi-cho 大隅町 …… 11 G3
Ōsumi Kaikyō 大隅海峡 …… 11 G5
Ōsumi Shotō 大隅諸島 …… 11 F6
Ota-cho 織田町 …… 22 A7
Ōta-machi 太田町 …… 28 C4
Ōta-shi 太田市 …… 25 H3
Ōta-mura 大田村 …… 13 H4
Ōtake-shi 大竹市 …… 14 D6
Ōtaki-machi 大多喜町 …… 24 E5
Ōtaki-mura 王滝村 …… 20 E3
Ōtaki-mura 大滝村 …… 30 D3
Ōtaki-mura 大滝村 …… 40 A2
Ōtama-mura 大玉村 …… 27 F5
Otari-mura 小谷村 …… 23 E5
Otaru-shi 小樽市 …… 30 D2
Ōtawara-shi 大田原市 …… 25 I5
Ōtō-machi 大任町 …… 44 D3
Ōtō-mura 大塔村 …… 18 D4
Otobe-cho 乙部町 …… 30 B5
Otofuke-cho 音更町 …… 31 I2
Ōtoineppu-mura 音威子府村 …… 32 B1
Ōtone-machi 大利根町 …… 25 G4⑨
Ōtoyo-cho 大豊町 …… 17 G3
Ōtsu-shi 大津市 …… 19 F4
Ōtsuchi-cho 大槌町 …… 28 C6
Ōtsuki-cho 大月町 …… 16 D6
Ōtsuki-shi 大月市 …… 21 H4
Ōuchi-machi 大内町 …… 17 H2
Ōuchi-machi 大内町 …… 28 C2
Ōuchiyama-mura 大内山村 …… 18 D5
Ōuda-cho 大宇陀町 …… 35 H5
Ōura-cho 大浦町 …… 11 E4
Owani-machi 大鰐町 …… 29 F3
Owariasahi-shi 尾張旭市 …… 38 D3
Owase-shi 尾鷲市 …… 18 D5
Ōya-cho 大屋町 …… 19 G1
Ōyabe-shi 小矢部市 …… 22 C5
Oyama-cho 小山町 …… 21 H4
Ōyama-machi 大山町 …… 13 G5
Ōyama-machi 大山町 …… 22 D5

Oyama-shi 小山市 …… 25 H4
Ōyama 大山 …… 40 C5
Ōyamada-mura 大山田村 …… 19 F5
Ōyamazaki-cho 大山崎町 …… 35 G2
Ōyano-machi 大矢野町 …… 13 F7
Ōyodo-cho 大淀町 …… 35 H6
Ōyodo-gawa 大淀川 …… 11 H2
Ōzato-son 大里村 …… 69 A6
Ozegahara 尾瀬ヶ原 …… 25 I3
Ōzu-machi 大津町 …… 13 G6
Ōzu-shima 大津島 …… 14 C7
Ōzu-shi 大洲市 …… 16 D4

P

Pippu-machi 比布町 …… 32 C4

R

Rankoshi-cho 蘭越町 …… 30 C3
Ranzan-machi 嵐山町 …… 40 C1
Rausu-cho 羅臼町 …… 33 I3
Rebun-cho 礼文町 …… 32 E1
Rebun-tō 礼文島 …… 32 E1
Reihoku-machi 苓北町 …… 12 E7
Rifu-cho 利府町 …… 27 G3
Rikubetsu-cho 陸別町 …… 33 F5
Rikuzentakata-shi 陸前高田市 …… 28 B6
Rishiri-cho 利尻町 …… 32 E2
Rishiri-tō 利尻島 …… 32 E2
Ritto-cho 栗東町 …… 19 F4
Rokkasho-mura 六ヶ所村 …… 29 G5
Rokkō-san 六甲山 …… 19 F3
Rokugō-machi 六郷町 …… 28 C3
Rokugō-cho 六郷町 …… 76 A1
Rokunohe-machi 六戸町 …… 29 F5
Rokusei-machi 鹿西町 …… 22 C4
Rubeshibe-cho 留辺蘂町 …… 33 E4
Rumoi-shi 留萌市 …… 32 A3
Rusutsu-mura 留寿都村 …… 30 D3
Ryōkami-mura 両神村 …… 40 A1
Ryōnan-cho 綾南町 …… 17 G2④
Ryōtsu-shi 両津市 …… 26 B4
Ryōzen-machi 霊山町 …… 27 G4
Ryūgasaki-shi 竜ヶ崎市 …… 41 H2
Ryūgatake-machi 竜ヶ岳町 …… 11 F1
Ryūhoku-machi 竜北町 …… 13 F7
Ryūjin-mura 龍神村 …… 18 C3
Ryūō-cho 竜王町 …… 19 G5
Ryūō-cho 竜王町 …… 76 A1
Ryūyō-cho 竜洋町 …… 39 I7

S

Sabae-shi 鯖江市 …… 19 I5
Sada-cho 佐田町 …… 15 F3
Sada-misaki 佐田岬 …… 16 B5
Sadamitsu-cho 貞光町 …… 17 H3
Sadoga-shima 佐渡島 …… 23 G1
Sadowara-cho 佐土原町 …… 11 H2
Saeki-cho 佐伯町 …… 15 D6
Saeki-cho 佐伯町 …… 15 I4
Saga-cho 佐賀町 …… 16 E6
Saga-shi 佐賀市 …… 12 E5
Sagae-shi 寒河江市 …… 27 F3
Sagami-gawa 相模川 …… 40 C5
Sagami-ko 相模湖 …… 40 B4
Sagamihara-shi 相模原市 …… 40 D5
Sagamiko-machi 相模湖町 …… 40 B4
Sagami Nada 相模灘 …… 24 C3
Sagami Wan 相模湾 …… 24 C3
Saganoseki-machi 佐賀関町 …… 13 I5
Sagara-cho 相良町 …… 21 G6
Sagara-mura 相良村 …… 11 G1
Sai-mura 佐井村 …… 29 I4
Saigawa-machi 犀川町 …… 44 E3
Saigō-cho 西郷町 …… 14 B1

Saigō-son 西郷村 …… 13 H7
Saihaku-cho 西伯町 …… 15 G3
Saijō-cho 西城町 …… 15 G4
Saijō-shi 西条市 …… 17 F3
Saikai-cho 西海町 …… 12 D5
Saiki-shi 佐伯市 …… 13 I5
Saita-cho 財田町 …… 17 G2
Saito-shi 西都市 …… 11 H1
Saji-son 佐治村 …… 15 I3
Saka-cho 坂町 …… 14 E6
Sakado-shi 坂戸市 …… 40 D2
Sakae-machi 栄町 …… 26 C5
Sakae-machi 栄町 …… 41 I2
Sakae-mura 栄村 …… 23 G5③
Sakahogi-cho 坂祝町 …… 38 D1
Sakai-cho 坂井町 …… 22 A6
Sakai-machi 境町 …… 25 G3
Sakai-machi 境町 …… 41 F1
Sakai-mura 坂井村 …… 23 F6
Sakai-shi 堺市 …… 37 F6
Sakaide-shi 坂出市 …… 17 G2
Sakaigawa-mura 境川村 …… 76 B2
Sakaiminato-shi 境港市 …… 15 G2
Sakaki-machi 坂城町 …… 21 F1
Sakakita-mura 坂北村 …… 23 F6
Sakamoto-mura 坂本村 …… 11 F1④
Sakashita-cho 坂下町 …… 20 E4
Sakata-shi 酒田市 …… 28 A2
Sakauchi-mura 坂内村 …… 20 B4
Sakawa-cho 佐川町 …… 17 F4
Sakekawa-mura 鮭川村 …… 28 A3
Sakishima Shotō 先島諸島 …… 4 C2
Sakito-cho 崎戸町 …… 12 C6
Saku-machi 佐久町 …… 21 G2
Saku-shi 佐久市 …… 21 G2
Sakugi-son 作木村 …… 15 E4
Sakuma-cho 佐久間町 …… 17 F5
Sakura-jima 桜島 …… 11 F3
Sakura-shi 佐倉市 …… 11 I3
Sakurae-cho 桜江町 …… 14 E4
Sakuragawa-mura 桜川村 …… 41 J1
Sakurai-shi 桜井市 …… 35 H5
Sakurajima-cho 桜島町 …… 11 F3
Sakuto-cho 作東町 …… 15 I4
Samani-cho 様似町 …… 31 I5
Sambongi-cho 三本木町 …… 27 G2①
Sambu-machi 山武町 …… 41 J4
Samegawa-mura 鮫川村 …… 27 G7
Samizu-mura 三水村 …… 23 F5
Samukawa-machi 寒川町 …… 40 D6
Sano-shi 佐野市 …… 25 H4
Sampoku-machi 山北町 …… 26 D3
Sanada-machi 真田町 …… 21 G1
Sanagōuchi-son 佐那河内村 …… 17 I3
Sanbe-san 三瓶山 …… 15 E3
Sanda-shi 三田市 …… 34 D2
Sandankyō 三段峡 …… 14 D5
Sangawa-cho 寒川町 …… 17 H2
Sangō-cho 三郷町 …… 35 G4
Sanjō-shi 三条市 …… 26 C5
Sankō-mura 三光村 …… 13 G4
Sannai-mura 三内村 …… 28 B4
Sannan-cho 山南町 …… 19 F2
Sannohe-machi 三戸町 …… 29 F5
Sanriku-cho 三陸町 …… 28 B6
Santō-cho 山東町 …… 19 G2
Santō-cho 山東町 …… 19 G5
Sanwa-cho 三和町 …… 15 G5
Sanwa-cho 三和町 …… 12 D7
Sanwa-machi 三和町 …… 25 G4
Sanwa-mura 三和村 …… 23 G4
Sanyō-cho 山陽町 …… 14 B6
Sanyō-cho 山陽町 …… 15 I4
Saori-cho 佐織町 …… 38 B3

Sapporo-shi 札幌市	30	E2
Sarabetsu-mura 更別村	31	I 3
Saroma-cho 佐呂間町	33	F3
Saroma-ko サロマ湖	33	F3
Sarufutsu-mura 猿払村	33	G1
Sasaga-mine 笹ヶ峰	17	F3
Sasaguri-machi 篠栗町	44	B3
Sasakami-mura 笹神村	26	D5
Sasayama-cho 篠山町	19	F3
Sasebo-shi 佐世保市	12	D5
Sashiki-cho 佐敷町	69	A6
Sashima-machi 猿島町	44	F1
Sata-cho 佐多町	11	F5
Sata-misaki 佐多岬	11	F5
Sato-mura 里村	10	E2
Satomi-mura 里美村	25	I 6
Satoshō-cho 里庄町	15	H5
Satsuma Hantō 薩摩半島	11	F3
Satsuma-cho 薩摩町	11	F2
Satsunan Shotō 薩南諸島	4	E6
Satte-shi 幸手市	41	F1
Sawara-cho 砂原町	30	D5
Sawara-shi 佐原市	25	F6
Sawata-machi 佐和田町	26	A4
Sawauchi-mura 沢内村	28	C4
Saya-cho 佐屋町	38	B3
Sayama-shi 狭山市	40	D2
Sayo-cho 佐用町	15	J4
Saza-cho 佐々町	12	D5
Sechibaru-cho 世知原町	12	D5
Sefuri-mura 脊振村	44	A5
Sefuri-san 背振山	12	E4
Seidan-cho 西淡町	34	A6
Seihi-cho 西彼杵町	12	D6
Seika-cho 精華町	35	G3
Seinaiji-mura 清内路村	21	F4
Seirō-machi 聖籠町	26	D4
Seiwa-mura 勢和村	18	E6
Seiwa-son 清和村	13	G6
Seki-cho 関町	19	F5
Seki-shi 関市	20	C4
Sekigahara-cho 関ヶ原町	20	B4
Sekigane-cho 関金町	15	H3
Sekijō-machi 関城町	25	G4
Sekikawa-mura 関川村	26	D4
Sekinomiya-cho 関宮町	19	G1
Sekiyado-machi 関宿町	41	F1
Sekizen-mura 関前村	16	E2
Semboku-machi 仙北町	28	C3
Semine-cho 瀬峰町	27	H2
Semmaya-cho 千厩町	28	B5
Senchō-machi 千丁町	13	F7
Sendai-gawa 川内川	10	E2
Sendai-shi 仙台市	27	G3
Sendai-shi 川内市	11	E2
Senhata-machi 千畑町	28	C4
Senkaku Shotō 尖閣諸島	4	D2
Sennan-mura 仙南村	28	C3
Sennan-shi 泉南市	34	D6
Sera-cho 世羅町	15	F5
Seranishi-cho 世羅西町	15	F5
Setaka-machi 瀬高町	44	B7
Setana-cho 瀬棚町	30	B4
Seto-cho 瀬戸町	15	I 5
Seto-cho 瀬戸町	16	C4
Seto-ōhashi 瀬戸大橋	17	G2
Seto-shi 瀬戸市	20	D5
Setoda-cho 瀬戸田町	15	F6
Setouchi-cho 瀬戸内町	10	B2
Settsu-shi 摂津市	37	H3
Shakotan-cho 積丹町	30	C1
Shari-cho 斜里町	33	H4
Shariki-mura 車力村	29	G3
Shibakawa-cho 芝川町	21	G5

Shibata-machi 柴田町	27	G4
Shibata-shi 新発田市	26	D4
Shibayama-machi 芝山町	41	J3
Shibecha-cho 標茶町	33	G5
Shibetsu-cho 標津町	33	I 4
Shibetsu-shi 士別市	32	C3
Shibukawa-shi 渋川市	25	H2
Shibushi-cho 志布志町	11	G3
Shibushi Wan 志布志湾	11	G4
Shichigahama-machi 七ヶ浜町	27	H3
Shichigashuku-machi 七ヶ宿町	27	F4
Shichijō-machi 七城町	70	E4
Shichimen-zan 七面山	21	G4
Shichinohe-machi 七戸町	29	G5
Shichiri-nagahama 七里長浜	29	G3
Shido-cho 志度町	17	H2
Shiga-cho 志賀町	19	G4
Shiga-kōgen 志賀高原	23	G5
Shiga-mura 四賀村	23	F6
Shigaraki-cho 信楽町	19	F5
Shigenobu-cho 重信町	16	E3
Shihoro-cho 士幌町	31	I 2
Shiiba-son 椎葉村	13	G7
Shiida-machi 椎田町	13	G3
Shijonawate-shi 四条畷市	37	I 3
Shika-machi 志賀町	22	C4
Shikabe-cho 鹿部町	30	D5
Shikama-cho 色麻町	27	G2
Shikamachi-cho 鹿町町	12	C5
Shikano-cho 鹿野町	15	I 2
Shikano-shima 志賀島	12	E3
Shikaoi-cho 鹿追町	31	I 2
Shikatsu-cho 師勝町	39	H1
Shiki-shi 志木市	40	E3
Shikishima-cho 敷島町	76	A1
Shikotan-tō 色丹島	9	I 2
Shikotsu-ko 支笏湖	30	E3
Shima-cho 志摩町	18	D7
Shima-machi 志摩町	12	E4
Shimabara Wan 島原湾	13	F6
Shimabara-shi 島原市	13	F6
Shimabara Hantō 島原半島	12	E6
Shimada-shi 島田市	21	F6
Shimagahara-mura 島ヶ原村	19	F5
Shima Hantō 志摩半島	18	D6
Shimamaki-mura 島牧村	30	B3
Shimamoto-cho 島本町	37	I 1
Shimane-cho 島根町	15	F2
Shimane Hantō 島根半島	15	F2
Shimanto-gawa 四万十川	16	E6
Shima spa 四万温泉	25	I 1
Shimaura-tō 島浦島	13	I 6
Shime-machi 志免町	44	B3
Shimizu-cho 清水町	18	D2
Shimizu-cho 清水町	22	A7
Shimizu-cho 清水町	31	H2
Shimizu-cho 清水町	76	D7
Shimizu-shi 清水市	21	G5
Shimo-mura 下村	22	D5①
Shimobe-cho 下部町	21	G4
Shimoda-machi 下田町	29	F5
Shimoda-shi 下田市	21	I 6
Shimodate-shi 下館市	25	G5
Shimofusa-machi 下総町	41	I 2
Shimogō-machi 下郷町	26	E6
Shimoichi-cho 下市町	35	H6
Shimoji-cho 下地町	4	C3⑨
Shimojō-mura 下条村	21	E4
Shimokamagari-cho 下蒲刈町	15	E6
Shimokawa-cho 下川町	32	C2
Shimokita Hantō 下北半島	29	H5
Shimokitayama-mura 下北山村	18	C4
Shimokoshiki-son 下甑村	10	D3
Shimonita-machi 下仁田町	25	G2

Shimonoseki-shi 下関市	14	A7
Shimosuwa-machi 下諏訪町	21	F2
Shimotsu-cho 下津町	18	D2
Shimotsuma-shi 下妻市	25	G5
Shimoyama-mura 下山村	20	D5
Shimukappu-mura 占冠村	31	G2
Shin-machi 新町	25	G3⑧
Shinano-gawa 信濃川	26	C4
Shinano-machi 信濃町	23	F5
Shinasahi-cho 新旭町	19	G4
Shinchi-machi 新地町	27	H4
Shingō-cho 神郷町	15	G4
Shingō-mura 新郷村	29	F5
Shingū-cho 新宮町	19	F1
Shingū-machi 新宮町	44	B2
Shingū-mura 新宮村	17	G3
Shingū-shi 新宮市	18	C4
Shinichi-cho 新市町	15	H5④
Shinji-ko 宍道湖	15	F2
Shinji-machi 宍道町	15	F3
Shinjō-machi 新庄町	35	G5
Shinjō-shi 新庄市	28	A3
Shinjō-son 新庄村	15	H3
Shinkawa-cho 新川町	39	G2
Shinminato-shi 新湊市	22	D5
Shinnanyō-shi 新南陽市	14	C6
Shinsei-cho 真正町	38	B1
Shinshinotsu-mura 新篠津村	31	F2
Shinshiro-shi 新城市	39	G5
Shintō-mura 榛東村	25	H2②
Shintoku-cho 新得町	31	H2
Shintomi-cho 新富町	11	I 2
Shintone-mura 新利根村	41	I 2
Shintotsukawa-cho 新十津川町	32	B5
Shinuonome-cho 新魚目町	12	B6
Shinwa-machi 新和町	10	E1
Shinyoshitomi-mura 新吉富村	13	G4③
Shio-machi 志雄町	22	C4
Shiobara-machi 塩原町	25	J4
Shiogama-shi 塩釜市	27	H3
Shiojiri-shi 塩尻市	21	F2
Shiokawa-machi 塩川町	26	E5
Shiono-misaki 潮岬	18	B4
Shionoe-cho 塩江町	17	H2
Shiota-cho 塩田町	12	E5
Shioya-machi 塩谷町	25	I 4
Shioya-zaki 塩屋崎	27	H7
Shiozawa-machi 塩沢町	23	H5
Shippō-cho 七宝町	38	C3
Shirahama-cho 白浜町	18	B3
Shirahama-machi 白浜町	24	C5
Shirakami-sanchi 白神山地	29	F3
Shirakawa-cho 白川町	20	D4
Shirakawa-mura 白川村	20	C2
Shirakawa-shi 白河市	27	F7
Shirako-machi 白子町	41	I 5
Shiramine-mura 白峰村	22	B6
Shirane-machi 白根町	25	H5
Shirane-san(kusatsu) 白根山(草津)	25	H1
Shirane-san(Nikko) 白根山(日光)	25	I 3
Shirane-san 白根山	21	G3
Shiranuhi-machi 不知火町	13	F7
Shiranuka-cho 白糠町	33	F5
Shiraoi-cho 白老町	30	E4
Shiraoka-machi 白岡町	41	E1
Shirasawa-mura 白沢村	25	I 3
Shirasawa-mura 白沢村	27	G5
Shirataka-machi 白鷹町	27	F3
Shirataki-mura 白滝村	32	E4
Shiretoko-misaki 知床岬	33	I 2
Shiriuchi-cho 知内町	30	C6
Shiriya-zaki 尻矢埼	29	I 5
Shiroi-machi 白井町	41	H3
Shiroishi-cho 白石町	12	E5

124

Romaji	Kanji	Page	Grid
Shiroishi-shi	白石市	27	G4
Shirokawa-cho	城川町	16	D5
Shirone-shi	白根市	26	C5
Shirotori-cho	白鳥町	17	H2
Shirotori-cho	白鳥町	20	C3
Shirouma-dake	白馬岳	22	E5
Shiroyama-machi	城山町	40	C4
Shisaka-jima	四阪島	15	G6
Shishikui-cho	宍喰町	17	H4
Shishūshin-machi	信州新町	21	F1
Shisui-machi	酒々井町	41	I3
Shisui-machi	泗水町	70	E4
Shitada-mura	下田村	26	C5
Shitara-cho	設楽町	20	E5
Shiunji-machi	紫雲寺町	26	D4
Shiura-mura	市浦村	29	H3
Shiwa-cho	紫波町	28	C5
Shiwahime-cho	志波姫町	27	G1
Shiwaku Shotō	塩飽諸島	17	G2
Shizugawa-cho	志津川町	27	I2
Shizukuishi-cho	雫石町	28	D4
Shizunai-cho	静内町	31	G4
Shizuoka-shi	静岡市	21	G5
Shō-gawa	庄川	22	C6
Shōbara-shi	庄原市	15	F4
Shōboku-cho	勝北町	15	I3
Shōbu-machi	菖蒲町	40	E1
Shōdo-shima	小豆島	17	H1
Shōgawa-machi	庄川町	22	C5
Shōkawa-mura	荘川村	20	C2
Shōnai-cho	庄内町	13	H6
Shōnai-machi	庄内町	44	D3
Shōnan-machi	沼南町	41	G2
Shōō-cho	勝央町	15	I4
Shosanbetsu-mura	初山別村	32	B2
Shōwa-machi	庄和町	41	F1
Shōwa-machi	昭和町	28	D2
Shōwa-machi	昭和町	76	A2
Shōwa-mura	昭和村	24	E6
Shōwa-mura	昭和村	78	A5
Shūhō-cho	秋芳町	14	B6
Shūtō-cho	周東町	14	D6
Shuzenji-cho	修善寺町	21	H5
Sōbetsu-cho	壮瞥町	30	D4
Sobo-san	祖母山	13	H6
Sobue-cho	祖父江町	38	B2
Sodegaura-machi	袖ヶ浦町	41	G2
Soeda-machi	添田町	44	E3
Sōja-shi	総社市	15	H5
Sōka-shi	草加市	41	F3
Sōma-mura	相馬村	29	F3
Sōma-shi	相馬市	27	G4
Soni-mura	曽爾村	35	J5
Sonobe-cho	園部町	19	G3
Sōryō-cho	総領町	15	F4
Sosogi Coast	曽々木海岸	22	D3
Sotome-cho	外海町	12	D6
Sōunkyō	層雲峡	32	D4
Sōwa-machi	総和町	25	G4
Sōya-misaki	宗谷岬	33	G1
Soyō-machi	蘇陽町	13	G6
Sudama-cho	須玉町	21	G3
Sue-machi	須恵町	44	B3
Sue-mura	須恵村	11	A1
Sueyoshi-cho	末吉町	11	G4
Suga-jima	菅島	18	E7
Sugadaira	菅平	23	G6
Sugito-machi	杉戸町	41	F1
Suibara-machi	水原町	26	D5
Suifu-mura	水府村	25	I6
Suita-shi	吹田市	37	G3
Sukagawa-shi	須賀川市	27	F6
Suki-son	須木村	11	G2
Sukumo-shi	宿毛市	16	D6
Sumida-gawa	隅田川	42	G5
Sumita-cho	住田町	28	B6
Sumiyō-son	住用村	10	B2
Sumon-mura	守門村	26	C6
Sumoto-machi	栖本町	11	E1①
Sumoto-shi	洲本市	34	B6
Sunagawa-shi	砂川市	31	F1
Sunami-cho	巣南町	38	B1
Sunomata-cho	墨俣町	38	B2
Suō Nada	周防灘	13	H3
Suruga Wan	駿河湾	24	C1
Susa-cho	須佐町	14	C5
Susaki-shi	須崎市	17	F5
Susami-cho	すさみ町	18	B3
Susono-shi	裾野市	21	H5
Suttsu-cho	寿都町	30	C3
Suwa-shi	諏訪市	21	F2
Suzaka-shi	須坂市	23	G6
Suzu-misaki	珠洲岬	22	E3
Suzu-shi	珠洲市	22	D3
Suzuka-shi	鈴鹿市	38	A5
Suzuka-tōge	鈴鹿峠	19	F5

T

Romaji	Kanji	Page	Grid
Tabayama-mura	丹波山村	25	F2
Tabira-cho	田平町	12	C4
Tabuse-cho	田布施町	14	D7
Tachiarai-machi	大刀洗町	44	C5
Tachibana-cho	橘町	14	D7
Tachibana-machi	立花町	13	F5
Tachibana Wan	橘湾	12	D7
Tachikawa-machi	立川町	28	A2
Tachikawa-shi	立川市	40	D3
Tadami-gawa	只見川	26	D6
Tadami-machi	只見町	26	D6
Tadaoka-cho	忠岡町	34	E5
Tado-cho	多度町	38	B3
Tadotsu-cho	多度津町	17	G2
Taga-cho	多賀町	19	G5
Tagajō-shi	多賀城市	27	H3
Tagami-machi	田上町	26	C5
Tagawa-shi	田川市	44	D3
Tagokura-ko	田子倉湖	26	D6
Tahara-cho	田原町	20	D6
Taiei-machi	大栄町	41	J2
Taihei-mura	大平村	13	G4④
Taiji-cho	太地町	18	B4
Taiki-cho	大樹町	31	I4
Taima-cho	当麻町	35	G5
Taimei-machi	岱明町	13	F6
Taira-mura	平村	22	C6
Tairadate-mura	平舘村	29	H4
Taisei-cho	大成町	30	B5
Taisetsu-zan	大雪山	32	D4
Taisha-machi	大社町	14	E2
Taishakukyō	帝釈峡	15	G4
Taishi-cho	太子町	19	F1
Taishi-cho	太子町	35	G5
Taishin-mura	大信村	27	F6
Taishō-cho	大正町	16	E5
Taiwa-cho	大和町	27	G2
Taiyō-mura	大洋村	25	G6
Taiyū-mura	大雄村	28	C3
Tajima-machi	田島町	26	E6
Tajiri-cho	田尻町	20	D5
Tajiri-cho	田尻町	27	H2
Takachiho-cho	高千穂町	13	H6
Takachihokyō	高千穂峡	13	H6
Takachihono-mine	高千穂峰	11	G2
Takagi-mura	喬木村	21	F4
Takahagi-shi	高萩市	25	I6
Takahama-cho	高浜町	19	H3
Takahama-shi	高浜市	38	D5
Takahara-yama	高原山	25	I4
Takaharu-cho	高原町	11	G2
Takahashi-shi	高梁市	15	H4
Takahata-machi	高畠町	27	F4
Takaishi-shi	高石市	37	F7
Takajō-cho	高城町	11	H2
Takaki-cho	高来町	12	E6
Takakuma-san	高隈山	11	G3
Takamatsu-machi	高松町	22	C5
Takamatsu-shi	高松市	17	H2
Takami-yama	高見山	18	E5
Takamiya-cho	高宮町	15	E4
Takamori-machi	高森町	13	G6
Takamori-machi	高森町	21	F4
Takanabe-cho	高鍋町	11	H1
Takane-cho	高根町	21	G3
Takane-mura	高根村	20	E2
Takanezawa-machi	高根沢町	25	H5
Takano-cho	高野町	15	F4
Takanosu-machi	鷹巣町	28	E3
Takao-san	高尾山	40	C4
Takaoka-cho	高岡町	11	H2
Takaoka-shi	高岡市	22	C5
Takaono-cho	高尾野町	11	F2
Takarabe-cho	財部町	11	G3
Takarazuka-shi	宝塚市	36	E2
Takasago-shi	高砂市	34	A3
Takasaki-cho	高崎町	11	G2
Takasaki-shi	高崎市	25	H2
Takasato-mura	高郷村	26	E5
Takase-cho	高瀬町	17	G2
Takashima-cho	高島町	12	D7
Takashima-cho	高島町	19	G4
Takashima-cho	鷹島町	12	D4
Takashimizu-machi	高清水町	27	G2
Takasu-cho	鷹栖町	32	C4
Takasu-mura	高鷲村	20	C3
Takata-machi	高田町	44	B7
Takatō-machi	高遠町	21	F3
Takatomi-cho	高富町	20	C4
Takatori-cho	高取町	35	H5
Takatsuki-cho	高月町	19	H5
Takatsuki-shi	高槻市	37	I1
Takayama-mura	高山村	23	G6④
Takayama-mura	高山村	25	H2
Takayama-mura	高山村	20	D2
Takayanagi-machi	高柳町	23	G4
Take-shima	竹島	11	F5
Take-shima	竹島	6	D3
Takebe-cho	建部町	15	I4
Takefu-shi	武生市	19	I5
Takehara-shi	竹原市	15	F6
Takeno-cho	竹野町	19	H1
Takeo-shi	武雄市	12	E5
Takeshi-mura	武石村	21	F2②
Taketa-shi	竹田市	13	H6
Taketomi-cho	竹富町	4	C2
Taketoyo-cho	武豊町	20	C6
Taki-cho	多伎町	15	E3
Taki-cho	多気町	18	E6
Takikawa-shi	滝川市	32	B5
Takine-machi	滝根町	27	G6
Takino-cho	滝野町	34	C2
Takinoue-cho	滝上町	32	D3
Takisawa-mura	滝沢村	28	D5
Takko-machi	田子町	29	F5
Tako-machi	多古町	25	F6①
Taku-shima	度島	12	C4
Taku-shi	多久市	12	E5
Takuma-cho	詫間町	17	G2
Tama-shi	多摩市	40	D4
Tamagawa-cho	玉川町	16	E3
Tamagawa-cho	田万川町	14	C5
Tamagawa-mura	玉川村	27	G6

Tamagawa-mura 玉川村	40	C1	Tenryū-shi 天竜市	21	F6	Tomisato-machi 富里町	41	I3
Tamagusuku-son 玉城村	69	A7	Tensui-machi 天水町	70	·C5	Tomiura-machi 富浦町	24	D4
Tamaho-cho 玉穂町	76	A2	Teradomari-machi 寺泊町	26	B5	Tomiya-cho 富谷町	27	G3
Tamaki-cho 玉城町	18	E6	Terai-machi 寺井町	22	B5	Tomiyama-machi 富山町	24	D4
Tamamura-machi 玉村町	25	H2	Teshikaga-cho 弟子屈町	33	G5	Tomiyama-mura 富山村	21	E5
Tamana-shi 玉名市	13	F6	Teshio-cho 天塩町	32	A1	Tomizawa-cho 富沢町	21	G5
Tamano-shi 玉野市	15	H5	Teshio-gawa 天塩川	32	B1	Tomobe-machi 友部町	25	H5
Tamanoura-cho 玉之浦町	12	A7	Tessei-cho 哲西町	15	G4	Tomochi-machi 砥用町	70	E7
Tamari-mura 玉里村	25	G5	Tetsuta-cho 哲多町	15	G4	Tomogashima Suidō 友ヶ島水道	18	D2
Tamatsukuri-machi 玉造町	25	G6	Toba-shi 鳥羽市	18	E7	Tomonoura 鞆の浦	15	G6
Tamayama-mura 玉山村	28	D5	Tobe-cho 砥部町	16	E4	Tonaki-son 渡名喜村	4	D4
Tamayu-cho 玉湯町	15	F2①	Tobishima-mura 飛島村	38	C4	Tonami-shi 砺波市	22	C5
Tamba-cho 丹波町	19	G3	Tōbu-machi 東部町	21	G1	Tonan-mura 都南村	28	D5
Tambara-cho 丹原町	16	E3	Tochigi-shi 栃木市	25	H4	Tondabayashi-shi 富田林市	35	G5
Tanabe-cho 田辺町	35	A3	Tochio-shi 栃尾市	26	C6	Tone-gawa 利根川	25	F5
Tanabe-shi 田辺市	18	C3	Toda-shi 戸田市	43	J3	Tone-machi 利根町	41	H2
Tanagura-machi 棚倉町	27	G7	Todoga-saki 魹ヶ崎	28	C7	Tone-mura 利根村	25	I3
Tanashi-shi 田無市	43	I1	Todohokke-mura 法華村	30	E6	Tōno-shi 遠野市	28	C6
Tanega-shima 種子島	11	G6	Tōei-cho 東栄町	21	E5	Tonoshō-cho 土庄町	17	H1
Taneichi-machi 種市町	29	F6	Toga-mura 利賀村	22	C6	Tōnoshō-machi 東庄町	25	F6
Tango-cho 丹後町	19	H2	Togakushi-mura 戸隠村	23	F5	Torahime-cho 虎姫町	19	H5
Tanigawa-dake 谷川岳	25	I2	Togakushi-yama 戸隠山	23	F5	Tori-shima 鳥島	9	H3
Tanigumi-mura 谷汲村	20	C4	Tōgane-shi 東金市	41	I4	Toride-shi 取手市	41	H2
Tannan-cho 丹南町	34	D1	Togauchi-cho 戸河内町	14	D5	Torigoe-mura 鳥越村	22	B6
Tannno-cho 端野町	33	F4	Togi-machi 富来町	22	C4	Toriya-machi 鳥屋町	22	C4
Tano-cho 田野町	11	H2	Togitsu-cho 時津町	12	D6	Tosa-cho 土佐町	17	F4
Tano-cho 田野町	17	G5	Tōgō-cho 東郷町	11	E2	Tosa-shi 土佐市	17	F4
Tanohata-mura 田野畑村	28	D6	Tōgō-cho 東郷町	11	I1	Tosashimizu-shi 土佐清水市	16	E6
Tanoura-machi 田浦町	11	F1	Tōgō-cho 東郷町	15	I2	Tosayama-mura 土佐山村	17	F4
Tantō-cho 但東町	19	H2	Tōgō-cho 東郷町	38	D4	Tosayamada-cho 土佐山田町	17	G4
Tanuma-machi 田沼町	25	H4	Togura-machi 戸倉町	21	F1	Toshi-jima 答志島	18	E7
Tanushimaru-machi 田主丸町	13	F5	Tōhaku-cho 東伯町	15	H2	Toshima-mura 十島村	5	F5
Tanzawa-yama 丹沢山	40	B5	Tōhoku-machi 東北町	29	G5	Toshima-mura 利島村	24	B3
Tappi-zaki 竜飛崎	29	H3	Toi-cho 戸井町	30	D6	Tosu-shi 鳥栖市	13	F4
Tara-cho 太良町	12	E5	Toi-cho 土肥町	21	H6	Totsukawa-mura 十津川村	18	C4
Tara-dake 多良岳	12	E6	Toi-misaki 都井岬	11	H4	Tottori-shi 鳥取市	15	I2
Taragi-machi 多良木町	11	G1	Tōin-cho 東員町	38	B4	Tōwa-cho 東和町	14	E7
Tarama-son 多良間村	4	C2	Tōjinbo 東尋坊	22	A6	Tōwa-cho 東和町	27	H1
Tarami-cho 多良見町	12	D6	Tōjō-cho 東城町	15	G4	Tōwa-cho 東和町	28	C5
Tarō-cho 田老町	28	D7	Tōjō-cho 東条町	34	C2	Tōwa-machi 東和町	22	G5
Tarui-cho 垂井町	38	A2	Tokachi-dake 十勝岳	32	C5	Tōwa-son 十和村	16	E5
Tarumizu-shi 垂水市	11	G3	Tokachi-gawa 十勝川	31	J3	Towada-ko 十和田湖	29	F4
Tashiro-cho 田代町	11	G4	Tōkai-mura 東海村	25	H6	Towada-shi 十和田市	29	F5
Tashiro-machi 田代町	29	E3	Tōkai-shi 東海市	38	D4	Towadako-machi 十和田湖町	29	F5
Tate-yama 立山	22	E6	Tōkamachi-shi 十日町市	26	D7	Tōya-ko 洞爺湖	30	D3
Tatebayashi-shi 館林市	25	G4	TokaraRettō 吐噶喇列島	5	F5	Toyama-shi 富山市	22	D5
Tateiwa-mura 舘岩村	26	D7	Tokashiki-son 渡嘉敷村	4	D4⑤	Tōya-mura 洞爺村	30	D3
Tateshina-machi 立科町	21	G2	Toki-shi 土岐市	39	E2	Tōyō-cho 東洋町	17	H4
Tateshina-yama 蓼科山	21	G2	Tokigawa-mura 都幾川村	40	C1	Tōyō-mura 東陽村	13	F7⑫
Tateyama-machi 立山町	22	D5	Tokiwa-machi 常葉町	27	G5	Tōyo-shi 東予市	16	E3
Tateyama-shi 館山市	24	D4	Tokiwa-mura 常盤村	29	G3	Toyoake-shi 豊明市	38	D4
Tatomi-cho 田富町	76	A2	Tokoname-shi 常滑市	20	C6	Toyoda-cho 豊田町	39	I6
Tatsugō-cho 龍郷町	10	C1	Tokoro-cho 常呂町	33	F3	Toyohama-cho 豊浜町	15	F6
Tatsukushi 竜串	16	E6	Tokorozawa-shi 所沢市	40	D3	Toyohama-cho 豊浜町	17	G3
Tatsuno-machi 辰野町	21	F3	Tokuji-cho 徳地町	14	C6	Toyohashi-shi 豊橋市	20	E6
Tatsuno-shi 龍野市	19	F1	Tokuno-shima 徳之島	10	A3	Toyohira-cho 豊平町	14	E5
Tatsunokuchi-machi 辰口町	22	B6	Tokunoshima-cho 徳之島町	10	A4	Toyokawa-shi 豊川市	20	E6
Tatsuruhama-machi 田鶴浜町	22	C4	Tokushima-shi 徳島市	17	I3	Toyokoro-cho 豊頃町	31	J3
Tatsuta-mura 龍田村	38	B3	Tokuyama-shi 徳山市	14	C6	Toyoma-machi 登米町	27	H2
Tatsuyama-mura 龍山村	21	F6	Tokyo Wan 東京湾	24	E4	Toyomatsu-son 豊松村	15	G4
Tawaramoto-cho 田原本町	35	H4	Tōma-cho 当麻町	32	C4	Toyonaka-cho 豊中町	17	G2
Tazawa-ko 田沢湖	28	D4	Tomakomai-shi 苫小牧市	31	F3	Toyonaka-shi 豊中市	37	G3
Tazawako-machi 田沢湖町	28	D4	Tomamae-cho 苫前町	32	A2	Toyone-mura 豊根村	21	E5
Tega-numa 手賀沼	41	G2	Tomari-mura 泊村	30	·C2	Toyono-cho 豊能町	35	F2
Temmahayashi-mura 天間林村	29	G5	Tomari-mura 泊村	15	I2	Toyono-machi 豊野町	23	F5
Tendō-shi 天童市	27	F3	Tombara-cho 頓原町	15	F3	Toyono-mura 豊野村	70	D6
Tenei-mura 天栄村	27	F6	Tomi-son 富村	15	H3	Toyooka-mura 豊岡村	39	I5
Tenkawa-mura 天川村	35	H7	Tomiai-machi 富合町	70	D6	Toyooka-mura 豊丘村	21	F4⑥
Tenmei-machi 天明町	13	F6	Tomie-cho 富江町	12	B7	Toyooka-shi 豊岡市	19	H1
Tennō-machi 天王町	28	D2	Tomigusuku-son 豊見城村	69	D5	Toyosaka-cho 豊栄町	15	F5
Tenri-shi 天理市	35	H4	Tomika-cho 富加町	38	D1	Toyosaka-shi 豊栄市	26	C4
Tenryū-gawa 天竜川	21	E7	Tomioka-machi 富岡町	27	H6	Toyosato-cho 豊郷町	19	G5①
Tenryū-kyo 天竜峡	21	F5	Tomioka-shi 富岡市	25	G2	Toyosato-cho 豊里町	27	H2
Tenryū-mura 天龍村	21	F5						

Toyoshina-machi 豊科町 ········· 21 E2
Toyota-cho 豊田町 ············· 14 A6
Toyota-mura 豊田村 ············· 23 F5
Toyota-shi 豊田市 ············· 20 D5
Toyotama-cho 豊玉町 ··········· 12 C1
Toyotomi-cho 豊富町 ··········· 33 G2
Toyotomi-mura 豊富村 ··········· 76 B2
Toyotsu-machi 豊津町 ··········· 13 G3①
Toyoura-cho 豊浦町 ············· 14 A6
Toyoura-cho 豊浦町 ············· 30 D3
Toyoura-machi 豊浦町 ··········· 26 D4
Toyoyama-cho 豊山町 ··········· 39 H1
Tozawa-mura 戸沢村 ············· 28 A3
Tsu-shi 津市 ················· 38 A6
Tsubame-shi 燕市 ············· 26 C5
Tsubata-machi 津幡町 ··········· 22 C5
Tsubetsu-cho 津別町 ··········· 33 F4
Tsuchiura-shi 土浦市 ··········· 41 I1
Tsuchiyama-cho 土山町 ··········· 19 F5
Tsuda-cho 津田町 ············· 17 H2
Tsuga-machi 都賀町 ············· 25 H4
Tsugaru Hantō 津軽半島 ········· 29 H3
Tsugaru Kaikyō 津軽海峡 ········· 29 I3
Tsugawa-machi 津川町 ··········· 26 D5
Tsuge-mura 都祁村 ············· 18 E4⑩
Tsugu-mura 津具村 ············· 20 E5
Tsuiki-machi 築城町 ············· 13 G7
Tsukechi-cho 付知町 ············· 20 E4
Tsukidate-cho 築館町 ··········· 27 G1
Tsukidate-machi 月館町 ··········· 27 G5
Tsukigase-mura 月ヶ瀬村 ········· 35 I3
Tsukigata-cho 月形町 ··········· 31 F1
Tsukigata-mura 月潟村 ··········· 26 C5
Tsukiyono-machi 月夜野町 ········· 25 I2
Tsukuba-san 筑波山 ············· 25 G5
Tsukuba-shi つくば市 ··········· 41 H1
Tsukude-mura 作手村 ··········· 20 E6
Tsukui-machi 津久井町 ··········· 40 C4
Tsukumi-shi 津久見市 ··········· 13 I5
Tsuma-mura 都万村 ············· 14 B1
Tsumagoi-mura 嬬恋村 ··········· 25 H1
Tsuna-cho 津名町 ············· 34 B5
Tsunagi-machi 津奈木町 ········· 11 F1
Tsunan-machi 津南町 ··········· 23 G5
Tsunezumi-mura 常澄村 ··········· 25 H6
Tsuno-cho 都農町 ············· 11 I1
Tsuno-shima 角島 ············· 14 A5
Tsuru-shi 都留市 ············· 21 H4
Tsuruda-machi 鶴田町 ··········· 11 F2
Tsuruga-shi 敦賀市 ············· 19 H5
Tsurugashima-machi 鶴ヶ島町 ······· 40 C2
Tsurugi-machi 鶴来町 ··········· 22 B6
Tsurugi-san 剣山 ············· 17 H3
Tsurui-mura 鶴居村 ············· 33 G6
Tsurumi-machi 鶴見町 ··········· 13 I5
Tsuruoka-shi 鶴岡市 ··········· 26 E2
Tsuruta-machi 鶴田町 ··········· 29 H3
Tsushima Kaikyō 対馬海峡 ········· 12 C2
Tsushima-cho 津島町 ··········· 16 D5
Tsushima-shi 津島市 ··········· 20 D5
Tsushima-tō 対馬島 ············· 12 C1
Tsutsuga-son 筒賀村 ··········· 14 D5
Tsuwano-cho 津和野町 ··········· 14 C5
Tsuyama-cho 津山町 ··········· 27 H2
Tsuyama-shi 津山市 ··········· 15 I3
Tsuyazaki-machi 津屋崎町 ········· 44 B2

U

Ube-shi 宇部市 ··············· 14 B7
Ubuyama-mura 産山村 ··········· 71 G4
Uchihara-machi 内原町 ··········· 25 H6
Uchiko-cho 内子町 ············· 16 D4
Uchinada-machi 内灘町 ··········· 22 B5
Uchinomi-cho 内海町 ··········· 17 H1

Uchinoura-cho 内之浦町 ········· 11 G4
Uchita-cho 打田町 ············· 34 E7
Uchiumi-mura 内海村 ··········· 16 D6
Uchiura-machi 内浦町 ··········· 22 D3
Udono-mura 鵜殿村 ··········· 18 C5
Ue-mura 上村 ··············· 11 G1
Ueda-shi 上田市 ············· 21 G1
Ueki-machi 植木町 ············· 13 F6
Ueno-mura 上野村 ············· 25 G2
Ueno-shi 上野市 ············· 19 F5
Ueno-son 上野村 ············· 4 C3⑧
Uenohara-cho 上野原町 ········· 77 E1
Ugo-machi 羽後町 ············· 28 B3
Uguisuzawa-cho 鶯沢町 ········· 27 G1
Uji-shi 宇治市 ··············· 19 F4
Uji Guntō 宇治群島 ··········· 10 C4
Ujiie-machi 氏家町 ············· 25 I5
Ujitawara-cho 宇治田原町 ········· 35 H2
Ukan-cho 有漢町 ············· 15 H4
Uken-son 宇検村 ············· 10 B2
Ukiha-machi 浮羽町 ··········· 13 F5
Uku-jima 宇久島 ············· 12 B5
Uku-machi 宇久町 ············· 12 B5
Umaji-mura 馬路村 ············· 17 H4
Ume-machi 宇目町 ············· 13 I6
Umi-machi 宇美町 ············· 44 B3
Unakami-machi 海上町 ··········· 25 F6
Unazuki-machi 宇奈月町 ········· 22 E5
Unoke-machi 宇ノ気町 ··········· 22 C5
Unzen-dake 雲仙岳 ············· 12 E6
Uoshima-mura 魚島村 ··········· 17 F2
Uozu-shi 魚津市 ············· 22 D5
Urabandai-kōgen 裏磐梯高原 ····· 27 F5
Uradome coast 浦富海岸 ········· 15 J2
Urado Wan 浦戸湾 ············· 17 F4
Uragawara-mura 浦川原村 ······· 23 G4
Urahoro-cho 浦幌町 ··········· 33 F7
Urakawa-cho 浦河町 ··········· 31 H4
Urasoe-shi 浦添市 ············· 10 A6
Urausu-cho 浦臼町 ············· 31 F1
Urawa-shi 浦和市 ············· 41 E2
Urayasu-shi 浦安市 ··········· 43 G7
Ureshino-cho 嬉野町 ··········· 18 E6
Ureshino-machi 嬉野町 ········· 12 D5
Urizura-machi 瓜連町 ··········· 25 H6
Uruma-mura 売木村 ··········· 20 E5
Uryū-cho 雨竜町 ············· 32 B4
Usa-shi 宇佐市 ············· 13 H4
Ushibori-machi 牛堀町 ········· 25 G6
Ushibuka-shi 牛深市 ··········· 10 E1
Ushiku-shi 牛久市 ············· 41 H1
Ushimado-cho 牛窓町 ··········· 15 I5
Ushiro-yama 後山 ············· 15 J3
Ushizu-cho 牛津町 ············· 12 E5⑨
Usuda-machi 臼田町 ··········· 21 G2
Usui-machi 臼井町 ············· 44 C4
Usui-tōge 碓氷峠 ············· 23 G2
Usuki-shi 臼杵市 ············· 13 I5
Utano-cho 莵田野町 ··········· 35 I5
Utanobori-cho 歌登町 ··········· 32 C1
Utashinai-shi 歌志内市 ··········· 32 B5
Utatsu-cho 歌津町 ············· 27 I1
Utazu-cho 宇多津町 ··········· 17 G2
Uto-shi 宇土市 ··············· 13 F6
Utsukushigahara 美ヶ原 ········· 23 F7
Utsumi-cho 内海町 ············· 15 G6
Utsunomiya-shi 宇都宮市 ········· 25 H4
Uwa-cho 宇和町 ············· 16 D5
Uwajima-shi 宇和島市 ··········· 16 D5

W

Wachi-cho 和知町 ············· 19 G3
Wada-machi 和田町 ············· 24 D5
Wada-mura 和田村 ············· 21 G2

Wadayama-cho 和田山町 ········· 19 G2
Wadomari-cho 和泊町 ··········· 4 E5①
Waga-cho 和賀町 ············· 28 C4
Wagi-cho 和木町 ············· 14 D6
Wajiki-cho 鷲敷町 ············· 17 I3
Wajima-shi 輪島市 ············· 22 C3
Wakakusa-cho 若草町 ··········· 76 A2
Wakamatsu-cho 若松町 ········· 12 B6
Wakamatsu-shima 若松島 ········· 12 B6
Wakami-machi 若美町 ··········· 28 D2
Wakamiya-machi 若宮町 ········· 44 C2
Wakasa-cho 若桜町 ··········· 15 J3
Wakasa Wan 若狭湾 ············· 19 H3
Wakayama-shi 和歌山市 ········· 18 D2
Wakayanagi-cho 若柳町 ········· 27 H1②
Wake-cho 和気町 ············· 15 I4
Waki-cho 脇町 ··············· 17 H3
Wakinosawa-mura 脇野沢村 ······· 29 H4
Wakkanai-shi 稚内市 ··········· 33 F1
Wakō-shi 和光市 ············· 43 J3
Wakuya-cho 涌谷町 ··········· 27 H2
Wanitsuka-san 鰐塚山 ··········· 11 H2
Wanouchi-cho 輪之内町 ········· 38 B2
Wara-mura 和良村 ············· 20 D3
Warabi-shi 蕨市 ··············· 41 E3
Washima-mura 和島村 ··········· 26 B5
Washimiya-machi 鷲宮町 ········· 25 G4⑩
Washūzan 鷲羽山 ············· 15 H5
Wassamu-cho 和寒町 ··········· 32 C3
Watarai-cho 度会町 ············· 18 E6
Watari-cho 亘理町 ············· 27 G4
Wazuka-cho 和束町 ··········· 35 H3

Y

Ya-shima 八島 ··············· 16 C4
Yabakei-machi 耶馬溪町 ········· 13 G4
Yabakei 耶馬溪 ··············· 13 G4
Yabe-machi 矢部町 ············· 13 G6
Yabe-mura 矢部村 ············· 13 F5
Yabu-cho 養父町 ············· 19 G1
Yabuki-machi 矢吹町 ··········· 27 F6
Yabutsukahon-machi 藪塚本町 ··· 25 H3⑩
Yachiho-mura 八千穂村 ········· 21 G2
Yachimata-machi 八街町 ········· 41 I4
Yachiyo-cho 八千代町 ··········· 14 E5
Yachiyo-cho 八千代町 ··········· 34 B1
Yachiyo-machi 八千代町 ········· 25 G4
Yachiyo-shi 八千代市 ··········· 41 H3
Yaeyama Shotō 八重山諸島 ······· 4 C2
Yagi-cho 八木町 ············· 19 F3
Yahaba-cho 矢巾町 ··········· 28 C5
Yahagi-gawa 矢作川 ··········· 39 F3
Yahiko-mura 弥彦村 ··········· 26 C5
Yahiko-yama 弥彦山 ··········· 23 H3
Yaita-shi 矢板市 ············· 25 I5
Yaizu-shi 焼津市 ············· 21 G6
Yakage-cho 矢掛町 ············· 15 H5
Yake-dake 焼岳 ··············· 22 D7
Yake-yama 焼山 ··············· 23 F5
Yaku-cho 屋久町 ············· 11 F7
Yaku-shima 屋久島 ············· 11 F7
Yakumo-cho 八雲町 ··········· 30 C4
Yakumo-mura 八雲村 ··········· 15 F3②
Yakushi-dake 薬師岳 ··········· 22 D6
Yamada-cho 山田町 ··········· 11 G2
Yamada-machi 山田町 ··········· 25 F6
Yamada-machi 山田町 ··········· 28 C7
Yamada-mura 山田村 ··········· 22 C5
Yamada-shi 山田市 ············· 44 D4
Yamae-mura 山江村 ··········· 11 G1
Yamaga-machi 山香町 ··········· 13 H4
Yamaga-shi 山鹿市 ············· 13 F5
Yamagata-machi 山方町 ········· 25 I6

127

Yamagata-mura 山形村 ………… 22 E7
Yamagata-mura 山形村 ………… 28 E6
Yamagata-shi 山形市 …………… 27 F3
Yamagawa-cho 山川町 ………… 11 F4
Yamaguchi-mura 山口村 ……… 20 E4
Yamaguchi-shi 山口市 ………… 14 B6
Yamakawa-cho 山川町 ………… 17 H3
Yamakawa-machi 山川町 ……… 44 B7
Yamakita-machi 山北町 ……… 40 B6
Yamakoshi-mura 山古志村 …… 26 C6
Yamakuni-gawa 山国川 ……… 13 G3
Yamakuni-machi 山国町 ……… 13 G4
Yamamoto-cho 山元町 ………… 27 G4
Yamamoto-cho 山本町 ………… 17 G3
Yamamoto-machi 山本町 ……… 28 E2
Yamanakako-mura 山中湖村 … 76 D3
Yamanaka-machi 山中町 ……… 22 B6
Yamanashi-shi 山梨市 ………… 21 H3
Yamanobe-machi 山辺町 ……… 27 F3
Yamanokuchi-cho 山之口町 … 11 H3
Yamanouchi-machi 山ノ内町 … 23 G5
Yamaoka-cho 山岡町 ………… 20 E4
Yamasaki-cho 山崎町 ………… 19 G1
Yamashiro-cho 山城町 ………… 17 G3
Yamashiro-cho 山城町 ………… 35 H3
Yamate-son 山手村 …………… 15 H5
Yamato-cho 大和町 …………… 14 D7
Yamato-cho 大和町 …………… 20 C3
Yamato-cho 大和町 …………… 44 A5
Yamato-machi 山都町 ………… 26 E5
Yamato-machi 大和町 ………… 23 H4
Yamato-machi 大和町 ………… 44 B7
Yamato-mura 大和村 ………… 25 H5⑤
Yamato-mura 大和村 ………… 76 C2
Yamato-shi 大和市 …………… 40 D5
Yamato-son 大和村 …………… 10 B2
Yamatokōriyama-shi 大和郡山市 35 G4
Yamatotakada-shi 大和高田市 … 35 G5
Yamatsuri-machi 矢祭町 ……… 25 I6
Yamauchi-cho 山内町 ………… 12 D5
Yamazoe-mura 山添村 ………… 35 I4
Yame-shi 八女市 ……………… 13 F5
Yamizo-san 八溝山 …………… 25 I5
Yamoto-cho 矢本町 …………… 27 H2
Yanadani-mura 柳谷村 ………… 16 E4
Yanagawa-machi 梁川町 ……… 27 G4
Yanagawa-shi 柳川市 ………… 44 B6
Yanagida-mura 柳田村 ……… 22 D3
Yanahara-cho 柵原町 ………… 15 I4
Yanai-shi 柳井市 ……………… 14 D7
Yanaizu-cho 柳津町 …………… 38 B2
Yanaizu-machi 柳津町 ………… 26 E5
Yao-shi 八尾市 ……………… 37 I5
Yaotsu-cho 八百津町 ………… 20 D4
Yariga-take 槍ヶ岳 …………… 22 E6
Yasaka-cho 八栄町 …………… 19 H2
Yasaka-mura 八坂村 …………… 23 E6
Yasaka-mura 弥栄村 …………… 14 D4
Yasato-machi 八郷町 ………… 25 G5
Yashima-machi 矢島町 ………… 28 B2
Yashio-shi 八潮市 …………… 41 F3
Yashiro-cho 社町 …………… 34 C2
Yasu-cho 夜須町 …………… 17 G4
Yasu-cho 野洲町 …………… 19 G5
Yasu-machi 夜須町 …………… 44 C4
Yasuda-cho 安田町 …………… 17 G4
Yasuda-machi 安田町 ………… 26 D5
Yasugi-shi 安来市 …………… 15 G2
Yasuoka-mura 泰阜村 ………… 21 F4
Yasutomi-cho 安富町 ………… 19 H1
Yasuura-cho 安浦町 …………… 15 F6
Yasuzuka-machi 安塚町 ……… 23 G4
Yatomi-cho 弥富町 …………… 38 B4
Yatsuga-take 八ヶ岳 …………… 21 G3

Yatsuka-cho 八束町 …………… 15 G2
Yatsuka-son 八束村 …………… 15 H3
Yatsuo-machi 八尾町 ………… 22 D5
Yatsushiro-cho 八代町 ………… 76 B2
Yatsushiro-shi 八代市 ………… 13 F7
Yatsushiro kai 八代海 ………… 11 F1
Yawahara-mura 谷和原村 …… 44 G1
Yawata-machi 八幡町 ………… 28 A2
Yawata-shi 八幡市 …………… 35 G2
Yawatahama-shi 八幡浜市 …… 16 D4
Yayoi-machi 弥生町 …………… 13 I5
Yobuko-cho 呼子町 …………… 12 D4
Yodo-gawa 淀川 ……………… 37 H3
Yodoe-cho 淀江町 …………… 15 G2
Yogo-cho 余呉町 …………… 19 H5
Yoichi-cho 余市町 …………… 30 D2
Yoita-machi 与板町 …………… 26 B5
Yōka-cho 八鹿町 …………… 19 G1
Yōkaichi-shi 八日市市 ………… 19 G5
Yōkaichiba-shi 八日市場市 …… 25 F6
Yokawa-cho 吉川町 …………… 34 C2
Yokkaichi-shi 四日市市 ……… 38 B4
Yokogawa-cho 横川町 ………… 11 F2
Yokogoshi-mura 横越村 ……… 26 C4①
Yokohama-machi 横浜町 ……… 29 H5
Yokohama-shi 横浜市 ………… 42 C4
Yokoshiba-machi 横芝町 ……… 25 F6
Yokoshima-machi 横島町 …… 70 C5
Yokosuka-shi 横須賀市 ……… 41 E7
Yokota-cho 横田町 …………… 15 G3
Yokote-shi 横手市 …………… 28 C3
Yokoze-machi 横瀬町 ………… 40 B1
Yomitan-son 読谷村 …………… 69 A5
Yomogita-mura 蓬田村 ……… 29 G4
Yonabaru-cho 与那原町 ……… 69 A6
Yonago-shi 米子市 …………… 15 G2
Yonaguni-cho 与那国町 ……… 4 C1
Yonaguni-jima 与那国島 …… 4 C1
Yonagusuku-son 与那城村 …… 69 B5
Yone-yama 米山 ……………… 23 G4
Yoneshiro-gawa 米代川 ……… 28 E2
Yoneyama-cho 米山町 ………… 27 H2
Yonezawa-shi 米沢市 ………… 27 E4
Yono-shi 与野市 …………… 40 E2
Yonouzu-mura 米水津村 ……… 13 I6
Yorii-machi 寄居町 …………… 40 B1
Yorishima-cho 寄島町 ………… 15 H5
Yōrō-cho 養老町 …………… 38 A2
Yoron-cho 与論町 …………… 10 C4
Yoshida-cho 吉田町 …………… 11 F3
Yoshida-cho 吉田町 …………… 15 E5
Yoshida-cho 吉田町 …………… 16 D5
Yoshida-cho 吉田町 …………… 21 G6
Yoshida-machi 吉田町 ………… 26 C5
Yoshida-machi 吉田町 ………… 40 A1
Yoshida-mura 吉田村 ………… 15 F3
Yoshii-cho 吉井町 …………… 12 D5
Yoshii-cho 吉井町 …………… 15 I4
Yoshii-cho 芳井町 …………… 15 G5
Yoshii-gawa 吉井川 …………… 15 I4
Yoshii-machi 吉井町 ………… 13 F4
Yoshii-machi 吉井町 ………… 25 G2
Yoshikawa-machi 吉川町 …… 23 G4
Yoshikawa-machi 吉川町 …… 41 F2
Yoshikawa-mura 吉川村 ……… 17 G4
Yoshimatsu-cho 吉松町 ……… 11 F2
Yoshimi-machi 吉見町 ………… 40 D1
Yoshinaga-cho 吉永町 ……… 15 I4
Yoshino-cho 吉野町 …………… 17 H2
Yoshino-cho 吉野町 …………… 35 H6
Yoshino-gawa 吉野川 ………… 17 I3
Yoshinodani-mura 吉野谷村 … 22 B6
Yoshioka-mura 吉岡村 ……… 25 H2③
Yoshitomi-machi 吉富町 ……… 13 G4②

Yoshiumi-cho 吉海町 ………… 16 E2
Yoshiwa-mura 吉和村 ………… 14 D5
Yōtei-zan 羊蹄山 …………… 30 D3
Yotsukaidō-shi 四街道市 …… 41 H4
Yuasa-cho 湯浅町 …………… 18 C2
Yubara-cho 湯原町 …………… 15 H3
Yūbari-shi 夕張市 …………… 31 F2
Yūbetsu-cho 湧別町 …………… 33 E3
Yuda-machi 湯田町 …………… 28 C4
Yudanaka spa 湯田中温泉 …… 23 G5
Yufu-dake 由布岳 …………… 13 H4
Yufuin-cho 湯布院町 ………… 13 H5
Yugawa-mura 湯川村 ………… 26 E5②
Yugawara-machi 湯河原町 …… 24 D2
Yuge-cho 弓削町 …………… 17 F2
Yui-cho 由比町 ……………… 21 G5
Yuki-cho 湯来町 …………… 14 D5
Yuki-cho 油木町 …………… 15 G4
Yuki-cho 由岐町 …………… 17 I3
Yūki-shi 結城市 ……………… 25 G4
Yukuhashi-shi 行橋市 ………… 44 E2
Yumesaki-cho 夢前町 ………… 34 A1
Yuni-cho 由仁町 …………… 31 F2
Yunomae-machi 湯前町 ……… 11 G1
Yunotani-mura 湯之谷村 …… 26 C6
Yunotsu-machi 温泉津町 ……… 14 E3
Yura-cho 由良町 …………… 18 C2
Yuri-machi 由利町 …………… 28 B2
Yusuhara-cho 梼原町 ………… 16 E5
Yutaka-machi 豊町 …………… 15 F6
Yūtō-cho 雄踏町 …………… 39 H7
Yuu-cho 由宇町 …………… 14 D6
Yūwa-machi 雄和町 …………… 28 C3
Yuya-cho 油谷町 …………… 14 A5
Yuza-machi 遊佐町 …………… 28 B2
Yuzawa-machi 湯沢町 ………… 23 H5
Yuzawa-shi 湯沢市 …………… 28 B3
Yuzukami-mura 湯津上村 …… 25 I5

Z

Zama-shi 座間市 …………… 40 D5
Zamami-son 座間味村 ………… 4 D4⑥
Zanpa-misaki 残波岬 ………… 10 A6
Zaō-machi 蔵王町 …………… 27 G3
Zaō-zan 蔵王山 …………… 27 F3
Zentsūji-shi 善通寺市 ………… 17 G2
Zushi-shi 逗子市 …………… 40 E7